TOO FAR ON A WHIM

MARITIME CURRENTS:
HISTORY AND ARCHAEOLOGY
Series Editor

Gene Allen Smith

Editorial Advisory Board

John F. Beeler
Alicia Caporaso
Annalies Corbin
Ben Ford
Ingo K. Heidbrink
Susan B. M. Langley
Nancy Shoemaker
Joshua M. Smith
William H. Thiesen

Too Far on a Whim

*The Limits of High-Steam
Propulsion in the US Navy*

TYLER A. PITROF

THE UNIVERSITY OF ALABAMA PRESS
Tuscaloosa

The University of Alabama Press
Tuscaloosa, Alabama 35487-0380
uapress.ua.edu

Copyright © 2024 by the University of Alabama Press
All rights reserved.

Inquiries about reproducing material from this work should
be addressed to the University of Alabama Press.

Typeface: Adobe Text

Cover image: Starboard bow view of USS Somers (DD-381) on September 28, 1938, at New York; source: Naval History and Heritage Command, Photo No. NH 66340
Cover design: Lori Lynch

Cataloging-in-Publication data is available from the Library of Congress.
ISBN: 978-0-8173-2191-8 (cloth)
ISBN: 978-0-8173-6140-2 (paper)
E-ISBN: 978-0-8173-9494-3
The views expressed in this book are those of the author and do not necessarily reflect the official position of the Department of the Navy, the Department of Defense, or the US government.

For Amanda, Max, and Elle.

Contents

List of Illustrations / ix
Acknowledgments / xi
Introduction / 1

PART I. Genesis of the High-Steam Navy, 1918–1941 / 17
1. The Rise of Steam Power / 19
2. The Through Ticket to Manila / 36
3. Crossroads / 49
4. Robinson, Bowen, and American High Steam, 1932–1938 / 62
5. Bowen versus the World / 81
6. Full Steam Ahead / 105

PART II. High Steam at War, 1939–1945 / 111
7. The Shipyard Revolution / 113
8. Riding the Wildcat / 122
9. The "Battle of the Fuel Oil," 1941–1945 / 133
10. The Impact of High Steam on the Pacific War / 152
Conclusion. Bowen's Legacy / 171
Notes / 177
Bibliography / 207
Index / 213

Illustrations

Figures

Figure I.1. Rear Admiral Harold G. Bowen Sr. / 5

Figure 1.1. The Reaction Turbine / 23

Figure 1.2. The Impulse Turbine / 24

Figure 1.3. The Reduction Gear / 32

Figure 4.1. *Clemson*-class destroyer USS *Goff* (DD-247) / 66

Figure 4.2. Rear Admiral Samuel M. Robinson / 68

Figure 4.3. USS *Mahan* (DD-364) / 71

Figure 4.4. Locked-Train, Double-Reduction Gear / 73

Figure 4.5. USS *Somers* (DD-381) / 75

Figure 4.6. Babcock & Wilcox "Type M" Boiler / 76

Figure 5.1. No Time for Interruptions / 86

Figure 5.2. Admiral Thomas C. Hart / 88

Figure 5.3. Captain William R. Purnell / 90

Figure 5.4. Rear Admiral Harry L. Brinser / 95

Figure 6.1. Cross-Compounded Turbine "Set" for an *Allen M. Sumner*-class Destroyer / 107

Tables

Table 3.1. High-Steam Propulsion in Interwar Destroyers Outside the United States / 60

Table 4.1. Power and Fuel Characteristics of the Mid-1930s US Navy / 65

Table 4.2. US Destroyer Classes of the Interwar Period, 1918–1939 / 78–79

Table 5.1. Comparative Costs of Destroyer Construction / 100

Table 7.1. US Destroyer Production, 1932–1945 / 115

TABLE 7.2. Destroyer Delays Reported to BuShips, June 11, 1941, and February 2, 1942 / 119

TABLE 9.1. *FTP 136* Fuel Consumption Variables (1940) / 136

TABLE 9.2. 1,850-ton DDs from *FTP 136* / 137

TABLE 9.3. Example Use of *FTP 136* Tables / 138

TABLE 9.4. *Somers*-class Data from *FTP 218* / 144–45

TABLE 9.5. CL-49 Data from *FTP 218* / 146–47

TABLE 9.6. Sample Calculations from *FTP 218* / 148

TABLE 10.1. Fleet Oilers Available to the US Navy in Late 1941 / 159

TABLE 10.2. Destroyer Escort Classes of the US Navy, 1943–1945 / 168

TABLE 10.3. US Navy Oiler Classes Acquired During World War II / 169

Acknowledgments

This book is the product of more than a decade of research and writing. As such, it could not exist without the support and encouragement of numerous individuals. Chief among these is Jon Sumida, who originally put me on high steam's trail and pushed me to pursue the story as far and as long as it took. Colleen Woods, David Sicilia, Patrick Chung, and David Rosenberg all provided valuable feedback on this manuscript as well as advice on where additional pieces of the puzzle might lie.

In my pursuit of elusive evidence, the wonderful archivists charged with the care of the US Navy's records at the National Archives in Washington, DC, and College Park, Maryland, went above and beyond in their efforts to help, for which I am eternally grateful. In the refinement of the narrative and injection of personal stories, numerous individuals affiliated with the United States Naval Academy (USNA) proved invaluable. These included Tom McCarthy, B. J. Armstrong, Marcus Jones, Matthew Dziennik, and the bulk of the USNA history department. It was also through the academy that I received the support of and ability to interview members of the class of 1957, many of whom had worked directly with World War II–vintage propulsion systems.

Last but definitely not least, I owe thanks to my family. My parents and sister were immensely supportive throughout my work on this project, and my father, Larry, often served as my editor and sounding board. The support of my wife, Amanda, and the joy of my two children, Max and Elle, were ultimately what kept me going to the finish line.

Too Far on a Whim

Introduction

> Steam, while it has given increased certainty and quickness of movement to fleets, has also imposed upon them such fetters, by the need of renewing their fuel, that naval enterprises can no longer have the daring, far-reaching sweep that they once had.
>
> —Alfred Thayer Mahan, *Naval Strategy*

On October 20, 1938, two young naval officers nervously made their way to the rear of the Navy Department complex in Washington, DC. Charles Hardesty and Carl Dalton were US Navy lieutenants then serving as chief engineers aboard two of the navy's newest warships: the destroyers USS *Somers* (DD-381) and USS *Warrington* (DD-383). They had been summoned to appear before a board that included five admirals, a captain, and a commander. Their singularly unenviable task was to explain to these officers—among the most distinguished in the US Navy—exactly how they operated their ships' machinery and to review every difficulty they had encountered in doing so.

Despite the circumstances Hardesty and Dalton found themselves in, they had not been brought in as a result of any wrongdoing of their own. Instead, their presence before the General Board of the Navy was the climax of an increasingly public conflict between the navy's engineers and combat officers over the new high-pressure and high-temperature steam propulsion system that powered their ships. At stake was the adoption of this high-steam system for *all* new ships, which was pushed primarily by the US Navy's de facto engineer-in-chief, Vice Admiral Harold G. Bowen Sr., from his position at the head of the Bureau of Engineering. Bowen asserted that this system promised vast increases in fuel economy that would prove invaluable to any future operations in the Pacific Ocean. The problem was that this economy was gained only through a substantial increase in the cost and complexity of propulsion machinery. This and the breakneck pace at which these changes were implemented badly rankled many in the navy, who questioned whether the new machinery was effective and rugged enough to actually do the job it was intended for. The escalation of this dispute with the discovery of major design flaws in newly built destroyers was ultimately what brought Hardesty and Dalton before Admiral Thomas C. Hart's general board in late 1938.

After more than a month of investigation, the board concluded that it was trapped in a Socratic paradox: it knew only that it knew nothing. The available data on high steam was simply too complex for the level of education the general line officers of the board possessed. Instead, the navy had little choice but to trust the word of its one subject matter expert—Admiral Bowen. "A decision and recommendation," the board reported to Secretary of the Navy Claude Swanson at the end of 1938, "can not be made by the board after careful deliberation. The Board is reduced to rendering an opinion based on opinions . . . [but] the Navy Department has gone too far on a whim to walk back on a hunch."[1]

Despite these inauspicious beginnings, the Hart board's words guaranteed that high steam would be the rule, rather than the exception, in all major warships built for the US Navy between 1939 and 1945. Postwar scholarship—on the rare occasions that this topic is discussed at all—has lauded this decision, universally asserting that vast improvements in cruising radius attributable to high steam were critical to US operations in the Pacific theater of World War II. This view of high steam as a great success relies almost entirely on the postwar account of Admiral Bowen. His 1954 book *Ships, Machinery, and Mossbacks: The Autobiography of a Naval Engineer* remains to this day the only easily accessible entryway into the highly complex subject of mid-century military steam propulsion.[2] As the resident subject matter expert, Admiral Bowen was instrumental in the development of this technology by the US fleet. However, as an engineering officer who found himself marginalized in the aftermath of high steam's adoption, Bowen had a clear motive for painting himself as the martyr for a pure cause. A complete reliance on his partisan account of high steam thus poses significant problems for modern scholarship.

This book therefore seeks to do what the general board could not: assess the overall impact that the adoption of a high-steam propulsion system had on the US Navy. To do so, it delves into the technical records of the navy's contentious bureau system, as well as those of the general board, the chief of naval operations, and the individual ship designers and builders. The story assembled through this effort traces the development of high steam from its beginnings ashore through the conclusion of World War II. In light of what this investigation reveals, this book argues that while high-steam developments did improve the endurance of navy warships, faulty operational assumptions made by Bowen and his bureau meant that the system often failed to achieve more than two-thirds the endurance expected of it once war broke out. This shortfall rendered the range data upon which all warship movements were planned utterly useless. To make matters worse, the improvements that were obtained were accompanied by substantial production and training problems. All of these issues snowballed after 1940 in a manner that placed severe limits on the pace of naval operations in the Pacific theater of World War II—precisely the bottleneck that high steam's adoption had been intended (and claimed) to avoid!

With these discoveries, it becomes clear that high-steam propulsion is not only a critically overlooked factor in American World War II naval planning but also an example of technological progressivism gone awry. It is clear from the archives that during the "high-steam controversy," there was little consideration given to either the situational nature of the fuel-economy advantages the system offered or its far-reaching administrative consequences. This is in large part due to the increased complexity of these technological systems, which by the early twentieth century had moved beyond the easy understanding of nonspecialists. The result was that experts like Admiral Bowen, who were relied upon to help leaders make important design and policy decisions, found themselves wielding tremendous power and influence that far exceeded their official limits.

This story of the American high-steam system is thus a cautionary tale for us today. In our era of enormous defense budgets and the well-entrenched military-industrial economy, innumerable organizations are charged with regularly producing the next great technical breakthrough. In this context, high steam provides an eye-opening example of how far off the rails things can go if we lose sight of *why* innovations are pursued in the first place and instead unquestioningly pursue technological innovation for its own sake.

THE ENGINEER, FUEL EFFICIENCY, AND HIGH STEAM

> The EDO [engineering duty only] is like a mule, no pride of ancestry and no hope of posterity.
>
> —Rear Admiral Robert S. Griffin, quoted in Harold G. Bowen, *Ships, Machinery, and Mossbacks*[3]

While understanding the machinery itself is important to this study, equally significant are the men who operated steam propulsion systems during the early twentieth century. These engines were not at all like modern internal combustion motors found in the common automobile. Instead, they required careful operation by a number of specialized "enlisted" sailors overseen by a pair of officers. Each individual sailor had a variety of tasks that ranged from managing water levels and burner configuration to operating the maze of steam valves and throttles. This was reflected by their various titles, with machinist mates, motor machinist mates, firemen, water tenders, and metalsmiths being the most prominent. For their own part, the officers overseeing these men—the engineer officer and assistant engineer officer—were charged with understanding every task that they might assign and with being able to do it themselves. As we shall see, this requirement and the structure of officer education in the mid-twentieth century often resulted in the engineering enlisted men ("snipes") teaching their officers how to run a propulsion plant rather than the other way around.[4]

All of these individuals should be our star sources for learning about how fuel efficiency was managed in the early days of steam propulsion. Sadly, the voices of enlisted personnel are mere ghosts in the record. While a handful of autobiographical accounts exist (such as that of water tender Frederick T. Wilson's experience on the Asiatic station between 1899 and 1901), the majority of these men were either illiterate or made no record of their experiences. Accordingly, there has been virtually no scholarly study of enlisted personnel beyond Frederick Harrod's groundbreaking 1978 study *Manning the New Navy*. We therefore must rely primarily on other sources, discussed below, and supplement them with these sparse accounts wherever possible. This, plus the recorded evolution of enlisted training efforts at the National Archives, is the best option we have for understanding how these men lived and worked.[5]

Unlike those of enlisted men, the voices of mid-century officers thankfully *can* be found. Their accounts primarily take the form of technical submissions to the *Journal of the American Society for Naval Engineers* (now the *Naval Engineers Journal*), published since 1889. Additionally, for the early twentieth century, the words of marine engineers are recorded regularly in other communications, such as the memoirs of high-ranking officers of World War II. These men were junior members of the navy in the first decades of that century, when the turbine was revolutionizing steam propulsion. Admiral Bowen was one such officer (figure I.1).

Harold Gardiner Bowen Sr. was born in Providence, Rhode Island, on November 6, 1883. He was the first member of his family to join the navy, securing an appointment to the United States Naval Academy in Annapolis,

Maryland, in late 1901. After his graduation in 1905, Bowen quickly discovered his affinity for propulsion engineering, while posted aboard the (hapless) destroyer USS *Hopkins* (DD-6).[6] In recognition of his interests and abilities, the navy sent him to Columbia University for a master of science in mechanical engineering, which Bowen completed in 1914. During his stint at Columbia, Bowen married Edith Brownlie, in September 1911.

With his master's degree in hand, Bowen was designated "engineering duty only" (EDO) and posted to a series of increasingly important engineering positions. Between 1914 and 1922, these jobs included chief engineer of the armored cruisers USS *Tennessee* (ACR-10) and USS *Pittsburgh* (ACR-4) and of the battleship USS *Arizona* (BB-39). He then spent the 1920s alternately ashore at the Mare Island and Puget Sound Navy Yards and afloat as part of the Battle Fleet command staff. In 1931, Bowen entered what would become the defining period of his life when he was appointed assistant chief of the Bureau of Engineering (BuEng) in Washington, DC. Initially under the watch of Rear Admiral Samuel M. Robinson

FIGURE I.1. Rear Admiral Harold G. Bowen Sr., chief of the Bureau of Engineering from 1935 to 1939. Image 80-G-603565 courtesy of the Naval History and Heritage Command.

and then in his own right as bureau chief from 1935 to 1939, Bowen seized the opportunity presented by renewed US naval construction to push an agenda of propulsion modernization.[7]

Prior to the 1930s, learning the intricacies of their positions allowed naval engineers to determine the best configurations for their own ship's power plant in different conditions. Usually, the best speed for general purposes was around 12 to 15 knots (varying depending on the type of ship), as horsepower requirements above that range rose exponentially with each additional knot added. These speeds generally allowed the shutting down of the majority of a ship's boilers and were thus preferred for long-distance cruising due to the fuel that this practice saved.[8]

In 1932, Admirals Robinson and Bowen initially reached out to the design firm Gibbs & Cox—who had never designed a warship for the US Navy—for their experience in working with contractors that were well-versed in higher-pressure and higher-temperature steam. This partnership took advantage of developments in steam power generation technology that had appeared over the previous twenty years in electric utilities and civilian shipping. As Bowen later argued, the goal was to produce warships with dramatically improved fuel economy and power-to-weight ratios, providing them with far greater operational ranges and speeds than had previously been the case. This was achieved through the creation of a uniquely American high-steam propulsion *system* that combined new inventions with a more traditional boiler-turbine-condenser design.

Built around an air-encased, water-tube boiler, and cross-compound impulse turbine arrangement for each propeller shaft, the American high-steam system required special alloys such as carbon molybdenum steel to handle the 650 PSI, 850°F steam that the boiler's controlled-type superheater produced.[9] Exhaust gases were vented past the water being fed to the boiler in an economizer, preheating the liquid and making additional use of waste heat. Each turbine set contained a high-pressure, low-pressure, and cruising turbine section designed to make the best use of the steam produced for various operational speeds. Each of these turbines was linked to its respective propeller shaft via a complex double-reduction gear to permit the optimum respective rotational speeds for the turbines and propeller. Overall, this system was an innovative solution to the operational problems posed by the Washington Naval Treaty, which banned the United States from building up refueling bases in the Pacific Ocean.[10]

Essentially, this transformation of the marine steam propulsion system represented an attempt by designers to supplement traditional means of producing fuel economy with a number of novel mechanical innovations. The addition of components specialized for long-range operation, such as the cruising turbine, fundamentally changed the way that high fuel efficiency was obtained. Sadly, it is extremely difficult to find firsthand accounts of this transition from the perspective of the engineering spaces rather than of Washington. By the time of high steam's standardization in the fleet, the voices of both junior officers and enlisted men who worked directly with propulsion systems become virtually nonexistent in the archival record. As we shall see, this is partly due to the structure of the US Navy's officer corps in the interwar era. After 1938, this force had been rapidly transformed from teams of highly skilled professional sailors working with machinery whose basic features were well-understood to a mix of inexperienced, temporary personnel who were unaware that they were dealing with new and imperfect equipment. The result is that their voices appear only in records concerning ship performance at the Bureau of Engineering and Bureau of Ships or in official reports of fuel usage, machinery derangements, and damage sustained at sea. In these sources, these men are often left unnamed.[11] In this context, it is not surprising that scholars have proven largely willing to take Bowen's account at face value on such a highly technical subject as high steam.

As mentioned above, Bowen argued at the time and subsequently in his autobiography that his actions while serving as BuEng chief were based on proven technology as well as a desire to keep up with what other national navies were doing in the interwar period. Simultaneously, he also claimed that the technology he was pushing would hand the United States a major technological advantage for the coming conflict that was clearly brewing in late 1938. His 1954 account of these details—which broadly matches the case he presented to the General Board of the Navy before World War II—is conceived and written in a way one might expect a subject matter expert to address a layperson. That is, it clearly underlines the goals and advantages of certain components of the high-steam system, without detailing how that system as a whole works. It is also utterly devoid of any shortcomings of or counterpoints to Bowen's own argument.

To critically examine Bowen's account of high steam, this book addresses four main questions that scholarship has so far left unanswered. First, what, exactly, was high steam, and where did this "proven" technology come from? While we have scratched the surface of this subject in the preceding paragraphs, we don't really know what any of that technical description of high steam means without the context of what it was replacing or how it developed ashore. Second, why was this system unique to the US Navy—how was adopting high steam simultaneously already "proven" yet also cutting-edge? Third, why was there such a contentious debate over high steam if it was such a purely beneficial innovation, as Bowen argues? Finally, how might we go about answering these questions without a single technical source that is as comprehensive as Admiral Bowen's autobiography?

In answering these questions, this book represents an initial foray into a previously imperviously dense subject that this author hopes will receive much more attention in the future. Yet it is important to note not only what this book *is* but also what it *is not*. Specifically, the following pages represent more than a decade of research and writing and yet only scratch the surface of high steam's impact on day-to-day operations in World War II itself. This is because *Too Far on a Whim*'s primary purpose is to place high steam and its previously unknown shortcomings in the context of the 1930s command culture that produced it. In doing so, it strives in part to provide insight into the interwar technological decision-making process for those attempting to make similar choices today. This is, in other words, a necessary first step. A wartime operational study—which is a significant and lengthy project in and of itself—is not the intent here but should instead be the primary focus of a future work.

HIGH STEAM IN MODERN SCHOLARSHIP

> I would be derelict in my duty if I did not invite your attention to the fact that there is a great schism in the marine engineering profession of the United States. Some of the elements of this schism are so deep and so fundamental that, in my opinion, it is a vital necessity that the General Board shall consider them in their deliberations.
>
> —Rear Admiral Harold G. Bowen Sr. to the General Board of the Navy[12]

While the development of high-steam technology and its impact on World War II has never been studied in detail, it is not wholly unknown to modern scholarship. That being said, the current narrative has been developed only in relatively brief sections of general works or alluded to in more specialized ones. In all of these works, high steam is treated as a "black box"—it is considered only in the context of its input and output while its inner workings are not understood. This approach glosses over the advantages or problems generated by individual components of the high-steam system in favor of overly reductionist comparisons of speed and range (itself a problematic concept at sea) between national navies' ships.

The former category of sources, which includes works by the historians Norman Friedman, David C. Evans and Mark R. Peattie, and Albert A. Nofi, present a consensus that vast improvements in cruising radius attributable to high steam, particularly in the case of the US Navy's destroyer force, made long-range operations in the Pacific theater feasible. This was done by cutting down on fuel usage, refueling time, and the additional bases that otherwise would have been required to fight the Imperial Japanese Navy.[13]

On the other hand, specialized scholarship that speaks to our subject by Rear Admiral Worrall Reed Carter, Thomas Wildenberg, and, most recently, Thomas Heinrich provides a slightly different angle. While the works by these authors generally do little more than mention high steam as tangentially related to their stories, they make admirable contributions to our knowledge of Navy procurement and logistics during the interwar period and World War II—particularly to how high steam was supposed to fit into these processes. They also occasionally provide less than glowing appraisals of Admiral Bowen's activities from the perspective of his fellow flag officers.[14]

All of these modern accounts of high steam rely almost entirely on *Ships, Machinery, and Mossbacks*, the autobiographical work of Admiral Bowen published in 1954. Bowen's account is not an operational history but rather a story of how high steam came to be adopted through his own heroic efforts, supplemented by anecdotal accounts from a handful of other individuals about how important this technology was. While Bowen was undeniably instrumental in the development of this technology for the US fleet, what we have discussed so far likely does not appear adequate for problematizing his account. What *should* tip the scales of our opinion is the fact that the adoption and apparent success of high steam did not end up being the major boost to Bowen's career that the admiral himself seems to have expected. Instead, by 1941—by which time high steam had clearly become the standard propulsion system for all major warship classes in the navy—Bowen had effectively been sidelined due to his adversarial management style. Bowen therefore had an axe to grind in 1954; in the interest of justifying his actions and boosting his own legacy, the admiral had a clear motive to emphasize the benefits of high steam and to downplay or even entirely ignore its shortcomings. He therefore cannot be exclusively relied upon for our consideration of the impact of high steam on the US Navy.

For the purposes of this study, replacing Bowen's voice is not a simple matter of finding a single piece of evidence. Instead, a better representation of the truth requires connecting the critical remarks made in fleet-wide publications with the statistical record of high steam's performance in World War II. When compared to the expectations detailed in the 1938 general board study of the subject, the difference becomes startlingly clear; changes in tactics and ordnance cannot have accounted for the apparent loss of basically one-third of the modern fleet's operating radius. While newer American ships did possess superior range in comparison with older designs, this was also the case with some contemporary foreign warships that did *not* employ high steam.

This study of high steam primarily focuses on interwar-era engineering operations, but it also speaks to the few works that concern themselves with the challenge of meeting rapidly changing personnel requirements that accompanied the coming of World War II. The scramble of the US Navy's Bureau of Navigation (or Bureau of Naval Personnel after 1942) to meet the escalating manpower requirements of global war has been touched upon by numerous modern-day scholars who have focused on general mobilization in the United States.[15] However, only two works focus specifically on the development of the US Navy's officers in any period. The first of these, Peter Karsten's *The Naval Aristocracy: The Golden Age of Annapolis and the Emergence of Modern Navalism*, attempts to depict the evolution and nature of US naval officers between 1845 and 1920. The first study of its kind, Karsten's work is unfortunately limited by the unreliable nature of his sources (primarily scattered personal correspondence) and the sweeping generalizations he attempts to draw from them.[16] Nevertheless, it is useful to us here, for it intersects with the second work of relevance: Donald Chisholm's much more recent *Waiting for Dead Men's Shoes: Origins and Development of the US Navy's Officer Personnel System, 1793–1941*. Representing a monumental effort on the part of Chisholm to trace the officer corps as the product of interaction between the US Navy and Congress, the general nature of this work (and its ending point in 1941) unfortunately prevents it from giving the field of engineering anything more than cursory treatment. Nevertheless, *Waiting for Dead Men's Shoes* contains tantalizing glimpses into an ongoing conflict between the Navy and the entire concept of the dedicated engineer. The present work seeks to provide more insight into this persistent source of friction.[17]

The adoption of high steam requires an examination of the state of American shipbuilding in the 1930s and 1940s and, as such, touches upon the complex subject of industrial mobilization. This is perhaps the most heavily populated field that this study explores, and as a result there are a gratifying number of valuable works upon which the information that follows relies. While too great in number to cover in detail, these include works by authors such as the aforementioned Thomas Heinrich, Alan S. Milward, and Paul A. C. Koistinen.[18] These books are the foundational references for American industrial mobilization in World War II and previous wars upon which this study's naval production research has been based. While an adequate understanding of the trials and travails of propulsion-component production can be obtained through this work alone, any broader implications for the US economy are beyond the scope of this examination. The reader is well-advised to consult the aforementioned authors for further information on this important and complex topic.

Finally, any study of the development of marine propulsion in the United States is inextricably linked with scholarship dedicated to the development of the electrical utility industry. There are a number of important and useful studies in this category. These include Louis C. Hunter's *A History of Industrial Power in the United States*.[19] For the beginnings of steam power itself in the early eighteenth century up through the 1920s, Hunter's work manages to touch upon almost every major field affected by the development of the steam-powered engine. His study is therefore a critical reference for the early development of marine propulsion and the coincidental evolution and advancement of the steam boiler. Picking up where Hunter leaves off is Thomas P. Hughes's *Networks of Power: Electrification in Western Society, 1880–1930*.[20] Focused exclusively on the development of the electric utility industry, this work paints a thorough portrait of the evolving needs, desires, and equipment of this important area of study. It therefore forms a critical frame of reference for the spread of power-generation technology to marine propulsion (and vice versa) as well as the ever-changing goals of the electrical utility industry that eventually led to its adoption of high-pressure and high-temperature steam. This latter point is ultimately rounded out by Richard F. Hirsch's *Technology and Transformation in the American Electric Utility Industry*, which focuses extensively on the developing executive culture of that titular industry and, by extension, its driving motivations.[21] Together, these works provide the critical background to Admiral Bowen's oft-cited source for American high-steam knowledge and serve as the foundation for our discussion of that subject.

HIGH STEAM AND THE US NAVY

> The quickest way to learn engineering was to get ordered to a rundown ship as Chief Engineer.
>
> —Rear Admiral Harold G. Bowen Sr., *Ships, Machinery, and Mossbacks*[22]

Telling the high-steam story without relying on Admiral Bowen's narrative requires us to first establish the environment within which the system was produced and then to explain how that technology worked (or rather, didn't work) in the Pacific environment, for which it was designed. As such, this book is divided into two parts: Genesis of the High-Steam Navy, 1918–1941, and High Steam at War, 1939–1945.

Part I begins with an exploration of the development of steam power so as to lay the foundation for the later transformation of that system. Chapter 1 briefly recounts the very beginnings of steam power, from its earliest eighteenth-century form as the "atmospheric engine" to the early years of commercial high-steam experimentation in the 1920s. In doing so, it touches upon the development of the two best-recognized components of the steam engine itself: the boiler and the reciprocating (later-turbine) engine. The genesis of this machinery and its importance to both the development of the electric utility industry ashore and marine propulsion afloat must be established before any understanding can be formed regarding the special conditions that naval designers found themselves in after 1922.

Chapter 2 covers these special conditions by exploring the transformation of the US Navy's strategic mission with the American acquisition of the Philippines in 1899. This (along with events in Hawaii and California) brought the United States into direct conflict with the rapidly industrializing Empire of Japan, a rivalry that would lead to one of the longest-lasting (and most successful) war planning efforts in modern history. In the aftermath of World War I and the 1922 signing of the Washington Naval Treaty, this effort became the navy's center of strategic gravity. The challenge of moving the entire fleet across the vast Pacific Ocean to confront a Japanese attack on the Philippines made the prospect of increased range that *could* be provided by high-pressure, high-temperature steam—so recently adopted by merchant shipping—highly attractive to Admiral Bowen and the Bureau of Engineering.

Bowen was not alone in spotting potential advantages to be had in elevated steam pressures and temperatures. Chapter 3 explores the various forays into this field conducted by the British, Japanese, French, and German navies in order to set the stage for why the US Navy's propulsion experience has for so long been considered unique. While these nations each investigated high steam for different reasons, knowledge of the mere existence of their efforts formed an additional motivation for Admiral Bowen to investigate high-pressure, high-temperature steam.

Accordingly, chapter 4 covers that effort via an exploration of the activities of Bowen and Admiral Samuel M. Robinson, who was his boss at BuEng between 1931 and 1935. Upon becoming the navy's de facto engineer-in-chief with Robinson's departure, Bowen used his position to quickly develop and embrace what would become the United States' ubiquitous high-steam propulsion system of World War II.

Unsurprisingly, Bowen's aggressive and uncompromising methods on high steam eventually triggered a bureaucratic turf war with other organizations who believed him to be recklessly gambling with the future of the navy. Firmly believing himself to be on the winning side of a long-simmering conflict between US Navy engineers and general line officers, the admiral took the issue of high steam before the General Board of the Navy, in the manner of a Supreme Court hearing, in 1938. This investigation, run by a collection of soon-to-be-famous and infamous names, attempted to consider the full spectrum of implications that accompanied a general adoption of high-steam technology. The findings of the general board represent an accurate picture of the operational vision of which high steam was a part. The hearing itself and the fallout from the general board's effective endorsement of high steam therefore make up the conclusion of Part I in chapters 5 and 6, respectively.

Part II of this book examines the consequences of high steam's adoption on US operational planners and on the United States' industrial mobilization efforts once naval expansion began in 1940. These consequences, despite the claims of prior historians, were decidedly negative. Chapter 7 addresses the extensive and complex production difficulties that high steam's material requirements caused with US Navy contractors, resulting in substantial delays in the completion of numerous critically needed destroyers in the early years of World War II. These effects were so dangerous to the navy that Bowen's predecessor, Admiral Robinson, was placed in charge of an entirely new organization dedicated to sorting them out. Along those same lines, chapter 8 addresses the partially foreseen manpower and training problems the navy encountered while attempting to crew its new high-steam ships once the war began and the navy was working with drafted sailors instead of volunteers. Both of these chapters reveal the narrow and misguided nature of Bowen's claims during the 1938 general board hearing that high steam was a pure advantage for these areas. However, the real danger arose from the limits these early issues placed on naval expansion once the war had begun.

Chapter 9 investigates how the introduction of high-steam machinery seriously undermined traditional methods of calculating warship operating ranges at economical speeds. Ignorance of this paradigm shift—and of how it amplified preexisting problems with calculations at *all* speeds—left the navy totally unprepared for the discovery that the environment for which high steam's economy measures were designed did not exist. The result was that a dark cloud of uncertainty obscured the true range of the majority of modern American warships at *any* speed after 1941—an uncertainty that persisted until new range tables could be compiled and distributed, which occurred only as the war was ending in 1945. Chapter 10 then performs an initial exploration of the ramifications of this revelation, examining the dangerous limits that production shortages, uncertain ranges, and unexpected needs for high-speed fleet oilers placed on the pace of US naval operations in the Pacific theater of World War II. Finally, the last chapter concludes by briefly examining high steam's impact on and presence within the postwar US Navy.

WEIGHTS, MEASURES, AND TERMINOLOGY OF THE WORLD WAR II US NAVY

Before we can proceed with our examination of the American high-steam system, there are a few subjects that must be touched upon in order to provide a proper framework of reference. Steam propulsion can be a very complicated subject for the layperson, so it is this author's hope that the following will be able to serve as something of a handy reference manual to which the reader might easily return at need.

Three universal measurements can be used to compare the parameters of different types of steam systems: the pressure of their steam, the temperature of their steam, and the power output of their engines. The pressure and temperature are measured in this work in pounds per square inch (PSI) and degrees Fahrenheit (°F), respectively, and are determined at the final output location of the heat source (usually a boiler) before any is siphoned off for auxiliary purposes. The power output is rated in horsepower (HP) or, in the case of ships, *shaft* horsepower (SHP). In either case, this is the actual force exerted by the output mechanism of the engine itself, be it a rocker-arm, crankshaft, or rotor.

What is referred to in this work as "high steam" is a system of major components. While considering the steam pressures and temperatures of the 1930s and 1940s in the full stream of history might indicate their relatively low state compared to more modern technology, "high-pressure and high-temperature steam" is quite a mouthful that, even at the time, was typically abbreviated. Accordingly, it is much easier to refer to "high steam" or "the high-steam system" than it is to continually reference a litany of inventions all combined in the name of increased steam pressure and temperature. The reader will therefore be asked to consider the term "high steam" as a callback to an ever-increasing list of items that will be well-defined as they are added, particularly in the American case.

The idea of high steam is often posed in opposition to that which it replaced, hereafter referred to as "low steam." As one might expect, this concept is shorthand for an older method of steam propulsion that had fewer major components but many smaller ones. It was the baseline standard for many navies around the world before the advent of high steam and serves as the primary point of comparison against innovations. Both of these subjects will be elaborated upon as they arise within this study.

Between 1842 and 1966, the US Navy was organized according to the "bureau system." This referred to the division of administrative responsibility among individual bureau chiefs and their staffs who nominally reported to the secretary of the navy (SecNav). These organizations operated entirely independently of one another, naturally lending themselves to the development of territoriality and frequent bureaucratic infighting. This shortcoming was amplified by the lack of the SecNav's actual executive authority over bureau activities. For the majority of the interwar period, between 1918 and 1939, the US Navy had nine bureaus: Bureau of Yards and Docks, Bureau of Supplies and Accounts (BuS&A), Bureau of Ordnance (BuOrd), Bureau of Equipment and Recruiting, Bureau of Construction and Repair (BuC&R), Bureau of Engineering (BuEng), Bureau of Navigation (BuNav), Bureau of Aeronautics, and the Bureau of Medicine and Surgery. Many of these organizations by the 1930s had shifted roles substantially, such as the Bureau of Navigation's responsibility for the recruitment and training of personnel.

Of particular interest to us for comparing vessels are displacement, speed, and distance. *Displacement* is a subject that was historically difficult to standardize. The literal meaning of the term is the weight of a ship in *long tons* (hereafter referred to only as *tons*), or imperial tons of 2,240 pounds (907.18 kilograms), calculated by the volume of water displaced at a given load. This was the internationally recognized unit of measure for ship size for the first half of the twentieth century, which bears the majority of our focus in this book. The difficulty comes in agreeing upon what the particular load state for determining "official" warship displacement was. Three primary types are often encountered in a work such as this one: "full load," "deep load," and "standard load." *Full load* is generally accepted to refer to the displacement of a vessel when loaded with all the passengers, cargo, fuel, water, and other materials required to be in full preparation for a voyage, thereby increasing draft to the level painted as the waterline. *Deep load* adds to the former full ammunition magazines and the usage of any extra fuel storage space available. *Standard load* is something of an anomaly for this period; the Washington Naval Treaty of 1922 established this term to refer to warships that were complete, fully manned, fully provisioned, and fully armed for sea but *without* fuel or reserve feedwater for the boilers. While "full load" is generally the term to describe the size of a civilian vessel, "standard load," or simply *tons standard* is the primary means of describing vessel size in this study unless otherwise indicated, as these were the terms by which things were done during the interwar period and World War II in the US Navy.

Ship speed to this day is most commonly measured in *knots*, where each knot (KT) corresponds to one nautical mile (NM) per hour. Developed in the age of sail by measuring speed via actual knots tied in a rope, 1 knot, or one nautical mile, per hour corresponds to 1.15 standard miles per hour (1.852 kilometers per hour). This unit remains the best means for measuring nautical speed thanks to its close relationship with navigation; a vessel passing along a meridian travels approximately one minute of latitude per hour for each knot of speed. Accordingly, *operational range* has traditionally been expressed as the total distance a vessel can sail before needing to refuel in nautical miles, as is often the case in this work.

PART I

Genesis of the High-Steam Navy, 1918–1941

Throughout most of the nineteenth century, steam power generation and propulsion relied upon engines built around pistons. Powerful steam engines therefore required large amounts of available space and often created excessive vibration. Beginning in the 1890s, these machines were gradually replaced by the smoother running and more easily scalable turbine engines, which instead relied directly upon rotational power from start to finish. Developments in boiler technology and the incremental improvement of the early reaction turbine ensured that most power plants and most modern major warships were so-powered by the outbreak of World War I in 1914.

Following the conclusion of this conflict, the continuing expansion of the electric utility industry into regional grids in the United States and Europe gradually resulted in the development of a boiler-turbine system that harnessed steam at previously unattainable temperatures and pressures. This was carried out in the pursuit of economies of scale. Simultaneously, the continuing search for speed and comfort among commercial shipping companies generated a similar, if markedly different-minded, interest in the new "high steam" among naval designers. Advances in both of these fields gradually attracted the attention of the major navies of the world in the 1920s and 1930s, but in most cases the experiments they carried out were either inconclusive or plagued with operational difficulties. Existing scholarship asserts that only the US Navy fully succeeded in developing and adopting a practical high-steam system during this period.

Histories of the Pacific theater of World War II, particularly those that touch upon warship design, have often portrayed the US Navy's sophisticated steam-propulsion system as a significant operational advantage.

Specifically, the higher steam pressures and temperatures in ships equipped with this high-steam system were said to have given all major US warships of that period exceptionally long operational ranges. This, in conjunction with the development of underway refueling, enabled the Navy to undertake long-range operations that would not have otherwise been feasible. The development of this propulsion system in the decade prior World War II is known to have had its difficulties, some of which were a source of contention within the navy bureau system in the 1930s. This eventually forced significant administrative change following high steam's submission to the General Board of the Navy for study in 1938. That high steam became the primary means of propulsion for the US Navy in World War II despite these events has since been portrayed as a triumph for progressive Navy engineers over a conservative administrative system. However, recent scholarship has proven that the tale of the ossification of and aversion to innovation by the US Navy's top brass between 1920 and 1940 is, in fact, a myth.[1] As a result, Part I of this work seeks to reexamine the maturation of the high-steam system in the US Navy in this light and thereby understand the operational vision from which it developed. In doing so, the advantages, disadvantages, and compromises of that system will become clear. This, in turn, will facilitate an exploration of high steam's impact on operations in the Pacific War in Part II.

Chapter 1

THE RISE OF STEAM POWER

The concept of high steam originated with the American electrical utility industry in the early twentieth century. The cross-pollination of ideas in this manner was not unusual for the time; the electrical utility and transportation industries frequently pursued advances in steam technology that were so similar that any study of one of these subjects is incomplete without the inclusion of the other. As steam power originated onshore, it is there that we must begin our story. However, it is important to keep in mind that each of these steam specializations operated under the influence of different motivations, requirements, and laws. As such, they looked for different strengths and ignored different weaknesses in the equipment developed for their particular purposes. This held true not only for the electrical industry and marine propulsion but also for civilian and military shipping—and even for different navies—depending on operational requirements. The steam engine as a means of electrical power generation evolved to emphasize reliability, small size, and the lowest possible manpower requirements. Fuel efficiency and relative operating efficiency were only secondary concerns that would be dealt with by dramatic increases in both equipment power and load size—economies of scale. The rise of high steam in the electric utility industry in the 1920s was therefore in accordance with these priorities.

The adaptation of the steam engine to marine propulsion presented a number of challenges similar to those faced by the early electrical utility industry. However, it is clear that taking the steam engine to sea required a fundamental reshuffling of design priorities. Ships required a means to transform mechanical energy produced by a steam engine into locomotion. They needed a way to guarantee a *sustainable* supply of safe heat to produce their steam. Finally, they had to compensate for accelerated corrosion at sea. As a result, the desirability of a high power-to-weight ratio and the maximum attainable fuel efficiency often superseded reliability (or "uptime") concerns in marine steam engines. Additionally, the employment of steam power for locomotion added a number of specialized jobs to ships that were not commonly needed ashore. These tasks, such as individual "throttlemen," whose sole job was to respond to ordered changes in speed, varied in number and complexity depending on the specific purpose of a given ship.[2]

By the early twentieth century, cargo vessels emphasized fuel economy and machinery size, while passenger "liners" searched for power and raw speed. After 1920, both high steam and a competitor technology—steam turbo-electric propulsion—seemed to offer even greater potential. The head-to-head competition between these two new alternatives that ensued in the civilian realm was ultimately what drew the attention of Admiral Bowen's bureau, BuEng, to high steam in the early 1930s.

PRINCIPLES OF STEAM POWER

At its essence, any steam system consists first of a *boiler*—a metal pressure vessel that serves to heat a water source to the boiling point in order to produce steam. The heat for this process has been produced by various fuels throughout history, including wood, coal, oil, and, more recently, nuclear fission. This heat is transferred to the water within the boiler through one of various methods. The earliest of these was the "haystack" boiler that had a simple combustion chamber below a dome containing water.[3] The steam produced by this process was then transported by piping from the boiler to an engine. Thomas Newcomen's "atmospheric engine," the first such steam engine invented in 1712, consisted of a balance beam linked on one end to a piston with an unsealed cylinder. When the piston began to rise, a valve between the boiler outlet and the cylinder opened, allowing steam to enter. Once the arm reached its highest point, the valve closed. The cylinder was then cooled with water, condensing the steam and forming a vacuum. Atmospheric pressure would then force the piston down via the open cylinder end, performing mechanical work and starting the process over again.[4]

Naturally, the amount of work that could be done merely through the use of atmospheric pressure was limited. Thus, despite the preventative efforts of James Watt in the United Kingdom during the mid-to-late eighteenth century, the use of steam at pressures above that of the atmosphere gradually developed.[5] In later steam engines, it was expanding steam rather than atmospheric pressure resulting from a condensation-induced vacuum that actually moved the piston. Like any gas, steam naturally and forcefully expands in a vacuum, expending heat and pressure in doing so. It is this phenomenon that was later harnessed to force a piston open, the steam's subsequent evacuation from the cylinder being performed by admitting it to the boiler flue at still above-atmospheric pressure. This was first perfected in 1800 by another Englishman, Richard Trevithick.[6] In some cases, the waste steam was sent to a *condenser* rather than being exhausted. There, it was cooled until it turned completely back into water, after which it was recycled into the boiler to restart the process (thus reducing external water supply requirements).[7]

For much of the nineteenth century, boilers were usually constructed of simple riveted wrought iron, unable to sustain pressures significantly higher than 40 PSI in non-atmospheric models. Despite this limitation, major gains in efficiency were made as the haystack boiler gave way to the flue boiler that ducted combustion exhaust through the water via a single pipe. This, in turn, gradually evolved into the *fire-tube boiler* after 1850. The fire-tube boiler dispensed with the single large flue in favor of numerous smaller ones. This increased the heating area available for the water and thereby dramatically improved heating efficiency.[8] Simultaneous with this development was the appearance of another idea that inverted the fire-tube principle: the *water-tube boiler*. In this design, the majority of the boiler was again given over to the flue, but piping carrying the feedwater was trunked through the flue rather than the other way around. In the same way that fire-tube boilers significantly improved heating efficiency by increasing the heating area, water-tube boilers therefore represented an efficiency increase of another order of magnitude. Boilers of this design, however, were significantly more expensive and difficult to produce and maintain and therefore did not come into their own until late in the nineteenth century.[9] Innovations of both types were critical for providing a *consistent* flow of steam to the engine, rather than the uneven, jerky movement that often resulted with older boiler types.

Like early boilers, nineteenth-century engines were made of riveted wrought iron and changed gradually in the pursuit of greater efficiency. For example, an additional cylinder was added to the basic balance-beam concept as early as 1805. This made use of the steam exhausted from the first cylinder in the second, larger cylinder—effectively using the same steam twice (though to a reduced effect the second time).[10] This was the earliest version of the *compound engine*, and this principle would later be applied to a third cylinder in what became known as the *triple-expansion engine* in the 1870s (these are also referred to as *reciprocating* engines from here forward, primarily referring to *vertical* types).[11] Other types of engines were developed from these basic ideas that further improved valves or the power stroke of the engine itself for additional increases in efficiency, such as the Corliss engine in 1849 and the Porter-Allen engine in 1862.

It was in this environment of competing water- and fire-tube boiler designs and increasingly complex compound engines that the electric utility industry got started in the 1880s. While steam had already gone to sea as early as 1802, the birth of electrical power ashore accelerated developments in steam-power efficiency that both marine and electrical industries would utilize well into the next century.

THE BIRTH AND DEVELOPMENT OF THE ELECTRICAL UTILITY INDUSTRY

The half-century before high-steam technology came to the attention of the US Navy was also the defining formative period for electric utility industries in Europe and the Americas.[12] Throughout the 1880s, increasing demand for electrical power in urban areas and a reliance on DC transmission pressed young power companies to attempt to fit generating stations into increasingly crowded areas. Perhaps unsurprisingly, fitting enough capacity into small spaces to meet demand very quickly became a difficult engineering problem, with reciprocating engines exceeding about 5,000 horsepower (HP) being prohibitively large.[13] These difficulties were eased significantly in 1884 by the invention of the modern *turbine engine* by another Englishman, Sir Charles Parsons. Unlike the reciprocating engine, which acted through a cyclic stop-and-start motion, the turbine generated continuous rotary movement. Early turbines were *reaction turbines*, dependent on fixed-steam nozzles that exhausted steam into the blades of the turbine disc. Both the moving and alternating fixed rows of blades were designed to allow the steam moving through them to expand, imparting kinetic energy to the turbine disc while simultaneously lowering the pressure and temperature of the steam. This rotated the shaft and, by extension, directly turned the generator.[14] On average, these early turbines were capable of generating the same power as contemporary reciprocating engines at about one-third of the installation cost and one-tenth of the space (figure 1.1).[15]

Although the advantages of the turbine for power generation seem obvious, it did not immediately replace reciprocating engines. Turbines with

FIGURE 1.1. The reaction turbine. While not the first of its type invented, the reaction turbine created by Sir Charles Parsons was the first practical turbine engine that saw widespread adoption. Image NH 114985 courtesy of the Naval History and Heritage Command.

ratings above about 2,000 horsepower were completely untested prior to 1903 and were widely considered to be a significant safety risk. Additionally, the lifetime operating costs and overall efficiency of these early model turbines were inferior to contemporary reciprocating engines. As a result, onshore turbine use during the first decade of their existence was confined to very small power stations in Europe, particularly in the United Kingdom and Germany.[16] Two factors ultimately prompted the meteoric rise of the turbine engine for electricity generation: the invention of the compound *impulse turbine* by C. G. Curtis and the leap of faith taken by the Chicago Edison Company with its decision to order unprecedentedly large turbines in 1903.[17]

Unlike the pure reaction turbine, the impulse turbine relies on steam expansion within the nozzles (rather than the blades) to increase steam velocity. The blades themselves are curved, so that the change in direction of the steam jet forces a partial transfer of momentum to the rotating blades but the pressure remains constant.[18] Early impulse turbines consisted of only a single row of moving blades due to the nature of this effect, but Curtis designs added alternating rows of fixed and moving blades; the blades affixed to the turbine casing redirected the steam back onto the next row of moving blades to make further use of the initial velocity imparted by expansion in the nozzles. This process made significantly more efficient use of the energy contained in the steam, though this would again be improved later by a combination of impulse and reaction turbines on the same steam line (figure 1.2).[19]

While the aforementioned turbines that the Chicago Edison Company ordered were at the time not as efficient or cost-effective over their lifetimes as their reciprocating predecessors, the company was willing to take the risk on installing them as long as they were able to guarantee regular and consistent demand from their customers. In achieving this predictability, the turbine's own economies of space, weight, manpower, and startup cost would allow Chicago Edison to take on more customers without needing more space, thereby achieving an *economy of scale*. Additionally, due to its very nature, the turbine reaches its peak efficiency when running at a consistent and relatively high rate of revolutions per minute (RPM). Accordingly, to achieve an economy of scale and to guarantee a consistent high load for his turbines' efficiency, Chicago Edison needed to not only seek many customers but also diversify

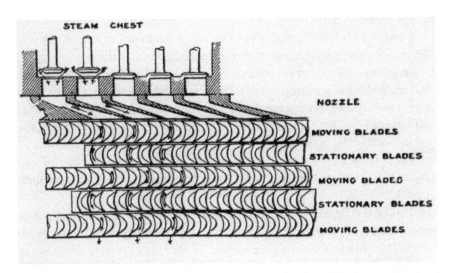

FIGURE 1.2. The impulse turbine. While C. G. Curtis developed the basic principle of the modern impulse turbine, Parsons himself adapted it only as the initial stages of his own turbine design before reverting to reaction sections. Image courtesy of Charles A. Parsons, *The Steam Turbine: The Rede Lecture, 1911*, 21–24.

the customers for each power station due to their different demands at different times of the day. By balancing these factors, a steady demand on the power station itself could be guaranteed and expansion properly planned.[20] This was ultimately to become the primary driving force behind technological change in the electrical utility industry through the 1930s and beyond.[21]

Simultaneously, around the beginning of the twentieth century, the American company Babcock & Wilcox became the champion of the water-tube boiler, whose popularity had rapidly grown. As noted previously, this boiler type had been around since the middle of the nineteenth century, but difficulties with its manufacture and high costs had long restricted its use. Advances in design had reduced the cost of water-tube installations to about twice that of a comparable fire-tube boiler by the 1890s, but what led to the rise of the former was the propagation of power stations throughout that decade.[22] Unlike fire-tube boilers, for power-generating purposes water-tube boilers did not require a large metal shell to contain the water and steam. Instead, the bulk of the boiler was given over to the flue itself and was often simply bricked-in—allowing the boiler to be more easily configured for whatever space was available. Additionally, the lack of a large metal pressure vessel not only eased maintenance access in these later designs but significantly improved safety (as there was less danger of a single, large, catastrophic loss of pressure via exterior damage). Finally, when paired with steam turbines, water-tube boilers proved significantly more flexible when the need to upgrade turbine size, capacity, or pressure arose to meet demands. In other words, the water-tube boiler was the perfect partner to the early turbine.[23]

By the 1920s, local pursuit of economies of scale was driving the development of many of America's regional power systems. Ever-increasing startup and operating costs in this pursuit were continuing to push the introduction of larger turbines and larger, even more diversified supply areas. Costs were, in fact, growing to the point of being prohibitively excessive. The result was the first instances of *rationalization* within the electrical utility industry: the search for the optimal combination of economic gains with a minimum input of economic resources. Developing electrical *grids* were reorganized so that new, more efficient generator systems carried the steady base loads, while older units were used only during peak hours. While this permitted greater tolerance of variances in demand on the electrical grid, it also substantially increased the need for labor during those peak hours.[24] The direct result was that the industry as a whole sought out innovation that promised both a more efficient use of capital and the reduction of labor demands.

This environment gave rise to the initial exploration of high-pressure, high-temperature steam in the American electrical utility industry.[25] The continuing demand for economies of power and size led the primary suppliers of boilers and turbines—Babcock & Wilcox, Westinghouse, General Electric, and others—to experiment with the theoretical increases in power to weight ratio promised by increases in the temperatures and pressures of steam in use.[26] The logic here is fairly straightforward; due to the fact that the energy produced by steam is proportional to its expansion within a turbine, a higher starting pressure should accordingly result in more energy from the same amount of steam. The catch was that such a change also promised to substantially alter the materiel requirements of the entire system.

At this stage, the most important motivators for the electrical utility industry's deployment of new and improved boilers and turbines are reasonably clear to us: good sustainability, a high power-to-weight ratio, and comparatively low manpower requirements. It was the further pursuit of these very qualities that gradually pushed steam pressures and temperatures higher into the 1930s and beyond.

However, by 1920, electrical supply had been an equal partner in the development of the steam-turbine system with maritime propulsion for twenty years. This partnership, stemming in large part from equal supply of boilers and turbines to either field by the very same manufacturers, had resulted in considerable technological overlap. The idea of high steam represented another instance of this transfer from shore to ship. However, though the principles of steam at sea were largely the same as those for power generation, the characteristics considered desirable for each led to a gradual divergence of the two systems.

SAILING AGAINST THE WIND

The advantages of steam propulsion over wind power were obvious from the beginning; breaking ships free from the whims of the wind and weather held out the promise of dramatically reduced travel times over long distances. Nevertheless, throughout the bulk of the nineteenth century, ocean-going ships remained dependent on wind for the majority of their motive power. The disadvantageous combination of low power-to-weight ratios and the poor fuel economy of early steam machinery, as well as the bulkiness of wood or coal fuel, meant that steam-powered ships were simply not economically viable.[27] Instead, the entry of steam power into the marine propulsion equation occurred on the interior waterways of the United States, where fuel was readily available.

The particular needs of marine propulsion dictated several significant alterations from land-based systems, even in this early form. Paradoxically, one of the most significant challenges was the acquisition of the water needed to make steam. While marine propulsion naturally had an unlimited water supply, shipping on *saltwater* presented serious challenges. Corrosion would not only reduce the efficiency of a propulsion system but also risked significant damage or even a highly destructive steam explosion. It was for this reason that land-based power stations were often located near freshwater sources that could satisfy their needs.

In addition to water requirements, marine propulsion also differed from shore-based power generation in that the piston itself needed to be connected to some form of propulsion without losing a significant amount of energy. In Robert Fulton's groundbreaking 1807 design, and for the majority of the nineteenth century thereafter, this took the form of a paddle wheel. While the quintessential river steamer would become recognizable by its one large paddle aft, the *North River Steamboat* foreshadowed ocean steamers to come with a pair of thinner paddle wheels on either side of the vessel roughly amidships. Initially, these were not directly linked to the piston. Rather, two vertical connecting rods linked the piston to an inverted-T lever beam, which, in turn, was connected by another rod to a crank on each paddle wheel's axle. This was soon simplified so that the first connecting rod directly cranked the axle—the first example of *direct drive* in marine propulsion.[28]

While paddle wheels were an adequate means of propulsion on inland waterways, the often-chaotic nature of ocean swells dramatically reduced their efficiency and increased vulnerability to damage. *Screw propellers*, the eventual successor to paddle wheels in nearly all types of ships, had been practically demonstrated as early as 1807. They did not effectively come into their own, however, until John Ericsson's arrival in the United States in 1839. The following year, the Swedish inventor was awarded a contract to design and build USS *Princeton*, a 1,000-ton screw sloop capable of a top speed of 13 knots.[29]

Screws such as the six-bladed model in use on *Princeton* were significantly more efficient than contemporary paddle wheels. Operating completely submerged, these devices were ideally suited to comparatively high rotational speeds—best lending them to the utilization of direct drive on a smaller engine placed low and aft within a ship. This led to the inversion of the piston and cylinder so that they acted directly on the crankshaft (now the propeller shaft). As we discussed in the previous section, this same period (1840–1860) witnessed the rapid rise of the fire-tube boiler and the compound engine, both of which rapidly made their way into naval designs. These factors, along with the rise of iron plating, resulted in a gradual but complete redesign of the oceangoing ship itself over the second half of the nineteenth century.

One of the most famous radical designs of the mid-nineteenth century is also one of the most instructive for our purposes: Ericsson's ironclad USS *Monitor*, designed and built rapidly for the US government in 1861–1862. *Monitor*'s engine drove a four-bladed screw and was powered by a pair of 40 PSI fire-tube boilers capable of generating steam for up to 8 knots. The ship had no auxiliary propulsion of any kind. Additionally, and unlike almost all other steam-driven vessels of the time, *Monitor* was fully enclosed by iron armor. This meant that the vessel's boilers (and the rest of the interior) lacked proper air circulation. This was remedied by an early example of steam-driven auxiliary machinery; the steam produced from *Monitor*'s boilers drove not only the main engine but also a pair of fans known as *blowers* that forced air through both the boilers and the interior of the ship. This became known as *forced draft*, and was the primary means of air circulation for all-metal steamers for the next half-century. Steam was also used to power *Monitor*'s bilge pumps and to rotate the ship's famous turret.

While *Monitor* was a unique design in many ways, the majority of the characteristics described above—direct-drive engine, screw propeller, fire-tube boilers, forced draft, and steam-driven auxiliary machinery—were to become universal among oceangoing steamers over the next few decades. To these innovations was added the marine surface condenser. Characterized by the large amount of cooling surface area achieved by running seawater through small tubes within the condenser itself, steam coming into contact with the tubes was not only kept separate from the corrosive effects of salt but also was more easily reused without much loss. This made the *closed feed system* possible, with only limited quantities of spare or distilled water required to be added throughout a given voyage, and even assisted open systems in keeping additional salt from being added to the feedwater during condensing. This was nothing short of a major breakthrough for naval engineering.[30]

THE MARINE TURBINE AND THE NEED FOR SPEED

By the 1890s, marine steam propulsion plants had evolved by necessity to be, on average, significantly more powerful and fuel efficient than their electric utility cousins. That state of affairs ended abruptly with the arrival of the turbine. While Parsons's invention first appeared in the 1880s, it did not make its way into the field of marine propulsion for another decade, and then only after a dramatic public stunt by Parsons himself. As was the case with utility reluctance to adopt turbines producing more than 2,000 horsepower, there was no automatic guarantee that the turbine would exceed existing marine engine designs in fuel economy, power, and reliability. In the end, the turbine would *not* beat the triple-expansion engine at its own game but instead would entirely change the terms of engine performance.

In 1893, Parsons founded the Parsons Marine Steam Turbine Company (later Parsons, Ltd.), based on his belief that the turbine represented the future of marine propulsion. To prove this, he and a group of investors designed and built the steam launch *Turbinia*, which was powered by a single water-tube boiler and three small reaction turbines of Parsons's design. The middle turbine operated at about 180 PSI, then exhausted into the two flanking turbines that operated at a lower pressure, making use of the same principle of expansion as other contemporary steam engines. The launch was capable of a top speed of 34.5 knots at a time when the average "high-speed" warship was unable to exceed 28 knots with engines running flat-out.[31] Though Parsons made the British Admiralty aware of *Turbinia*'s existence, he did not warn them that he planned to appear at the Royal Navy Review for Queen Victoria's Diamond Jubilee in the middle of 1897. There, he proceeded to race *Turbinia* between the assembled ranks of warships at speeds so high that the patrolling picket boats could not hope to catch him. The message to the world was loud and clear: the turbine promised speeds unprecedented in the history of marine propulsion.[32]

Parsons's primary challenge with his early turbine was the matter of economy and efficiency. In the case of older piston engines, the advanced forms of the compound and triple-expansion engine then in maritime service had achieved a considerable degree of economy across all speeds via their direct-drive connection to the propeller shafts. Turbines, and particularly early models, were most efficient only at *very* high rotational speeds. Power plants had dealt with this characteristic in part by searching for consistent loads to maintain this level of RPM, but an excessively high rotational rate of a propeller instead produces cavitation. This production of small vapor-filled cavities around the propeller blades reduces propeller efficiency and generates cyclic stress that results in excessive wear on the blades themselves. Parsons somewhat dealt with this issue in *Turbinia* by placing no fewer than *three* propellers on each of the three propeller shafts, but this only slightly mitigated the problem. Until this issue was resolved, turbines would have significant fuel economy deficiencies when compared to the reciprocating engines of turn-of-the-century vintage. They would also have to be quite large to reduce their rotor speed as much as possible.[33]

Despite the turbine's shortcomings, *Turbinia*'s sensational 1897 demonstration in the Solent prompted a serious investigation into the turbine's potential by both the Royal Navy and private investors. For the navy, the result was the equipping of two experimental torpedo-boat destroyers (themselves a very new class of warship) with turbines: HMS *Viper* (344 tons) and HMS *Cobra* (400 tons), both launched in 1899. While these vessels were highly inefficient from the standpoint of fuel and were quickly lost to unrelated accidents, at 36 knots they were substantially faster than any other torpedo-boat destroyers in the world.[34] In the commercial sector, the first turbine-powered vessel was *King Edward*, a highly successful excursion steamer built in 1901 that was of comparable size to *Viper* and *Cobra*. The single-shaft *King Edward* proved capable of 20.5 knots after modifications on her trials, seemingly proving once and for all that the turbine was suitable for all sorts of ships.[35]

It is principally with the arrival of the turbine that we begin to see divergence between military and commercial naval propulsion design. The raw power of the turbine with its accompanying high cost in fuel was immediately attractive for some military purposes, but its allure for civilian shipping was far more limited in scope. For the former, the commitment of the Royal Navy to the turbine with the battlecruiser concept and the legendary HMS *Dreadnought* in 1906–1907 indicated that nations needed to buy-in on speed or be left at the mercy of substantially faster foes. For commercial vessels, the speed of the turbine was at first promising only for what would become known as "express liners"—the high-speed passenger and mail trade. Since these vessels operated almost exclusively at high speeds, they alone were able to get the best economy out of their direct-drive turbines.[36]

Between 1907 and 1915, there were a number of minor advances in the design of turbines and water-tube boilers, primarily involving smoother steam circulation in the boilers, ease of maintenance, and increased room for steam expansion within the turbines. In general, the system continued to follow the same pattern set down by *Turbinia* (though without multiple propellers per shaft): a "high pressure" turbine would directly drive one propeller shaft, while its exhausted steam would drive one or more "low pressure" turbines on additional shafts. As before the rise of the turbine, service pressures continued to rise until they approached 280 PSI in World War I–era designs.

Two major innovations transformed the turbine system in the second decade of the twentieth century. The first was the gradual conversion from coal to oil fuel. Oil was naturally a more attractive fuel source than coal due to numerous factors, particularly its comparative superiority in energy content and ease of storage, transfer, and employment. Additionally, these advantages of oil meant that comparatively more fuel could be stored in the same amount of space, substantially improving endurance at a stroke. Only the lack of major oil reserves within national borders prevented the world's leading navy of the time, the British Royal Navy, from wholesale embracing oil fuel as quickly as others like the United States, which possessed significant reserves of its own.[37]

The advantages gained by the adoption of oil as the primary source of fuel were enhanced by the first major technical innovation of the marine turbine system that began appearing after 1910. This was the concept of the *reduction gear*: the interposition of a set of gearing between the turbine rotor and propeller shaft that allowed the turbine to rotate at a significantly higher speed than the shaft it was turning (figure 1.3). While this did not completely solve the question of how to operate a turbine and propeller at ideal speeds at all times, it substantially mitigated the inefficiencies of older direct-drive systems. It was also superior even to those vessels that had adopted the idea of an additional bypassable "cruising turbine" in an attempt to introduce some measure of economy at lower rotational speeds.[38] This carried the added benefit of allowing more than one turbine to be mated to the same propeller shaft, whereas previously their different rotational speeds would have prevented such a configuration. The idea of a multiple turbine-per-shaft arrangement is now referred to as a type of *cross-compounding* and would later become known as a turbine *set*. Unfortunately, the precision and strength of materials needed for the manufacture of such a system were difficult to come by at this stage in history. Therefore, the adoption of reduction gearing was slow initially, but over time it became the standard method of shaft linkage in navies around the world.[39]

The combination of the adoption of oil fuel, the reduction gear, and turbine "set" arrangements dramatically increased the efficiency of marine-turbine propulsion. Though it remained inferior to reciprocating engine

FIGURE 1.3. The reduction gear. By interposing gearing between the turbine rotor and the propeller shaft, each was able to rotate at a speed much closer to its ideal efficient speed. Initially connected only to cruising turbines, by the end of World War I, this principle had mostly supplanted cruising turbines in the world's navies. This particular reduction gear was built for a World War I–era destroyer. Image NH 115108 courtesy of the Naval History and Heritage Command.

systems with respect to raw endurance, by the end of World War I this no longer mattered much to the world's navies. Instead, further increases in the power and speed offered by turbine systems had displaced operating range as the primary objective of improvement in marine propulsion design.

Despite these developments, marine propulsion in military vessels around 1920 represented only incremental increases in pressure over those produced two decades earlier—about 270 PSI.[40] During this same time, when the marine-propulsion field had been attempting to recoup some of its losses in fuel efficiency so hard-won over the previous half-century, the electric-utility industry had begun commissioning equipment that depended on higher and higher pressures in the pursuit of economies of scale. Given their shared history and identical suppliers of electric utilities and commercial shipbuilders, it was therefore only a matter of time before the possibilities of higher-pressure turbine systems were seriously examined by naval designers.

WILLIAM F. GIBBS AND HIGH STEAM

Developments in civilian marine propulsion during the 1920s largely depended on the competing interests of range and speed; the former was most desirable in cargo vessels, while the latter was highly envied for passenger service. In this context, the decade before the Great Depression became a period of particular competition between traditional, single-reduction steam turbine systems and a relatively new innovation: the turbo-electric drive.

Turbo-electric systems have much more in common with their shore-based counterparts than most of the marine-power systems we have discussed. Their objective is not directly to move the ship but first and foremost to generate *power*. This power can be stored or used to operate auxiliary machinery but is primarily used to drive electric motors that themselves propel the ship. This avoidance of any direct linkage between turbine and propeller shaft allows each to operate at their ideal RPM without the need for any kind of reduction gearing. It also permits wide spacing between boiler, turbine, and motor rooms, thereby creating extra flexibility in hull design. However, both electric motors capable of matching geared turbine output for raw shaft horsepower and very high-pressure, very high-temperature steam (in excess of 280 PSI, 400°F) were the very cutting edge of propulsion technology in the early 1920s. As such, there were considerable teething problems with each, and it was not immediately clear which would be preferable for which purpose in the long run.[41]

Observing these developments in propulsion from afar was the American William Francis Gibbs. Although educated in law, Gibbs had long held a passion for naval design. He and his brother, Frederic, first became known in the maritime community when they proposed a 1,000-foot, 30-knot "superliner" design to the International Mercantile Marine Co. (IMM), a shipping trust founded by J. P. Morgan, in 1916. The eventual result was the founding of the naval design firm Gibbs Brothers in 1922.[42]

From the beginning, William Gibbs's ultimate goal was to build the swiftest civilian ship imaginable. Gibbs was obsessed with speed and was constantly on the prowl to learn how naval designers were pushing the envelope in this area.[43] Initially, this led to some enthusiasm first for diesel propulsion, then for the turbo-electric drive. As a result, both types of drives were fairly common in Gibbs Brothers designs of the 1920s.[44] Nevertheless, the first passenger liner actually *built* to one of William Gibbs's designs was SS *Malolo* in 1926, a single-reduction, single-screw ship that was capable of a surprising speed of 23 knots.[45]

In 1929, the Gibbs brothers hired experienced designer Daniel H. Cox and rebranded their company as Gibbs & Cox, Inc. With this name transformation came the general abandonment of diesel and turbo-electric propulsion designs in favor of high steam, which William seems to have become convinced was the optimum path to superior speed following *Malolo*'s success in service.[46] This shift was due in large part to some of the first successful examples of *double*-reduction gearing produced for naval purposes. As the name might imply, this set of gearing interposed an additional gear-and-pinion connection between the first and last stages of the single-reduction gear, drastically increasing the maximum RPM differential between a turbine and its associated propeller shaft. This, along with significant improvements in the design of the impulse turbine, dramatically improved the efficiency and decreased the size of the geared-turbine system—at least in theory.

The reader might recall that, even up through World War I, single-reduction gearing had remained problematic for the majority of manufacturers, and the implementation of an additional gear did nothing to alleviate these problems. Rather, the addition of this gearing substantially increased the precision and material requirements of marine-propulsion plants that utilized them. Despite these difficulties, in 1930 Gibbs & Cox designed four 17,000-ton *Santa Rosa*-class passenger vessels for the Grace Line that utilized steam at 375 PSI and 725°F.[47] Built at the Federal Shipbuilding and Drydock Company, these ships utilized General Electric–made compound impulse turbines that depended on their double-reduction gearing to operate at peak efficiency at this pressure. This was the entry of American shipping into the field of high steam.[48]

At the same time that the *Santa Rosa*-class passenger ships were beginning to enter service in 1932, the US Navy was beginning to commission its first class of post–World War I destroyers to replace the now twenty-year-old flush deck, 1,000-ton destroyers designed during that conflict. This design involved an attempt to increase the steam pressures in use in order to extend operational range. It was due to this pursuit, and having kept an eye on naval design activities of other nations, that Admiral Bowen and the navy's Bureau of Engineering quickly took notice of Gibbs & Cox's employment of high-pressure steam.[49] In 1933, after the contract winners for the next class of warships were determined to lack acceptable in-house design structures, Gibbs & Cox was contracted in their stead.[50] This began the transfer of machinery like the double-reduction gear from civilian to US Naval service.

As we shall see shortly, the environment of intense naval competition that characterized the 1930s led the various navies of the world down a variety of developmental paths. The majority of these did not lead to the successful large-scale use of high-steam propulsion systems. The US Navy has long appeared to be the exception to this rule. Yet despite the apparent compatibility with Gibbs & Cox's civilian experience, the different requirements of military service were to be the source of an increasing number of complications the navy was forced to compensate for in the late 1930s and early 1940s.[51] For while the navy wished to take advantage of the proven power and efficiency of a high-steam system, it wanted *both* qualities in large numbers and in a durable and compact package that would survive combat. The costs to achieve these goals would be much higher than anyone, including Admiral Bowen, anticipated.

Chapter 2

THE THROUGH TICKET TO MANILA

In 1884, the US Navy embarked on a crash course in modernization and construction, transforming itself from a relic of the late age of sail to a fully modern, steam-and-steel force. In the midst of this transformation, the New Navy was bloodied in a "splendid little war" with Spain—and had its strategic mission utterly transformed. For the first time in American history, the United States was obligated to defend territory *overseas*. In the case of the Philippines, this meant that radically new ideas were required to deal with the host of other powers in the Far East.

In 1905, the Imperial Japanese Navy annihilated the Russian Second Pacific Squadron at Tsushima and thereby became the most likely adversary for the United States in the Pacific. In the thirty-six years that followed, planning for a potential American-Japanese conflict evolved into the center of strategic effort for both navies. After 1918, their strategies, tactics, force design, and policy all stemmed from an overwhelming focus on solving the problems inherent in fighting a circum-Pacific war. For the United States, the ultimate question of this exercise was how (and even if) the navy could prevent a rapid Japanese conquest of the Philippines before the bulk of the American fleet could arrive from California. It was as part of this effort to build a fleet capable of swiftly deploying from the West Coast to the Philippines on the outbreak of war—initially dubbed the "Through Ticket to Manila"—that high steam was first embraced by Samuel Robinson, Harold Bowen, and the Bureau of Engineering.

THE BIRTH OF THE MODERN US NAVY, 1884–1900

Following the conclusion of the American Civil War, the US Navy was downsized, defunded, and left to its own devices. For a nation without any sort of permanent overseas commitments, this was not necessarily a catastrophic problem; the navy merely returned to the prosecution of its lifelong mission of commerce protection. As in the pre–Civil War era, this meant the shielding of American commercial interests from pirates and small-scale attacks wherever they might occur. While this required the deployment of ships to various stations around the world, it did not entail any real need to plan for combat with a first-class foreign navy. The lack of reliable, US-owned refueling stations also meant that this situation discouraged full conversion of the navy from sail to steam power on its slim postwar budget. The result was that when a crisis with Spain over Cuba arose in 1873, the US Navy consisted of only a handful of obsolete wooden sail-and-screw powered vessels and *Monitor*-derived coastal ironclads left over from the Civil War.[1]

In October 1873, the *Virginius*, an American-owned oceangoing paddle-wheel steamer, was captured while attempting to land reinforcements and munitions for Cuban revolutionaries seeking independence from the vestigial Spanish Empire. When the Spanish government began executing *Virginius*'s American crew on charges of piracy, a major diplomatic crisis between the United States and Spain ensued. In response, the US Navy attempted to rapidly concentrate a squadron of ships at Key West, Florida, for a show of force. The result was nothing less than a complete embarrassment for the Americans. Widespread propulsion breakdowns among the Navy's wooden hybrids and coastal ironclads initially prevented the squadron from assembling for several weeks. Once this had finally been accomplished, it quickly became clear that there were no established procedures for operating this mixed bag of vessels—each with substantially different armament and top speed—in concert with one another. Even if this had not been the case, the squadron of relics was completely outclassed by Spanish oceangoing ironclads.[2]

Although the *Virginius* Affair was resolved diplomatically, Congress ultimately responded to this revelation in 1883 with the authorization of the so-called ABCD ships: the protected cruisers USS *Atlanta*, USS *Boston*, USS *Chicago*, and the gunboat USS *Dolphin*. These vessels, which were followed in 1886 by the battleship USS *Texas* and armored cruiser USS *Maine*, were the first steel warships commissioned into the US Navy and therefore represented a crash course in pure steel-and-steam naval design and operations. The ABCD ships were powered by fire-tube ("Scotch Marine") boilers and compound engines, and *Maine* and *Texas* paired their boilers with state-of-the-art triple-expansion reciprocating engines, which had come into vogue by the late 1880s.[3] While these vessels overtly shared the same purpose of their earlier wooden cousins (i.e., the protection of US commercial interests from pirates), they were unique in that they were additionally intended to aid in the mission of coastal defense. The knowledge gained from the construction of these ships with an eye to foreign designs was then applied to the three much more advanced *Indiana*-class coastal battleships subsequently ordered in 1889, which were equipped with similar machinery to that aboard *Texas*.[4]

Although their low freeboard made the *Indiana*-class battleships unsuitable for blue-water combat, they were readily recognizable for what they were: weapons for employment against the best of what *any* enemy navy might be able to throw at them. This was a fact that did not escape congressional notice, and even as late as the 1880s this ran against the traditional American streak of isolationism that dominated much of Washington. These ships therefore faced considerable opposition from the more conservative elements in Congress, which saw the *Indiana*s as tools that could be easily turned to imperialistic pursuits by a motivated presidential administration. Nevertheless, the combat characteristics of foreign warships had improved so dramatically since the *Virginius* Affair that Congress eventually relented and authorized the navy to build three *Indiana*s for coastal defense—just in time for the long-foreshadowed war with Spain over Cuba to finally erupt.

The events of the War of 1898 were every bit as dramatic and momentous for the US Navy as they seemed to the public of the time. Spanish squadrons were overwhelmed and destroyed off Manila and Santiago by steel American warships that had been only a dream fifteen years earlier. But while the public focused on the long-awaited US "liberation" of Cuba, what wasn't as widely appreciated (or even desired) was the momentous significance of the additional inheritance from Spain of the Philippine islands. For it was the defense of the Philippines, not Cuba, that would utterly transform the mission of the US Navy for the next half century.

Forming the eastern edge of the South China Sea, the Philippines were ideally located for a colonial power looking to solidify its position in the all-important China trade. Commercial interest in China had been a significant feature of American commerce for more than a century by the time of the Spanish-American War. Maintaining the American Open Door policy there was part-and-parcel to the US Navy's commerce protection mission, and the result was that a squadron of American warships had been based at whatever friendly port in the region would have them in the decades before and after the American Civil War.[5]

In April 1898, the American Asiatic Squadron was based out of British-controlled Hong Kong, from which it sailed for Manila Bay to confront the Spanish on the outbreak of war. Commodore George Dewey's relatively easy victory there (and the foreign warships observing his activities thereafter) persuaded William McKinley's government to take advantage of the opportunity the Philippines offered to break free from dependence on the goodwill of other powers for operations in the region. Spain was thus compelled to cede control of the Philippines, along with Cuba, Puerto Rico, and Guam, to the United States in 1899. While the initial result was the continuation of the ongoing Filipino quest for full independence in the form of the 1899–1902 Philippine-American War, by 1903 the Americans had consolidated control of their own Asian outpost. Henceforth, responsibility for the islands' defense came to rest squarely on the shoulders of the US military.[6]

For a navy that had previously been designed with commerce protection and coastal defense in mind, the protection of the Philippines represented a fundamental shift in priorities. While the goodwill of other nations could generally be relied upon for refueling purposes by a navy whose primary mission was the suppression of piracy, they could not be relied upon in the event of actual war with a major navy. Manila is more than six thousand nautical miles from San Francisco; the *Indiana*-class battleships had a design range of only five thousand nautical miles.[7] Warships traveling to the "Asia Station" would either need to make numerous refueling stops en route at American bases or be planned from the keel-up to substantially increase their operating range. Essentially all major American warships of this era had been designed around a coastal defense mission that did not require long range. While new ships of all types were joining the fleet between 1900 and 1920, they did not quickly benefit from substantial design upgrades due to the length of the review and construction process. Instead, the fleet's range deficiency was addressed through the claiming of Wake Island in 1899 and the construction of coaling stations there and on the war prize of Guam soon thereafter.[8]

A third critical link in this supply chain was Hawaii, which had been the object of American interest for decades prior to the Spanish-American War. Nominally an independent island kingdom, Hawaii had come to be economically dominated by the American-owned sugar industry, which had rapidly expanded and thrived following the signing of a US-Hawaiian reciprocity treaty in 1876. In 1893, the minority white planters overthrew Queen Liliuokalani and petitioned the US government for annexation in part to ease tariffs on their sugar exports to the continent. While Grover Cleveland's election as president would derail this effort for four years, growing American interest in the islands as an economic stepping stone to Asia (and in Pearl Harbor as a naval base) meant that the archipelago's days of independence were almost certainly numbered.[9]

However, the McKinley administration that came into office in 1897 had another problem with which it had to contend in its resumption of the quest for Hawaiian annexation: the rising power and interests of Imperial Japan. While there were nearly seven thousand white residents in the Hawaiian Islands by the mid-1890s, immigration had brought some twenty-five thousand Japanese—mainly to serve as laborers on the white-owned sugar plantations. The renewed US annexation efforts in 1897 were thus met with emphatic protests by the Japanese government over both American rights to the islands and the heavy discrimination that Japanese nationals faced. Although diplomatic tensions ran high on this issue in 1897, they would be brushed aside by both parties the following year as matters of greater importance took priority. For the United States, it was the war with Spain. For Japan, it was the increase in German and Russian activity in northeastern China. Regardless, the Hawaiian Crisis is regarded as the first of a number of major diplomatic crises between these two rising powers.[10]

THE JAPANESE RIVALRY AND WAR PLAN ORANGE

American interest in preserving commercial access to the Far East with the "Open Door" was far from unique; China was a major theater for international competition in the late nineteenth century. Britain, France, Germany, Russia, and Japan all had significant interests of their own in the region. While relations between these powers were by rule somewhat chaotic, following the international suppression of the Boxer Rebellion between 1899 and 1901, several events occurred in rapid succession that had a lasting impact on the geopolitical situation. The first was the Anglo-Japanese alliance of 1902 leading to the acceleration of an ongoing naval technology transfer to the quickly industrializing Japanese. The second event was the shockingly decisive Japanese victory over the Russian Navy at Tsushima only three years later.

Japan was not considered one of the traditional great powers in 1905, but what it had accomplished in the previous fifty years was nothing short of remarkable. When American Commodore Matthew C. Perry's four-ship squadron arrived off Edo (Tokyo) in mid-1853, Japan was 250 years into the Tokugawa shogunate, a feudal-military dictatorship that had enforced strict isolationism (and late-medieval technology) for much of its existence. Perry's success in forcing the Japanese government at gunpoint to agree to trade concessions—which was quickly copied by the great powers—was essentially the swan song for the shogunate. Within fifteen years, the resulting "Meji Restoration," named for its consolidation of power under the Emperor Meji, was complete. In the course of the following four decades, Japan completely remade itself in the image of the great powers. By the dawn of the twentieth century, this process of societal transformation had catapulted Japan far enough into the industrial era that it no longer had to purchase all of its modern military equipment from foreign suppliers.[11]

However, in 1900, Japan was not yet self-sufficient enough to design and build the most sophisticated (and rapidly changing) military technology of the time: modern warships. Considerable foreign expertise was required to expedite the expansion of the Imperial Japanese Navy (IJN), which was seen as absolutely necessary to fully protecting the country from further Perry-like predatory treaties. While the United States, France, and Germany all supplied some equipment to the IJN, it eventually became clear that for maritime knowledge Japan would be best served by learning from that undisputed master of the seas since Trafalgar: Great Britain. Therefore, the beginning of the twentieth century found the IJN equipped with a preponderance of warships designed and built in British shipyards.[12]

Like its western models, during this period Imperial Japan sought to carve out its own sphere of influence in the Korean Peninsula and Manchuria at Qing China's expense. This quickly brought about a collision with Tsarist Russia, which had similar designs on the region. The result was the 1904–1905 Russo-Japanese War, when Japan shocked the world by completely destroying the Russian forces arrayed against it. The most significant action of this conflict was the climactic engagement of the naval campaign, the Battle of Tsushima, in late May 1905. In the course of this action, the Imperial Japanese Navy overwhelmed and destroyed the Russian Second Pacific Squadron—virtually the entire remaining force of Russian capital ships—in a single day.

Tsushima fundamentally altered both the balance of power in East Asia and the ways in which *all* of the major powers approached naval warfare.[13] The battle itself had primarily been an action between heavily armored battleships, with the largest guns of the Japanese fleet dealing the decisive blows. With Russian naval power in the region effectively destroyed, the Japanese had nearly complete control of local waters, securing their supply lines and providing them with the ability to move troops by sea wherever they pleased. These effects ensured that Tsushima came to be viewed internationally as the quintessential "decisive battle" in the same vein as Nelson's victory at Trafalgar had a century earlier: a model fleet engagement the likes of which must be sought in modern war. The resulting doctrinal importance of the Tsushima-like battle would wane in some major navies after the Battle of Jutland failed to prove decisive in 1916. But it would remain utterly central to the Imperial Japanese Navy throughout the interwar period as enshrined in its Kantai Kessen, or Decisive Battle Doctrine. All of Japan's naval war plans between the wars thus ultimately revolved around winning a single, climactic, and overwhelmingly decisive engagement.[14]

By 1906, the diplomatic situation in the Far East had thus fundamentally shifted. Russia had been eliminated as a military power in the region and would not come close to replacing its naval losses before the two revolutions of 1917. France and Germany commenced significant naval construction programs in the first decade of the twentieth century but concentrated the majority of their new forces in European waters as tensions there escalated. For its part, Britain, having secured an uneasy alliance with Japan and a mutual understanding with the United States, retired most of its elderly capital ships that had previously patrolled the Western Pacific. Their replacements, which were part of a major structural overhaul initiated following the investiture of Jackie Fisher as first sea lord in 1904, would remain in Europe with very few exceptions. This essentially left the United States and Japan as the only major naval powers in the Pacific theater, and it would not be long before these two once again found themselves at loggerheads.[15]

In 1906 and 1907, racial tensions between white landowners and immigrant Japanese laborers flared in California. Enraged by race riots and the passage of racial segregation laws there, the Japanese government began publicly airing its grievances with Washington. But unlike the crisis over Hawaii, Japan was flushed with its recent victory over Tsarist Russia—a major European power—and was now perceived as a much greater military threat to the United States than had previously been the case. While this confrontation would not actually lead to armed conflict, it permanently altered the US Navy's perception of Japan. For the first time, the USN was forced to seriously consider how it would manage a war with Japan in the *Western* Pacific over the Philippines, which was now US territory.[16]

The defense of overseas possessions acquired by the United States following the Spanish-American War quite simply required a degree of strategic analysis and planning that the existing navy bureaucracy was not equipped to carry out. While the navy's bureau system was capable of handling basic administration, it was unable to provide a united, strategic vision much beyond day-to-day tasks.[17] Such a job fell instead to the secretary of the navy, a political appointee whose ideas were not always likely to survive a single presidential administration.

In recognition of this fact and of widely publicized planning failures in the Spanish-American War, the McKinley administration in March 1900 established the General Board of the Navy. Composed primarily of a variable number of high-ranking flag officers as well as junior admirals or captains considered to be "promising," the basic motivation behind the general board's creation was to facilitate planning in the same way that a general staff did for armies. Politically, the extreme territoriality of the existing bureaus and their congressional allies ensured that the board would never rise above its nebulous mission to "advise the secretary." Yet—perhaps thanks in large part to the inclusion of Admiral Dewey—the general board quickly became an important strategic planning organization. In conjunction with the Naval War College in Newport, Rhode Island, the board guided the navy's nascent war planning process and resulting strategic direction throughout the first four decades of its existence. Throughout this period, the board's power became increasingly focused on directing technological development toward solving the navy's most difficult problems.[18]

In the spring of 1910, in the aftermath of the California crisis and the famous cruise of the Great White Fleet (itself begun as a rehearsal for the onerous task of moving the entire US fleet from the Atlantic to the Pacific to defend the Philippines), the general board undertook a formal study of how a war with Japan would unfold. This study was soon integrated into the larger color-coded US war planning process of the first half of the twentieth century. The United States was always known as "Blue" in these plans, while Japan was referred to as "Orange." Thus, the plan for war with Japan, which emerged from this initial general board study, became known as "War Plan Orange" or the "Orange Plan."[19]

From the beginning, the primary strengths of the opposing sides were clear to both American and Japanese planners. Japan had a consolidated geographic position—the home islands and strategic interests all lay in the same region of the Western Pacific—which meant that the Japanese fleet was nearly always concentrated or could be concentrated rapidly for major operations. On the other hand, while the US Navy was all but immune from any sort of Japanese surprise attack on its East Coast bases in 1910, it would take considerable time to concentrate the bulk of the fleet and move it to the Pacific (although the completion of the Panama Canal aided this process). Only the ultimate destruction of German naval power after World War I eventually allowed the United States to concentrate the bulk of its fleet on the West Coast in peacetime. Regardless, both sides expected that any Blue-Orange war would be initiated with a sudden, swift strike by Japan. Even after the move of the fleet to California, this supposition would remain—and would prove accurate in 1941.[20]

Regardless of how a war between the United States and Japan might start, the universal belief was that the ensuing fight would consist of three phases. In the first phase, Japan would move to occupy the Philippines quickly before the US fleet could interfere. How the United States attempted to respond to this action in the second phase of the conflict served as the primary variable in War Plan Orange. Whether the Philippines were occupied by Japan or held out for the arrival of reinforcements, both the United States and Japan assumed that the eventual arrival of the American fleet in the Western Pacific would result in a Tsushima-like decisive battle somewhere in the vicinity of the Ryukyu Islands in the third phase. If the United States was successful, the blockade and siege of Japan would then follow. Japanese planning efforts throughout the interwar period were dedicated toward the development of a means by which Japan might wear down the US fleet before it could arrive for the decisive battle. In 1942, this took the form of a defensive perimeter of interlocking air bases established during the opening phases of the Pacific War. The Americans were correspondingly focused on finding ways to preserve their strength for the final showdown . . . at least at first.[21]

While the basic structure of a Blue-Orange war was never particularly in doubt for either side, the middle phase of the American plan—that is, how (or if) the US fleet would relieve the Philippines and come to grips with the Japanese fleet—was vigorously debated. The general board in conjunction with the Naval War College concluded in its earliest studies that there were three primary options for this phase.

The first option was to construct a heavily fortified base (an "American Gibraltar," in reference to that idealized British bastion) that could hold out until the US fleet arrived. Such a base would ideally be well-defended from both its seaward and landward approaches and would be equipped with the substantial facilities necessary to carry out major maintenance and repair tasks, such as a dry dock capable of handling capital ships. This was an expensive proposition and relied upon the existence of a defensible port that could be fortified.[22]

Second was a gradual approach familiar to students of World War II history. Rather than incur the risks inherent in a mad rush to get the fleet across the Pacific in one movement, this option called for the United States to gradually conquer its way to the Philippines, seizing and fortifying new anchorages of its own in various Japanese-held island chains in the Pacific. While this approach was considered safer for the fleet, it also risked taking a *considerable* amount of time that the American public might not be willing to stomach before clamoring for a return to peace. Further complicating this plan before World War I was the fact that most suitable anchorages in the Central Pacific belonged to neutral powers like Imperial Germany. Proponents of this strategy have come to be referred to as "cautionaries."[23]

The third option was the reverse of the cautionary strategy: to rush the fleet to an improvised (rather than fortified) Philippine base as rapidly as possible in the hope that the fleet would move quickly enough (and local defenses would hold long enough) for the navy to arrive before Japan fully occupied the islands. This was the "Through Ticket to Manila" strategy (so-named for its initial 1923–1925 objective), whose proponents are retroactively known as "thrusters." While this strategy held a number of inherent dangers and challenges, its adherents claimed that the preservation of the Philippines as a base from which to sortie for the final, decisive battle was a means by which victory could be purchased much more cheaply in time, men, and material than any other method. It was also this cheapness, thrusters argued, that made the "Through Ticket" the only *politically* viable strategy to defeat Japan.[24]

Of these three approaches, both the general board and the Naval War College favored the "bastion" strategy in the initial studies of 1910–1911. With the bulk of the fleet based on the East Coast to counter European threats, this seemed to offer the only plausible way to hold out against the Japanese until the fleet could arrive in the Western Pacific. While a cursory investigation of Subic Bay in the Philippines had already proven it was unsuitable as a location for this base by the time the general board took up the subject, the belief was growing that Apra Harbor on Guam was ideally suited to the bastion role. Major investment in Apra was therefore advocated by the board, along with an accordingly significant buildup of Pearl Harbor in Hawaii. Both of these sites, the board argued, would be required for the Blue fleet to coal, repair, and otherwise resupply, ensuring that it would arrive in the Blue-Orange battle area of the Ryukyus prepared to fight—regardless of whether the Philippines had held out.[25]

World War I interrupted this planning process. While the United States was neutral until 1917, Japan joined the Entente in 1914 in fulfillment of its obligations under the Anglo-Japanese alliance. As the European participants in the Great War had the majority of their naval assets concentrated in Europe, the IJN represented the most powerful active force in the Pacific by a wide margin between 1914 and 1918. Germany's Pacific possessions in Micronesia and at Tsingtao in China were, as a result, occupied by Japanese forces in relatively short order. After the war was concluded, the islands seized in the Western Pacific—which included most of the Mariana islands surrounding Guam—were officially granted to Japan by the League of Nations as the South Seas Mandate.

The Japanese Mandate had serious implications for War Plan Orange. Lying directly in the path that any American fleet bound for Guam *or* the Philippines would have to take, the seized islands promised to be both a critical asset for Japanese planners and a dangerous obstacle for the United States. Should the islands be fortified preemptively, they might serve as a major source of the attrition attacks that the Japanese planned to make on American forces in the event of a Blue-Orange war. Proponents of the fortified western bastion approach to War Plan Orange therefore believed that the mandate further underscored the need to establish and fortify a secure base for the US fleet. However, the vast resources that this would require collided with a radically altered public attitude toward military spending in the immediate aftermath of the Great War. The result would permanently alter the US Navy and set the stage for high steam.[26]

THE WASHINGTON NAVAL TREATY

Despite growing international disgust with armed conflict following the end of World War I, the years immediately following the war featured a resumption of warship construction projects that had been authorized before 1914. This naval-arms race primarily featured complex and expensive battleships with ever-larger weapons that quickly began to overstrain the weakened postwar economies of Europe as well as the significantly smaller resources of Japan. This confluence of circumstances ultimately led diplomats from a large number of powers to the negotiating table in Washington in 1921.

The treaties produced by this conference and its successors (Washington in 1922, London in 1930, and London again in 1936) each defined substantial limitations that all of its signatories agreed to abide by until their next meeting. Most famous among the earliest agreements was undoubtedly the 5:5:3 battleship tonnage ratio between the United Kingdom, United States, and Japan. But equally—if not even more significant—were moratoriums on the construction of many types of warships and the institution of a complete ban on Pacific island fortifications.[27]

The ban on fortifications—which included "unfortified" refueling bases—was a powerful direct rebuke of proponents of the bastion strategy and ultimately doomed that approach altogether despite protestations that Japan might secretly fortify the mandate anyway.[28] In the renewed debate over the Orange Plan that followed, the offensive campaign plan instead came to be a political football exclusively passed between the thruster and cautionary camps. While a climactic naval battle to conclude the campaign remained a point of consensus despite the misgivings produced by the inconclusive Battle of Jutland, interwar-era War Plan Orange would be fundamentally characterized by disagreement over what speed of advance was militarily wise *and* politically viable. It would also complete the navy's turn toward technological solutions to strategic problems initiated by the general board. After 1923, this matter of solving the Orange Plan's operational and tactical problems would absorb all of the board's energy, while control of the Plan itself was ceded to the Joint Army and Navy Board.[29]

While the cautionaries briefly held sway in the immediate aftermath of the Washington Naval Conference, the greater political influence of the thrusters soon made itself known. Ironically, with the tremendous downsizing of the navy following the establishment of the Treaty system, this clout instead lay with the army. The early 1920s featured Leonard Wood's appointment as governor-general of the Philippines and General John "Black Jack" Pershing's investiture as chair of the Joint Board. Both of these men firmly believed in both the American empire and the ability of the reformed army to hold Manila until relieved by the navy's arrival. This argument, along with the sympathetic ear lent by the Republican administrations of the era, meant that after 1923 the "Through Ticket" strategy became the favored approach to a Blue-Orange war. Ultimately, this would not be the underlying logic behind the actual campaign carried out during the Pacific War, as the cautionaries would manage to upset the apple cart in 1934 after Admiral William H. Standley—a former cautionary war planner himself—was appointed chief of naval operations by the incoming

Roosevelt administration. However, the extreme logistical demands of the "Through Ticket" plan resulted in a number of enduring operational and design innovations that *did* become part of the war effort. Among these were experiments with underway refueling, the eventual expansion of the fleet logistical train, the development of large floating dry docks and rapid base-building methods, and the long operational ranges promised by high-steam propulsion.[30]

It was therefore in fulfillment of the needs of War Plan Orange that the Bureau of Engineering under Admirals Samuel Robinson and Harold Bowen began their push for greater range through their adoption of high steam in the early 1930s. To them, this approach was not unique for the times; all available evidence indicated that high steam was a hot commodity among other major navies. As we step into their shoes, we must therefore explore not only why they needed to find a way to increase the US fleet's range but also why *high steam* seemed to be the best way to do that. That is the subject of the next chapter.

Chapter 3

CROSSROADS

In the late 1920s and early 1930s, the success of high steam in the electrical utility industry prompted serious interest in applying the same technologies to merchant and warship propulsion. Initial experiments in merchant ships were carried out in pursuit of either high speed at a reasonable fuel cost or operating range at an economical machinery size. This represented a significant departure from the shore-based pursuit of raw production capacity for developing regional power grids. In the same way that the original adoption of the turbine had promised much greater speed, higher pressures and temperatures appeared to promise that speed with unprecedented fuel economy. However, just as translating power-generation equipment from a power plant to a civilian ship posed significant environmental challenges, moving high steam from a passenger liner to a warship had its own complications. These were evident in the experience of the various Washington Naval Treaty system signatories with high steam.

As was mentioned in the introduction and will be discussed in the next chapter, the American employment of elevated steam pressures and temperatures represented just one component of a complex overall system. For the United States, the intent was to leverage higher pressure and temperature steam into the longer operational reach that war planning for the Pacific made desirable. This was in part carried out by Admiral Bowen and his staff at BuEng under the belief that a number of foreign navies had already proven high steam to be both practical and desirable for similar reasons.

It was true that the British, Japanese, French, and German navies all experimented with significantly elevated steam temperatures and pressures in the interwar period, while the Italians alone did not.[1] However, each of these navies were motivated by radically different sets of strategic, operational, and tactical challenges, and as a result they approached high steam in the pursuit of *entirely different* advantages. Nevertheless, the collective trials and ultimate judgments passed by these nations in this technological field have a story to tell us about why the United States was the sole nation to make a full commitment to a fleshed-out system. A review of these stories will also provide us with useful perspectives on what actually went wrong with the American approach that cannot otherwise be divined from Admiral Bowen's account alone.

BRITAIN: DEFENDING AN EMPIRE

The British Royal Navy pioneered sending the turbine to sea aboard warships in the first years of the twentieth century. Early successes in this endeavor had been significant enough that Parsons, Ltd., the creator of the marine reaction turbine, went on to become one of the world's leading naval suppliers of the period.[2] However, the aftermath of World War I left the Royal Navy with a limited number of vessels with which it could meet its global commitments. As a result, Britain opted to retain its World War I–era propulsion systems with minor improvements throughout the interwar period in order to save money and guarantee reliability. While the British would eventually embrace significant increases in steam temperatures and pressures, this would not happen until 1942. It also came in isolation from other attendant technological improvements that other powers (specifically the US Navy) believed would offer better results.

Experimentation by the Royal Navy with components of what we might now recognize as a high-steam system began much earlier than other major navies—during its 1910–1911 building program. In this (and in many cases across the world thereafter), *destroyers* were chosen as the testbed for experimental technologies. These vessels were the smallest, newest, cheapest, and most numerous oceangoing warships present in major navies at this time.[3] The I-class destroyers authorized under this program featured partial single-reduction gearing and a concept known as *superheat* in an attempt to increase both the efficiency and durability of their propulsion systems, respectively. These vessels also contained early examples of military cross-compounding (the separation of main turbines into several separate sections *per shaft*, creating a turbine "set").[4]

Extremely high-pressure and high-temperature steam would not have been possible without the development of the superheat concept. In principle, this is a second heating of steam after it has been produced in a boiler. The intent is to remove all remaining liquid water in the system (thereby creating 100 percent "dry" steam) and then to boost the temperature above this point to the level desired. In the case of the I-class vessels, superheat was obtained by directing the already-generated steam back through the boiler one additional time.[5] This was known as *integral* superheat. The main deficiency of an integral-type superheater was that it proved difficult to carefully regulate the exact temperatures and pressures being emitted from the superheater outlet. Here, this issue was offset by the fact that dry steam was sought to reduce wear in the system, rather than to boost temperature. Steam in these vessels generated by their Yarrow straight-tube boilers reached around 220 PSI but had a variable temperature of more than 200°F.[6]

While one might expect the Royal Navy to have continued experimenting with superheat once it had been introduced, this did not occur. The excessive number of vessels built during World War I, coupled with the introduction of the Naval Treaty system after 1922 and Britain's worldwide network of naval bases, meant there was no immediate need for new vessels, nor were substantive improvements in vessel propulsion urgently required. The Royal Navy *did* build new destroyers and cruisers during this period, but the destroyers in particular exhibited only a gradual increase to 290 PSI in a few instances in the 1924 building program and 300 PSI in the A class of the 1927 program. Temperatures remained in the 200–300°F range, and single reduction gearing was retained. In fact, very few changes were made in Royal Navy propulsion at all outside of occasional experimentation with an extra "cruising" turbine intended to be used at intermediate speeds. This offered a limited increase in the fuel efficiency of some early Royal Navy destroyers but was often omitted from later designs as unnecessary due to gains in efficiency elsewhere.[7]

Part of the aforementioned A class of 1927 vintage was the Royal Navy's lone experiment with significantly increased temperatures and pressures of the interwar period: HMS *Acheron* (H45), a 1,350-ton standard, Parsons-powered, single-reduction vessel that was capable of generating 500 PSI and 750°F steam and possessing a range of approximately 4,800 miles at 15 knots.[8] Considered costly, unnecessary, and unreliable at the time, *Acheron*'s "Thornycroft Special" boilers actually resulted in a lower shaft horsepower and speed than the rest of the A class, albeit at a reduced displacement and roughly a 7 percent increase in fuel efficiency overall. *Acheron* otherwise did not exhibit any major advantages over its siblings, resulting in the much more conservative climb to 400 PSI in subsequent ships equipped with Admiralty three-drum boilers, until World War II was well underway.[9]

It was only with the loss of access to numerous bases and the increasing importance of range and overall fuel economy that British design priorities would begin to place an increasing emphasis on improving these qualities. In the attempt to increase the ranges of Royal Navy warships, particularly destroyers, the *Battle*- and *Weapon*-class destroyers of 1942 featured a leap to 500 PSI and 750°F, and the 1944-designed *Daring* could claim 650 PSI and 850°F.[10] However, by this point the Royal Navy had lost its technological edge in steam propulsion to the US Navy. Even as dramatic increases in steam pressures and temperatures were ultimately achieved, single-reduction gearing and integral-type superheaters and the hard limits to efficiency they represented were retained. As we shall see, the US Navy had by this stage experimented with a number of additional innovations intended to increase efficiency, power, and range that had long become central components of its high-steam system. This eventually led to a partial reliance on American machinery that saw many British vessels equipped not with Admiralty three-drum boilers but with those produced by Babcock & Wilcox.[11]

Ultimately, until World War II dramatically changed the circumstances of the Royal Navy, the British did not vigorously pursue high steam beyond the basic superheat concept due to a lack of perceived need and a sensitivity to the risks that such a change represented. Durability and reliability were the most important qualities sought by British designers, which in light of limited funding between the wars directed a focus on tried-and-true designs with only marginal improvements. The British experience with high steam in the interwar years can therefore be characterized as a disinclination to pursue what was perceived as unnecessary (and slight) improvements in range that would come only at an unpalatable increase in unit costs and operational risk.

JAPAN: PREPARING FOR THE DECISIVE BATTLE

As discussed in the previous chapter, the Imperial Japanese Navy (IJN) had, by the time of World War II, existed in its modern form for only about fifty years. During that time, the force had managed to advance from complete reliance on outdated, foreign-built weapons and machinery to license-built, then finally homegrown products that could in some areas even claim to be the best of their kind in the world. However, while the IJN was able to catch up to the state-of-the-art in steam propulsion as it stood in 1914, it was there that it largely remained until World War II. This was primarily because the Kantai Kessen (Decisive Battle Doctrine) initially predicted a final showdown between the IJN and USN off the Ryukyu islands, although this location gradually shifted outward toward the Marianas throughout the 1930s into 1940.[12] Nevertheless, the expectation of needing to fight only in relatively close proximity to the Japanese Home Islands led the IJN to view high steam as a high-risk, low-reward project with no relevance to the expected decisive battle. Instead, the Japanese fleet emphasized individual ship qualitative superiority and high tactical speed.[13]

In the category of propulsion, from 1914 through most of the Pacific War, the IJN relied on the *Ro-Gō Kampon* boiler, a cylindrical water-tube boiler that operated at 284 PSI using saturated steam, comparable to (though perhaps not as durable as) contemporary British designs.[14] While this opened the window for further experimentation such as that which the Royal Navy carried out with the *Acheron* in the 1927 program, the Japanese quest for higher tactical speed instead led them to increase the size and potential of their turbines. The effective culmination of their resulting superiority in this area was the *Nagato*-class (pre-treaty) battleships, capable of developing 80,000 shaft horsepower with their *Kampon* turbines. These vessels could reach up to 27 knots compared to the American battleship standard of 21 knots at that time.[15]

In addition to their desire for high-tactical speed in their capital ships, the Japanese also had a slightly different philosophy in regard to their destroyers and cruisers. While high speed was still considered extremely attractive, the decisive battle thinking that had grown out of Tsushima also valued the ability to use torpedo craft to "whittle down" any prospective (American) force before the decisive clash that would decide it all.[16] This would eventually result in focused experimentation with superheated steam in the early 1930s; the *Mogami*-class cruisers and *Hatsuharu*-class destroyers were designed to produce steam at 312 PSI and 572°F via integral-type superheaters. With limited but encouraging results in fuel consumption and durability, steam pressures and temperatures were increased again in the *Kagerō*-class destroyers and *Shōkaku*-class aircraft carriers in the late 1930s, which operated at 426 PSI and 662°F. With a very small number of exceptions (such as the destroyer *Shimakaze*), this remained the standard pressure and temperature for all new IJN vessels until the force's dissolution following World War II.[17]

Despite some experimentation with cruising turbines to improve low-power efficiency, the Japanese remained tied to unpredictable, integral-type superheaters and additionally maintained the British practice of utilizing single-reduction gearing for their turbines due to its relative simplicity. While this allowed for a higher turbine speed than would have been otherwise practical, it also continued to produce propeller speeds significantly above what would have been most efficient for both power and fuel. This limited the effectiveness of Japanese developments in fuel efficiency, though there were definite improvements in this category throughout the 1930s merely from the increases in pressures and temperatures.[18] While Japanese machinery continued to produce remarkably high horsepower ratings compared to its western counterparts, it did so by using significantly larger machinery than its US opponents, which left less hull-space for fuel bunkerage or other purposes. Thus, while remaining relatively conservative, IJN experimentation with higher steam pressures and temperatures was far ahead of their Royal Navy counterparts.

FRANCE: SPEED ABOVE ALL ELSE

Of special interest to us among the navies of the interwar period is the French Marine Nationale (MN, literally "national navy"), which utilized high-pressure steam in all major warships ordered after 1929. In keeping with the pattern we have observed in the British and Japanese navies, MN steam experiments were primarily carried out in destroyers. In this case, the technology was developed in the pursuit of increased speed and operational range and eventually included a number of innovations paralleled only by developments in the US Navy. The result was a well-known series of exceptionally large and fast ships of this type. However, while the French high-steam system seemed to hold significant promise, it never lived up to the range that expectations placed upon it and proved exceptionally fragile in operation. Development was also slowed by production delays and financial restrictions that impeded the entire French interwar shipbuilding program. This effort ceased after the German occupation began in 1940.[19]

France was unique in the interwar period for its employment of two types of destroyers with distinctly different roles. *Torpilleurs d'escadre* ("fleet torpedo boats" or TEs) were comparable to the destroyers of other nations and ranged between 1,300 and 1,500 tons standard. These vessels were designed primarily to make torpedo attacks and only secondarily intended to disrupt the attacks of enemy flotilla craft. *Contre-torpilleurs* ("anti-torpedo boats" or CTs), on the other hand, were very large destroyers of 2–3,000 tons standard. Ships of this type were specialized scouts and (as their name implied) armed well enough to protect the French Fleet from enemy torpedo craft. High speed was therefore of paramount importance for these vessels. While CTs were equipped with torpedoes, their employment against enemy capital ships came third in their list of design missions.[20]

While no new destroyers were built in France during World War I, the creation of the Treaty system in the early 1920s reordered national priorities. Thereafter, a heavy emphasis was placed on their construction. Destroyers were well-suited to the defensive strategy the Marine Nationale adopted at the end of 1922, and the existence of foreign destroyers that far outstripped the capabilities of the MN's existing 800-ton units underlined the need for powerful new designs.[21] This was the impetus for the ordering of the 2,126-ton *Jaguar*-class CTs and 1,320-ton *Bourrasque*-class TEs in 1922.

Jaguar and *Bourrasque* were excellent representations of French low-steam propulsion technology. All units of these classes utilized saturated steam at 260 PSI and 420°F that was produced by air-encased boilers, eliminating the need for pressurized firerooms. They also universally employed single-reduction gearing between their turbines and propeller shafts. However, it was there that the homogeneity ended. *Jaguar*-class CTs were equipped with two high-pressure turbines that operated in parallel for each propeller shaft and were also equipped with one low-pressure cruising turbine for each set. This equipment enabled speeds of up to 35 knots. The smaller *Bourrasque*s instead relied upon only one high-pressure and one low-pressure turbine per shaft and could reach a maximum speed of 33 knots. Each vessel in both classes had a different turbine design based upon the production license that its builder held at the time. Some of the turbines employed were Parsons or Breguet-Laval reaction turbines, while others were impulse turbines designed by Rateau-Bretagne, Zoelly-Fives-Lille, or Zoelly-Schneider. Despite their larger size and employment of cruising turbines, the *Jaguar*s had nearly the same projected range as their smaller cousins: 3,000 miles at 15 knots. In practice, this number proved impossible to reach; ranges instead proved closer to 1,500 miles at 15 knots.[22]

As the 1920s progressed, additional vessels were ordered with nearly identical steam conditions to *Jaguar* and *Bourrasque* but with different equipment. This included the 1,350-ton *L'Adroit*-class TEs in 1924 (which were essentially repeats of the *Bourrasque*s) and the 2,400-ton *Guepard*-, *Aigle*-, and *Vauquelin*-class CTs in 1925, 1928, and 1929. Although these later vessels increased steam pressure to 280 PSI, experimented with different turbine configurations, and narrowed their turbine designs to Parsons reaction and Rateau-Bretagne impulse, they also struggled to exceed a 3,000-mile range at 15 knots.[23] Thus, despite their impressive speeds (*Gerfaut* of the *Aigle*-class exceeded 41 knots on trials), the universally short ranges of these destroyers was considered to be a serious problem. This helped spur considerable interest in the high speed and lower fuel consumption seemingly promised by high steam.

In October 1928, it was decided that the last two units of the *Aigle* class would be completed with British integral superheater designs (sourced from Yarrow and Thornycroft, respectively). This allowed these ships to produce steam rated at 384 PSI and 617°F, with the hope of extending their range to 4,000 miles at 15 knots. *Milan*'s steam powered three Parsons reaction turbines per set—high pressure, intermediate pressure, and low pressure—and included a single cruising turbine clutched to the intermediate. *Epervier* instead used Rateau-Bretagne impulse turbines in a configuration identical to that of *Milan* except for a pair of independently geared cruising turbines clutched to each intermediate. This latter configuration proved tactically effective, propelling *Epervier* to 43 knots on trials, although the projected range of both ships only reached 3,100 miles at 15 knots.[24]

The follow-on 2,570-ton *Le Fantasque*-class CTs were ordered with identical machinery in 1930, as *Milan*'s and *Epervier*'s trial data took too long to obtain. This was due to a combination of political and economic factors that dramatically slowed French warship construction at the end of the 1920s.[25] The result was that while the *Le Fantasque*s were very fast (*Le Terrible* achieved more than 43 knots), their range topped out at around 2,900 miles at 15 knots. To make matters worse, the high speeds possible with this machinery could not be quickly reached. Trials revealed that it took forty-six minutes to safely raise steam for 39 knots, an unacceptably long time for a warship type that relied upon speed for its survival. Ignoring established procedure in the pursuit of speed risked significant damage, as the machinery in this class proved exceedingly fragile.[26]

Following the *Le Fantasque*s, France ordered just two additional destroyer classes before its defeat in 1940. The first of these was the *Mogador*-class CTs of 2,950 tons, ordered in 1932 and 1934. These vessels produced steam at 498 PSI and 725°F and operated Rateau-Bretagne impulse turbines in a high pressure, intermediate pressure, and double-low pressure configuration per shaft. They were aided by a pair of cruising turbines that operated by a Vulcan clutch. This system propelled *Mogador* to a maximum speed of more than 43 knots on trials and a still-disappointing range of 3,350 miles at 15 knots in service.[27] As in the *Le Fantasque* class, safety dictated a long period to raise steam for 40 knots (in this case fifty-two minutes), but this was safely bypassed in practice.[28] Additionally, the Vulcan clutch proved so unreliable that the cruising turbines were difficult to use. This, in turn, prompted proposals to remove them entirely from future classes.[29]

The *Le Hardi*-class TEs of 1,750 tons represented the final class of destroyer ordered by France before 1940, and only *Le Hardi* itself completed acceptance trials prior to that date. These vessels had identical steam conditions to *Mogador* but used revolutionary "Sural" boilers that were about half the size as those employed previously and capable of rapid increases in steam pressure.[30] The propulsion configuration was otherwise the same as in classes prior to *Mogador*: a high-pressure, intermediate-pressure, and low-pressure turbine set per shaft. These were accompanied either by a single cruising turbine (in ships employing Parsons reaction equipment) or two independently geared cruising turbines (in those built with Rateau-Bretagne impulse designs). *Le Hardi* achieved 40 knots on trials but was only able to manage a range of 3,100 miles at 10 knots.

Although many French destroyers of the interwar period were able to achieve extraordinarily high speeds in excess of 40 knots, it appears that the adoption of a high-steam system did not significantly aid in this development. The Marine Nationale adopted its ultimate steam conditions of 498 PSI and 725°F in only its final two destroyer designs, of which only three ships were fully completed prior to the middle of 1940. The concept of high steam had simply been embraced too late for it to have much of an opportunity to make a material difference.[31] In the classes that adopted elevated steam conditions of any kind—*Le Fantasque*, *Mogador*, and *Le Hardi*—perceived range deficiencies persisted. This was likely due at least in part to a continued reliance on single-reduction gearing. Additionally, while machinery fragility seems to have become less of an issue in later vessels like *Mogador*, keeping these vessels consistently functional remained a problem throughout their service lives.[32] Finally, while *Le Hardi*'s Sural boilers proved capable of raising steam for high speed much more quickly than predecessor designs, their high complexity required a capable engineering staff to operate and maintain them. Widespread adoption of this equipment would have required increased personnel requirements for the MN.[33]

Overall, the French high-steam system was chiefly limited by its fragility, reliance on integral-type superheaters and single-reduction gearing, and lack of turbine standardization. While this did not prevent the Marine

58 / CHAPTER 3

Nationale from achieving its primary goal of unmatched speeds, it contributed to the repeated failure of French designs to develop satisfactory operational ranges. That this latter problem persisted even after the adoption of complex cruising turbine arrangements designed to defeat it boldly underlines the fears of British naval designers and other opponents of high steam during the interwar period.

GERMANY: PLAYING CATCH-UP

While the Marine Nationale made a significant attempt to transform its propulsion systems, the German Reichsmarine (empire navy), or Kriegsmarine (war navy) after 1935, took even bolder steps toward change. German naval designers explored high-steam propulsion in the mid-1930s with the specific intent to reduce the size taken up by their vessels' machinery. This pushed the Germans to extremes of engineering that were not adopted by other nations prior to World War II's conclusion. It also resulted in severe difficulties with a class of five heavy cruisers and with the sixteen destroyers of the Type 34 and Type 34A class, ordered in 1934.[34]

During the interwar period, the German Navy had to consider three likely opponents: Poland, France, and Britain. While Poland was a minor naval power (with a handful of destroyers and submarines to its name), the French possessed a considerable force of powerful destroyers, and the Royal Navy posed an existential threat with its sheer numbers alone. As the post–Versailles Treaty German Navy was essentially starting from scratch, the common perception was that there was little option other than attempting to find a qualitative solution to the quantitative inferiority problem that German naval forces would face in nearly any conceivable near-term conflict. Additionally, at first it was believed that any new destroyers would be utilized only in the Baltic and North Seas as fleet escorts, increasing the importance of speed and survivability while reducing the need for extensive endurance.[35] While this outlook gradually changed through the late 1930s and World War II, the vast majority of the destroyers that entered service conformed to this early mindset.

The design philosophy behind Germany's World War II destroyers was thus a quest for a qualitatively superior fleet escort for short-range missions. This led designers to investigate high steam based on experience in the German commercial sector—particularly that of shipbuilders DeSchiMAG and Blohm and Voss.[36] The former had performed work with high-pressure (1,000 PSI) Wagner boilers in the passenger ship SS *Scharnhorst*, while the latter had subsequently installed an even higher-pressure (1,600 PSI) Benson boiler in the freighter *Uckermark* for the Hamburg America (HAPAG) line in 1930.[37] This machinery was significantly smaller than its lower-steam counterparts due to the pressures utilized, and such a saving of space could potentially allow the addition of more or at least smaller watertight compartmentalization and thus a higher degree of survivability in a warship. The attraction of this line of logic was overpowering for the German Navy when it began to rapidly rebuild in the mid-1930s. It therefore concluded that DeSchiMAG and Blohm and Voss's work definitively proved that these extremely high pressures were practical and moved directly to incorporate the technology in their designs before any extensive shore or sea testing could be carried out.[38]

The Type 34 and 34A destroyers that resulted from this effort were large for their time: around 2,200 tons standard. They operated on two sets of Wagner steam turbines that provided 70,000 shaft horsepower by design and promised a maximum speed of 38 knots. This power came at a cost: their range was only 1,530 or 1,900 miles at 19 knots. The key to their unique speed and small machinery was their six boilers. *Z1* through *Z8* possessed Wagner boilers that operated at a superheater outlet pressure of 1,028 PSI and a temperature of 460°F, while *Z9* through *Z16* possessed Benson boilers that operated at an eye-popping 1,616 PSI and 510°F.[39] Both sets of machinery were capable of achieving these pressures and temperatures by making use of integral-type superheaters. Superheat generated by such methods is inherently difficult to accurately regulate—a problem that was never entirely overcome by the Kriegsmarine.

German destroyers of World War II possessed not only state-of-the-art, high-pressure boilers but also a number of unique turbine configurations. All types were equipped with cross-compounded turbines (produced either by DeSchiMAG or Blohm and Voss) on each of their two propeller shafts. Though the exact turbine configuration differed in a number of ways even between Type 34 destroyers, it generally included a high-, an intermediate-, and finally a low-pressure turbine in a cross-compounded set. A few of these configurations included an additional independent cruising turbine meant to increase efficient use of steam at lower speeds, but, as with the French *Mogador*, the troublesome Vulcan clutch used to bypass this section at higher loads meant that it was excluded from all ships after *Z4*.[40]

With an abbreviated and disjointed testing period for equipment to be installed in the Type 34 destroyers, the reader might expect some teething problems with the propulsion equipment in question. Not only was this the case, but the onset of World War II immediately following the entry of the Type 34s into service meant that operating routines among the German Navy's engineers took abnormally long to develop. Additionally, this process was further complicated by the exceptionally complex piping both within and outside of the boilers of these vessels. To make matters worse, war service rapidly revealed that the superheater designs in both the Wagner and Benson boilers were not only difficult to regulate but also highly prone to corrosion due to difficulties in servicing the dense pipe "nests" within these ships.[41] All of these factors together produced a maintenance nightmare that had these vessels in port for repairs almost as often as they were at sea, earning the Type 34s a reputation of being notoriously unreliable.

The records of other high-steam warships of the German Navy—its torpedo boats, six Type 36 destroyers, *Admiral Hipper*-class heavy cruisers, *Scharnhorst*-class battleships, and *Bismarck*-class battleships—are a repeat

Table 3.1. High-Steam Propulsion in Interwar Destroyers Outside the United States

Nation	United Kingdom	Japan	France	Germany
Class	*Acheron*	*Kagerō*	*Le Hardi*	Z5 (Type 1934A)
Order Year	1928	1937	1935	1935
Tonnage (Standard)	1,350	2,000	1,770	2,200
Steam Conditions	750°F, 500 PSI	662°F, 426 PSI	725°F, 498 PSI	510°F, 1,616 PSI
Installed Power (SHP)	34,000	52,000	57,200	70,000
Estimated Range (NM)	4,800 @ 15 knots	5,000 @ 18 knots	3,100 @ 10 knots	1,530 @ 19 knots
Maximum Speed (Knots)	35	35	37	36

The increase of steam temperatures and pressures in use by navies around the world by the middle of the 1930s was a clear trend that the US Navy intended to follow. Note that *Acheron*, despite setting an example for the French, was only a one-off design. The Royal Navy relied upon 300 PSI, 300–400°F right up to 1942.

Sources: March, *British Destroyers*; Evans and Peattie, *Kaigun*; Jordan and Moulin, *French Destroyers*; Whitley, *Destroyer!*

of this tale. While the characteristics of each were slightly different (in a reflection of their different intended roles), the unreliability of German high-steam engineering continued to haunt each until the end of World War II. In the case of the *Scharnhorst*-class battleships, their objective of maintaining an extensive cruising range for commerce raiding without the need to carry excessive amounts of oil proved to be a failure for some of the same reasons.[42] The Kriegsmarine's struggle to plan coherently with an unreliable fleet thus seems to validate the lack of enthusiasm for high steam found in the Royal Navy and elsewhere.

The experiences of these four nations in the use of high-pressure, high-temperature steam during the 1920s and 1930s makes the US Navy's story seem all the more remarkable (table 3.1). Modern historiography asserts that the US Navy succeeded in fully harnessing this potential advantage for its ships in a manner that avoided the range and maintenance problems experienced by the French and the Germans. The characteristics of the US experience—what Admiral Bowen sought in pursuing high steam, and the challenges he faced in doing so—have been pointed to as difference makers in the limited literature on this subject. As we shall see, this has often been reduced to a quest for increased fuel economy, as opposed to the maintenance, tactical-speed, and machinery-size priorities of other navies. However, the Bowen narrative has never been subjected to a thorough analysis. Such an exercise reveals a story of unexpected twists and turns that alter our understanding not only of high steam itself but also of how the US Navy fought the Pacific War.

Chapter 4

ROBINSON, BOWEN, AND AMERICAN HIGH STEAM, 1932–1938

When the first *Farragut*-class destroyers were laid down in 1932—the US Navy's first such vessels since World War I—the Bureau of Engineering under Rear Admirals Samuel M. Robinson and Harold G. Bowen Sr. seized the opportunity to launch an American high-steam experiment. This was primarily a quest for markedly increased fuel economy at moderate and high speeds. While a propulsion redesign of this magnitude would inevitably result in a higher initial capital investment for each warship, the hope was that this would be offset by the promise of long-term savings on fuel and maintenance.

Unlike other national experiments, the adoption of higher steam pressures and temperatures in the US Navy was accompanied by the addition of a significant number of other technical innovations. It was the combination of all of these changes that came to be known as the American high-steam *system* by the end of the 1930s. However, the major components of this system entered service in a piecemeal fashion, leaving little time for proof-of-concept testing before each new, more complex configuration was fielded. As a result, a major conflict developed in 1938 between now-bureau head Admiral Bowen and a significant group of nonspecialized "general line" officers who accused the engineer-in-chief of recklessness in his continuing efforts to push the technological envelope.

GROWING US INTEREST IN HIGH STEAM

Although the Naval Treaty system's restrictions were not limited to the United States, its enforcement demonstrably transformed the manner in which the US Navy planned and prepared for future conflicts during the interwar period. In particular, the strict limitations on shipbuilding and tonnages pushed the General Board of the Navy (and the various bureaus that deferred to its judgment) to search for technological solutions for the operational problems confronting them.

As was discussed previously, in the early twentieth century, the US Navy was divided into different bureaus that made up the "bureau system," each bureau having a strictly defined role in day-to-day operations. In 1930, those bureaus with which we must concern ourselves include the Bureau of Engineering (all things dealing with propulsion), the Bureau of Ordnance (all things dealing with weapons), the Bureau of Construction and Repair (all things material *not* about engineering or weapons), and the Bureau of Navigation (somewhat misleadingly—things dealing with personnel, education, and training). As might be expected with any well-established bureaucratic system, these agencies had become fiercely territorial by the final decade before World War II, and their lack of cooperation in policy development and the production of new warships had the potential to cause serious problems.

Mitigating these issues had become the job of the General Board of the Navy. Originally, this body was established as an advisory panel for the secretary of the navy to which various studies (and particularly war-planning questions) could be charged, but by 1930 it had styled itself as the "authority without authority" on the overall doctrinal, technological, and design direction of the US Navy.[1] The board's precise makeup changed over time, but it typically consisted of some nine senior officers nearing the end of their careers who were capable of examining matters thoroughly and objectively. For a combination of reasons, this agency had a reputation in the immediate post–World War II period for having made somewhat backward decisions, but recent scholarship has proven just the opposite. Throughout the 1920s and 1930s, the general board called for technological or doctrinal change to solve problems whose traditional solutions had been blocked by the Treaty system. This was the mindset that informed much of the navy's executive leadership in the 1930s.[2]

In this environment and with knowledge of experimentation by other navies during the 1920s and early 1930s, the US Navy was well aware of developments in steam technology.[3] This subject logically fell under the purview of the Bureau of Engineering. In 1932, BuEng's chief, Admiral Robinson, opted to begin increasing steam pressures and temperatures in future warship designs for two reasons: first was the apparent success of high steam in merchant shipping (designed by Gibbs & Cox) and throughout the electrical utility industry, both of which obtained machinery from homegrown American companies; and second was the difficulty of the operational challenges that the navy's planners faced.

As explored in chapter 2, in the aftermath of the Spanish-American War, the United States did not possess the overseas bases or fortifications that war planners believed were necessary to protect the Philippines in the event of a conflict with Japan.[4] War Plan Orange, between 1922 and 1934, had therefore taken the form of the "Through Ticket to Manila" or "thruster" strategy of rushing the US fleet across the Pacific to an improvised Philippine base, as this was seen by the general board as the only politically and militarily viable option. The details of this strategy (and other war plans) were tested and refined in semi-regular exercises known as Fleet Problems throughout the interwar period. These wargames were meant to simulate actual wartime conditions as accurately as possible under the fiscal and material limitations of the interwar period.[5]

The provisions of War Plan Orange heavily influenced the thinking of the Bureau of Engineering during the 1930s. Such a campaign would strongly benefit from the availability of protected anchorages along the fleet's intended route (for repair and replenishment) and the improvement of warship operating ranges.[6] Even once a "cautionary" gradual campaign strategy came into favor in 1934 and after, these concerns continued to dominate US naval strategy right up to 1941. The result was a number of innovative projects designed to ease the difficulty of such an effort, such as floating dry docks and underway refueling.[7]

While some interwar developments were able to mitigate the problem of long transit distances, they did not directly deal with the limited operational range of the navy's ships. This would traditionally have been addressed purely through new construction specifically designed to remedy this deficiency, but only a handful of ships (all cruisers) were built between 1922 and 1932 due to the construction and tonnage limitations imposed by the Washington Naval Treaty. Fortunately, this was not a major obstacle for larger ships with deep bunkers, which could operate *if* sufficient fuel stocks and the ships to carry them were available at the war's outset.[8] Instead, Fleet Problem exercises quickly highlighted the restricted oil capacity of smaller ships. By 1927, this was considered to be a major shortcoming of the US fleet's destroyers.[9]

The range issue was particularly acute for these vessels because of their contradictory design requirements. They had to be fast for escorting, which mandated a huge power-to-displacement ratio. They had to be light for agility but could not be so lightly built that they lacked the strength to withstand the rigors of heavy seas or steaming at high speed. They had to be prepared for almost any task but had limited space for the electronics, guns, torpedoes, and fuel this required. Destroyers during the first half of the twentieth century presented a highly complex design conundrum—another reason that they were widely experimented on by all nations (table 4.1).[10]

The newest and most numerous class of destroyers the US Navy possessed prior to the building of the *Farragut*s was a World War I–era design that largely favored surface (torpedo) combat. This was the *Clemson* class, and its range repeatedly proved to be a thorn in the side of commanders attempting to carry out their exercise orders in the 1920s (figure 4.1). A typical example of this class displaced 1,215 tons standard and had a maximum speed of about 35½ knots when new. The class was powered by four Yarrow boilers (without superheat) feeding a pair of low-pressure turbines to a maximum of about 27,500 shaft horsepower (split over two propeller

Table 4.1: Power and Fuel Characteristics of the Mid-1930s US Navy

Type	Destroyer	Destroyer Leader	Aircraft Carrier	Battleship
Class Name	Benham	Somers	Yorktown	North Carolina
Build Year	1936	1935	1934	1937
Tonnage (Standard)	1,656	1,840	19,800	36,600
Installed Power (SHP)	50,000	52,000	120,000	121,000
Power Ratio (SHP/Ton)	30.19	28.26	6.06	3.30
Fuel Capacity (US Gal)	146,000	179,000	1,605,433	2,118,173
Maximum Speed (Knots)	38	36	33	28

A comparison of selected characteristics of the navy's building projects clearly demonstrates the dilemma of destroyer design. Specifically, destroyers required huge amounts of engine power, something that was difficult to obtain in vessels their size. This left little room for much else, including fuel. Note that the *Yorktown* class alone among these has an older plant with Parsons turbines.

Sources: Office of the Chief of Naval Operations, *FTP 136 Cruising Radii of US Naval Vessels from Actual Steaming Data, Change No. 2* (Washington, DC: Government Printing Office, 1940); Office of the Chief of Naval Operations, *FTP 218 War Service Fuel Consumption of U.S. Naval Surface Vessels* (Washington, DC: Government Printing Office, 1945); "Special Specifications for Propelling Machinery," ITEM S-18 (Ships & Ships' Machinery), Boxes 12–15, RG 19, NACP.

FIGURE 4.1. *Clemson*-class destroyer USS *Goff* (DD-247). A class of 156 ships completed between 1919 and 1922, the *Clemson*s were the most advanced destroyers in the US Navy until 1934. Image NH 64559 courtesy of the Naval History and Heritage Command.

shafts) and an estimated range of up to 5,600 miles at 12 knots (but dramatically less at higher speeds).[11] Built primarily by the "Big Three" shipyards of Bethlehem Shipbuilding (Bethlehem Steel), Newport News Shipbuilding, and New York Shipbuilding between 1919 and 1922, *Clemson*s were produced entirely on site with all requisite machinery and spares. This included their turbines, which were built to a simplified British design under license from Parsons, Ltd, similar to those produced directly by Parsons for the Royal Navy.[12]

Technical specifications of the *Clemson*'s low-steam installation were typical of those found in pre-1930s US destroyers; the overall system utilized saturated steam oil-burning boilers powering (mostly) reaction turbines linked by a single reduction gear to the propeller shafts.[13] The turbines themselves were (relatively) large, low-speed, and low-pressure machinery that possessed 17,500 blades and utilized steam ranging from 260 to 75 PSI. The use of saturated steam meant that steam generated by the boilers tended to be more corrosive due to the presence of residual moisture, making these propulsion plants less durable than their British counterparts.[14] Temperatures in use typically remained around 450°F.

While considered very capable because of their high-design speed and heavy-torpedo armament, the range of these destroyers proved to be a disappointment. Typical operational reports from the Fleet Problems of the 1920s *began* with an immediate need for refueling of the force's destroyers—not by choice but out of necessity. While this fueling process became more efficient as the years passed, it nevertheless required a considerable supply train to accompany any significant force. Additionally, the need to frequently refuel destroyers both slowed the pace of operations and limited the tactical options available to individual commanders, as they were forced to perpetually keep a close eye on their fuel supply. This was a serious challenge for a navy that planned to fight a war in the Pacific Ocean.[15] And, due to the highly complex nature of destroyer design, retrofitting different propulsion configurations into older ships was not a viable option. Thus, until new naval construction was authorized in 1930, the navy was severely handicapped.

THE HIGH-STEAM GAMBIT

It was with all of these factors in mind that Admiral Robinson's Bureau of Engineering was finally tasked with developing the engineering specifications for a new class of destroyers—the first since the implementation of the Treaty system—in 1932. The perception in BuEng at that time was that the relatively minor investment this order represented (eight small ships) offered an ideal opportunity for a modest technological experiment. They therefore mandated a moderate increase in steam conditions that were within the established theoretical limits of Parsons-designed equipment. This ability of Parsons machinery to meet BuEng's demands was critical in 1932; the shipyards upon which the navy traditionally relied—Bethlehem, Newport News, and New York—all utilized Parsons designs and badly needed work to stay in business in the era of the Great Depression.

Such a diplomatic and balanced approach was typical of Samuel M. Robinson (figure 4.2). Like Bowen, Robinson was a career engineer. Born in Texas in 1882, Robinson had attended the US Naval Academy from 1899 to 1903.[16] Following his initial posting to the Asiatic Fleet, Robinson took part in the Great White Fleet's long cruise aboard the battleship USS *Vermont* (BB-20) from 1907 to 1909. After his return, Robinson recognized his

FIGURE 4.2. Rear Admiral Samuel M. Robinson in 1935. Image NH 47178 courtesy of the Naval History and Heritage Command.

own attraction to engineering and successfully applied to become one of the original attendees of the navy's School of Marine Engineering, better known today as the Naval Postgraduate School.[17]

Robinson's post-1909 naval career quickly saw him propelled to the forefront of propulsion development in the service. He was closely involved with early experiments with turbo-electric propulsion in the 1910s before beginning a long association with the Bureau of Engineering that defined his interwar career. Robinson was first assigned to the design division of BuEng from 1914 to 1919 and was head of the same from 1921 to 1927. Following a four-year term as head of the Puget Sound Navy Yard, Robinson was promoted to rear admiral to begin the first of what would be two nonconsecutive terms as chief of the Bureau of Engineering in 1931.[18]

Robinson's appointment to the leadership of BuEng was fortuitous for the navy for a number of reasons; it is clear from his records alone that the newly minted admiral was intimately familiar with both the state of engineering in the navy and the process by which it had developed. But Robinson also had another quality that was far more difficult to pin down: he was the consummate bureaucratic diplomat. Years of experience with the navy's design bureaucracy in Washington clearly served as a lesson in patience and negotiation that Robinson took to heart. This was an invaluable tool for a design bureau chief in the interwar period, when referring to US naval design as "contentious" was something of an understatement.[19]

The US Navy's warship design process in the interwar period was complex at best and fraught with difficulties at worst. First, the general board would determine a new ship's purpose and desired characteristics. After their approval by the secretary of the navy, a directive to conduct design studies would then be passed to the Bureaus of Construction and Repair, Ordnance, and Engineering. Following competitive review of the resulting options, "contract designs" that contained a much higher degree of detail would be created by both BuC&R and BuEng, which covered their specific areas of responsibility. These were then used to solicit bids from private shipyards. Only once a contract had been awarded were actual working plans of the highest degree of detail drawn up by the design agent (usually a division or partner of the prime awardee) and precise specifications finalized. Following the Dallinger amendment to the Cruiser Bill of 1928, these contracts were frequently divided between both large and small private shipyards and government-owned navy yards, depending on the how reasonable the bids appeared.[20]

The fruit of this endeavor in 1932 was the *Farragut* class of destroyers. Displacing 1,365 tons standard, these vessels operated at 400 PSI and up to 650°F, providing an estimated maximum range in excess of 8,800 miles at 12 knots.[21] This range was possible due in part to the fact that these were the first American warships to employ three important components of what would become its high-steam system: a primitive superheater, basic economizers, and the division of the lone turbine-per-shaft arrangement into a cross-compounded set.

As previously described in the section on British experiments, the superheater is a critical component of high steam both for its removal of remaining liquid water and boosting of the original boiler-outlet pressures and temperatures. In the *Farragut*-class destroyers, this was accomplished through double-back piping similar to that employed by the British I-class and German Type 1934 destroyers. This style of superheat generally accomplished its task, but, as with the British and German models, it was difficult to regulate with precision in practice.[22]

Optimizing superheat required the adoption of *economizers*—a fancy term for what was effectively just feedwater preheating. Rather than directly injecting feedwater into the boilers to be transformed into steam, USS *Farragut* (DD-348)'s boilers first ran their feedwater through a heat exchanger supported by their own exhaust gases. This effectively reduced the amount of energy required to heat the water beyond its boiling point within the boilers and made use of exhaust heat that had previously been simply discharged.

The final innovation of the *Farragut*-class destroyers was the improvement of their turbine arrangement. This, too, was accomplished in a manner similar to what had been done with Britain's I class and Germany's Type 1934s. While superheated steam is all well and good, it is useless unless the turbines are capable of harnessing the additional energy. The Parsons-designed turbines installed in earlier US warships were intended to draw energy from a gradual drop in pressure and temperature as steam moved through the rotor. This was efficient only within a limited pressure range, as space for larger turbines (with larger ranges) was limited. *Farragut*'s turbines were meant to correct this problem through the division of each turbine into a *set* rather than a single unit per shaft. This consisted of two specialized turbines (still designed by Parsons): one for the initial use of steam from the boilers at the highest pressures and temperatures, and a larger secondary unit for the residual lower-pressure and lower-temperature steam. These were paired with the same reduction gear linking them to their respective propeller shafts, a significant improvement in energy utilization. The addition of cross-compounding ultimately completed the loop of the first iteration of high steam and provided the boost in range that *Farragut* possessed over the *Clemson*-class destroyers.[23]

While this initial class of destroyers represented an improvement over previous ships designed for the US Navy, their range increases were marginal when considered with respect to the long distances that would need to be traversed in the Pacific Ocean. After an identical machinery arrangement was designed for the *Porter*-class destroyer leaders that followed the *Farragut*-class destroyers, Robinson moved to further leverage the potential advantages of high steam in its next iteration. This innovation produced the *Mahan*-class destroyers, built beginning in 1934 (figure 4.3).

While *Farragut* was significant as an experiment with largely preexisting machinery, USS *Mahan* (DD-364) represented the first time that BuEng was willing to step out in an entirely new direction in its attempts to improve destroyer range. The *Mahan*-class destroyers were a 1,500-ton design (the maximum permitted under the London Naval Treaty of 1930) constructed in large part by smaller shipyards. These yards did not possess

FIGURE 4.3. USS *Mahan* (DD-364). The *Mahan*-class destroyers, the first warships designed by Gibbs & Cox, represented a significant departure from traditional propulsion design. Image NH 101658 courtesy of the Naval History and Heritage Command.

the in-house design and production capabilities of their larger counterparts previously relied upon by the navy. As previously discussed, this was the reason Gibbs & Cox was brought in as the primary design agent of US destroyers: to counteract the perceived deficiencies of these small contractors. As a result, the *Mahan*-class destroyers were universally fitted with a new turbine design: two sets of General Electric–built *impulse* turbines producing about 49,000 shaft horsepower. They were arranged so that each propeller shaft was linked by a double-reduction gear to a high-pressure turbine, a low-pressure turbine, and a declutchable cruising turbine. *Mahan*'s boilers, designed by Babcock & Wilcox, operated at 450 PSI and 650°F and gave the destroyer a prewar estimated range of 9,300 miles at 12 knots.[24]

As discussed earlier, up until construction of the *Mahan*-class destroyers, *reaction* turbines, designed by the British company Parsons, Ltd., were virtually ubiquitous in the US Navy. Thus, it should come as little surprise that one of the highest-profile components of high steam (and one that would prove to be the most industrially problematic) was the homegrown compound "Curtis" impulse turbine. To review, reaction turbines depend on a change in pressure within the blades to accelerate the rotor itself.

Impulse turbines require a pressure change in the (stationary) nozzle only. High-speed steam is directed against the blades, transferring the steam's velocity to the rotor. Compound impulse turbines, which used several stages of alternating fixed (pressure and direction-changing blades) and moving blades to gradually reduce the pressure and temperature of the steam in the system, were able to more efficiently make use of the extreme energy of high-pressure and high-temperature steam. Their simpler blades were also easier to manufacture, fewer in number, and less prone to damaging expansion at high operating temperatures.[25]

Additionally, as touched upon in the review of British developments in high steam, rising steam temperatures and pressures and the multiplying turbines needed to make use of them necessitated ever-increasing turbine size and length. This was because turbines are naturally more efficient at higher rotational speeds, while propellers are limited to much lower speeds for proper efficiency.[26] The concept of cross-compounding and the introduction of the single reduction gear early in the twentieth century tried to solve this problem. Neither had been a completely satisfactory solution. The introduction of compound impulse turbines and steam in excess of 600 PSI effectively upped the ante, as higher-pressure machinery again required a substantial increase in rotational speeds to maintain peak efficiency. While the other navies of the world settled with single-reduction designs, the United States renewed its search for a solution other than increasing turbine size.

From this effort emerged the initial concept of a locked-train (rigid) *double* gear-and-pinion reduction gear (figure 4.4). As mentioned earlier, single reduction gears had long proven to be problematic in both manufacture and maintenance. Double-reduction gearing, if proven reliable, represented a significant advantage in machinery size and efficiency.[27] It allowed for smaller turbines (since their rotor size was now far less of a factor in the rotation speed that they could be permitted to transmit to the propeller shaft) and by extension considerably smaller and less numerous internal blading. Additionally, this component opened the door for even higher steam pressures and temperatures.[28]

The multiturbine cross-compounding "set" arrangement established by the *Farragut*-class, along with the transition to compound impulse turbines and the development of the double-reduction gear, allowed for the inclusion of the single greatest fuel-saving concept of the entire American high-steam system: the declutchable cruising turbine. This was a turbine intended for operation only during long-distance travel and designed

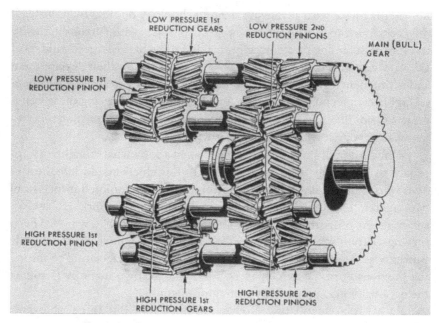

FIGURE 4.4. Locked-train, double-reduction gear. By interposing an additional pinion between the propeller shaft gear and turbine gear, significantly more efficient rotational speeds could be utilized by each. This, by extension, made the extremely high rotational speeds of impulse turbines fully practical for naval use for the first time. Image courtesy of the Bureau of Naval Personnel, *Principles of Naval Engineering*, 102.

to take advantage of a low-to-moderate rate of speed to aid the vessel in achieving unheard of operational range. It needed to be "de-clutched," or bypassed, in order to prepare the full turbine set for high-power operation. This procedure generally took a few minutes for experienced crews.[29] When employed properly, it allowed the entire propulsion system to be specially configured for fuel-efficient operation at multiple speeds (rather than at a single speed, as in older designs). The reader might recall that such an innovation had briefly been experimented with by the German Navy on *Z1*, *Z2*, *Z3*, and *Z4* but was proven to be both impractical in its design and unnecessary for the roles envisioned for German destroyers.[30] In principle, it was seen as a perfect match for the US Navy's destroyers in the Pacific.

The *Mahan*-class destroyers were a milestone in the development of the high-steam US Navy for a number of technical reasons but also for several equally important bureaucratic ones. By the mid-1930s, it was clear to those within the Bureau of Engineering that the "Big Three" shipyards were not keeping pace with advancing steam technology on their own. Instead, they continued to rely on their long-term contracts with Parsons in the interest of maintaining profit margins, making some of the largest builders of US Navy warships dependent on foreign technology for their development and maintenance.[31] For its part, Parsons was unwilling to share experimental high-steam technology with its American partners, placing these builders in a major dilemma should BuEng continue to raise propulsion requirements beyond that which Parsons was willing to meet.[32]

While Admiral Robinson may have taken a somewhat conciliatory approach to this problem, his first tenure as BuEng chief ended while the *Mahan*s were being built. In June 1935, Robinson was appointed inspector of naval materiel for General Electric and relocated to New York. His successor was none other than Rear Admiral Harold G. Bowen Sr., who had been serving as Robinson's assistant chief for the previous four years. Thus, while Bowen was familiar with what BuEng had collectively been up to during the previous term, he quickly moved to make his own mark by changing the organization's approach to contractor relations.

Rather than negotiating, Bowen informed the "Big Three" shipyards that their partnership with Parsons was in violation of the Espionage Act of 1917. These contracts, he argued, required Bethlehem, Newport News, and New York Shipbuilding to share crucial details of US warships with a foreign power—an illegal arrangement under this legislation.[33] They were given the choice to either forfeit their right to bid on future navy contracts or void their agreements with Parsons. While these yards chose to terminate their relationship with the British turbine manufacturer, they decided not to build their own versions of high-pressure and high-temperature steam plants. Instead, they sought a cheaper alternative: purchasing said plants from companies already proficient in the production of civilian and land-based steam power machinery. It was by these means that companies such as Babcock & Wilcox, General Electric, and Westinghouse became the primary boiler and turbine suppliers of the US Navy.[34]

While the 9,300-mile estimated range of the *Mahan* class would eventually be welcomed in the fleet, Bowen had not been satisfied by his predecessor's small victories. Instead, before *Mahan* had even been commissioned, he quickly moved to press for additional increases that shore-based technology seemed to promise.[35] Accordingly, following the Espionage Act episode in 1935, a new stage of development was ordered for the *Somers*-class destroyer leaders (figure 4.5). These vessels were to be capable of producing steam at 650 PSI and 850°F—a second increase of nearly 200

PSI before the original experiment aboard *Farragut* had been in service for a year.[36]

Somers-class destroyer leaders were effectively larger than normal US destroyers of the same general design, coming in at 1,840 tons standard. However, despite the size differential, the challenges of designing an effective propulsion system for this class remained. They contained all the innovations necessary for effective employment of high steam in the American model: a high-pressure and high-temperature impulse turbine set for each propeller shaft, double reduction gears, and a cruising turbine. The wild card in this design was the superheater. These were the first American warships to exchange integral systems for what came to be called *controlled* superheaters. While the former method of heating had accomplished its task utilizing double-back piping methods that ran steam through the boiler a second time, controlled superheat relied upon convection and conduction of heat from the combustion gases leaving the boiler rather than the boiler itself. By avoiding direct exposure of steam to the boiler, the amount of heat being passed could be precisely measured and controlled, eliminating

FIGURE 4.5. USS *Somers* (DD-381). This class of 1,800-ton destroyers were the first American warships capable of generating steam at 650 PSI and 850°F. Image NH 66340 courtesy of the Naval History and Heritage Command.

the danger of anomalous heat spikes damaging the delicate turbines.[37] Temperature boosting could be used far more aggressively in these vessels and the 1,600-ton *Benham* and *Sims* classes that followed, opening the door wider to additional increases in steam pressures and temperatures. The net result was that a steam plant such as this provided *Somers* with a significant estimated range advantage over every previous US destroyer class. Prewar data indicates that *Somers* was believed capable of nearly 9,800 miles at 12 knots, or 1.75 times the range of the *Clemsons*.[38]

With production of the *Somers* class and the designs that followed, the American system of high steam was elevated to a level where it would remain throughout World War II. Only one additional prewar high-steam innovation would emerge on a large scale after the completion of *Somers*: the air-encased boiler, providing *Gleaves*-class destroyers and their successors with reliable superheat control in the comfort of "open" (unpressurized) boiler rooms (figure 4.6).[39] The apparent success of this propulsion design

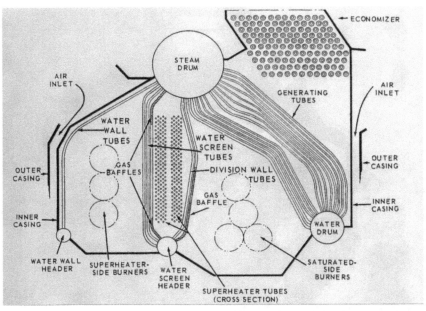

FIGURE 4.6. Babcock & Wilcox "Type M" Boiler. By 1938, the US Navy had begun to use advanced water-tube boilers of this type. These combined an economizer, controlled superheater, and outer casing to generate the 600 PSI, 850°F steam that BuEng specifications called for. Image courtesy of the Bureau of Naval Personnel, *Principles of Naval Engineering*, 249.

led to BuEng's proposal to use it in all larger types of warships then on the drawing board.

Stopping even at this stage was *not* the intention of Admiral Bowen. However, enhancements to the standard engineering plants being designed for US Navy ships were halted as a result of escalating tensions within the navy. This occurred during production of the first batch of *Gleaves*-class destroyers and their near-identical sister class, the *Bensons*. The collision of interests leading to this freeze had been brewing since design of the *Farragut* class and—while not helped by Bowen's adversarial management style—was the result of long-standing divisions in both the navy bureau system and officer corps. The resulting administrative fallout, combined with the emerging world crisis, prevented further major alterations to the system until after World War II (table 4.2).[40]

"THERE IS A SCHISM IN THE ENGINEERING PROFESSION"

The reader may recall that BuEng shared its design responsibilities with the navy's Bureau of Construction and Repair, which in the late 1930s was under the direction of Rear Admiral William G. DuBose. Many in this organization were alarmed by what they perceived as a single-minded and reckless pace of engineering advancement. BuC&R was effectively charged with designing all aspects of US Navy warships not related to engineering or ordnance, and they did not take lightly BuEng's radical shift to experimental technology under Admiral Bowen.[41]

Compounding matters was the troubled development process of the *North Carolina*-class battleships, the preliminary stage for which dragged on through some fifty design iterations between mid-1935 and mid-1937. As expensive, critical, and highly visible investments, it was perceived as crucial that these ships pack the best possible combination of speed, armor, and armament into the maximum displacement permitted them under the Treaty system (35,000 tons). Reducing weight by any means possible was thus the motivation behind many revisions to *North Carolina*'s design. While the developing high-steam system was only just putting to sea in a handful of destroyers during this time, the potential weight savings represented by impulse-turbine sets provided an opening for Bowen to propose a radical increase in this case to 1,200 PSI and 950°F. This, in effect, would be the straw that broke the camel's back.[42]

As the 1930s progressed, BuC&R's vocal opposition to Bowen's activities was joined by a considerable array of "straight" (nonspecialized) line

Table 4.2. US Destroyer Classes of the Interwar Period, 1918–1939

Build Year	Class Name	Tonnage (Standard)	Number Built	Range @ 12 Knots (NM)*	Steam Pressure (PSI)
1918	Clemson	1,215	162	5,629	275
1932	Farragut	1,365	8	8,865	400
1933	Porter	1,850	8	8,455	400
1934	Mahan	1,500	18	9,313	450
1935	Gridley	1,590	4	8,000	400
1935	Bagley	1,624	8	9,313	450
1935	Somers	1,840	5	9,778	600*
1936	Benham	1,656	10	8,529	600*
1937	Sims	1,570	12	8,176	600*
1938	Benson	1,620	30	8,000	600*
1938	Gleaves	1,630	66	8,176	600*
1941	Fletcher	2,050	175		600*
1943	Allen M. Sumner	2,200	58		600*
1944	Gearing	2,616	98		600*

The gradual changes pursued by the Bureau of Engineering are clearly visible in this layout. While the fleet escort standard cruising speed became 15 knots around 1936, all ranges are shown for 12 knots for comparative purposes. All data shown is as calculated in early 1940.

*Data marked with an asterisk is what was specified in the operating manual despite the fact that destroyers including and after Somers all had boilers capable of 650 PSI, 850°F.

Steam Temperature (°F)	Machinery
450 (Saturated)	One Turbine per Shaft, Single Reduction
650 (Integral Superheat)	Two Reaction Turbines per Shaft, Single Reduction, Economizers
650 (Integral Superheat)	Two Reaction Turbines per Shaft, Single Reduction, Economizers
650 (Integral Superheat)	Three Impulse Turbines per Shaft (Incl. Cruising), Double Reduction, Economizers,
650 (Integral Superheat)	Two Reaction Turbines per Shaft, Single Reduction, Economizers
650 (Integral Superheat)	Three Impulse Turbines per Shaft (Incl. Cruising), Double Reduction, Economizers
700 (Controlled Superheat)*	Three Impulse Turbines per Shaft (Incl. Cruising), Double Reduction, Economizers, Air-Encased Boilers
700 (Controlled Superheat)*	Three Impulse Turbines per Shaft (Incl. Cruising), Double Reduction, Economizers, Air-Encased Boilers
700 (Controlled Superheat)*	Three Impulse Turbines per Shaft (Incl. Cruising), Double Reduction, Economizers, Air-Encased Boilers
750 (Controlled Superheat)*	Two Reaction Turbines per Shaft, Single Reduction, Economizers
850 (Controlled Superheat)	Three Impulse Turbines per Shaft (Incl. Cruising), Double Reduction, Economizers, Air-Encased Boilers
850 (Controlled Superheat)	Three Impulse Turbines per Shaft (Incl. Cruising), Double Reduction, Economizers, Air-Encased Boilers
850 (Controlled Superheat)	Three Impulse Turbines per Shaft (Incl. Cruising), Double Reduction, Economizers, Air-Encased Boilers
850 (Controlled Superheat)	Three Impulse Turbines per Shaft (Incl. Cruising), Double Reduction, Economizers, Air-Encased Boilers

Sources: Bowen, *Ships, Machinery, and Mossbacks*, 62–70; Friedman, *U.S. Destroyers*, 462–65; Office of the Chief of Naval Operations, *FTP 136 Cruising Radii of US Naval Vessels from Actual Steaming Data, Change No. 2* (Washington, DC: Government Printing Office, 1940); "Special Specifications for Propelling Machinery," ITEM S-18 (Ships & Ships' Machinery), Boxes 12–15, RG 19, NACP.

officers. These included Rear Admiral Harry L. Brinser in his capacity as the head of the navy's Board of Inspection and Survey (INSURV) and, for a time, Rear Admiral Thomas C. Hart, while he served as chairman of the general board. Additionally, it should come as little surprise that the "Big Three" shipbuilding firms of Bethlehem Shipbuilding Corporation, New York Shipbuilding Corporation, and Newport News Shipbuilding and Drydock Company all favored the continuance of their contracts with Parsons for older, low-steam installations for cost reasons and said so publicly.[43] Bowen's 1935 threat to the "Big Three" to sever their Parsons contracts or face prosecution under the Espionage Act of 1917 therefore also fueled the showdown between the navy's technical specialists and generalists. The result of this increasing friction within the US Navy's warship building apparatus was a formal general board hearing on high steam in 1938.[44]

General board study 420–13, "Steam Conditions of Pressure," offers a rare glimpse into the state of US naval engineering in the late interwar period. It represents the single largest and earliest source documenting the process of high steam's development. It also casts a rare spotlight upon the junior officers responsible for the day-to-day operation of these new systems. The recorded words of these operators represent our best opportunity to understand the actual environment in which the navy was operating. It also helps explain why further high-steam progress at this crucial time was halted.

It is important to note that the crisis surrounding high steam was rooted in the general animosity between engineers and line officers that is traceable to the late nineteenth century. Our modern perspective has been excessively based upon the brief period directly preceding the hearings. This is due, in large part, to the writings of Admiral Bowen. Scholars have therefore tended to view the high-steam hearings dismissively, with an air of "progressives inhibited by reactionaries" more appropriate to the Salem witch trials. A critical examination of the general board hearings on the high-steam system is therefore necessary.

Chapter 5

Bowen versus the World

On October 18, 1938, Navy Secretary Claude Swanson directed his primary advisory organization, the general board, to begin a review of the utility and future of high-steam propulsion in the US Navy. In the months that followed, Admirals Bowen (BuEng), DuBose (BuC&R), and Brinser (Inspection and Survey) made their cases for and against high steam to the senior flag officers of the board. By the end of that year, the general board would advise Swanson that BuEng should be allowed to continue installing high-steam systems in new warships. But the board's endorsement was qualified. In their final statement, Admiral Hart and his fellows collectively asserted that further test data with the new machinery was required, though they conceded that the time for this might not be available given international tensions. Ultimately, the board's misgivings were reflected in the wry observation that with respect to its recommendation, "we have come too far on a whim to walk back on a hunch."[1]

This general board study is a major feature of Admiral Bowen's autobiography, *Ships, Machinery, and Mossbacks*, and is described by the author as being one of the great victories of his naval career despite the ambiguous ruling. There are a number of reasons for this, but Bowen's own dramatic testimony to the board shines a light on what he clearly believed to be the biggest: "I would be derelict in my duty if I did not hereby call your attention to the fact that there is a great schism in the marine engineering profession of the United States. Some of the elements of this schism are so deep and so fundamental that, in my opinion, it is a vital necessity that the general board shall consider them in their deliberations."[2] For Bowen, this was not merely a debate over a propulsion system. It was a collision of interests that was decades in the making.

This subtext—the conflict between the specialized propulsion engineers of BuEng and more general officers of the rest of the navy—is important not only because of its influence on the ship designs with which the United States fought a world war but also because of the *long* line of events that had given rise to it. To appreciate their significance and to understand why the normally progressive general board demurred on this issue, we must take a brief detour to explore the historical conflict surrounding engineering personnel in the US Navy. In doing so, we can better understand why Admiral Bowen's partisan account has been accepted without being challenged by serious scholarship.

WHO NEEDS ENGINEERS?

The US Navy formally came into existence in 1794, a period we now recognize as the twilight of the age of sail. Thus, while initial patterns of officer education generally mirrored apprenticeship practices common in the British Royal Navy over the previous centuries, change was on the horizon from the very beginning.

As the industrial revolution gradually spread to the United States in the first half of the nineteenth century, Congress initiated the professionalization of the US Navy's officer corps by establishing the US Naval Academy in Annapolis, Maryland, in 1845. At first, the perceived need for formal officer training was *not* a response to the rapid development of steam power in the preceding decades and no particular education was provided along these lines. Caring for the few unreliable and inefficient engines in the navy in the years just after the Naval Academy's founding therefore became the responsibility of specialist contractors trained in the private sector. These early naval engineers worked outside the existing chain of command and possessed no formal rank.

During the American Civil War, the advent of ironclad warships derived from the initial design of USS *Monitor* of 1862 elevated the importance of the naval engineer to a level that the navy brass could no longer ignore. The complete reliance of these ships on their engines for propulsion compelled the establishment of a permanent cadre of Annapolis-trained engineers in 1866.[3] This specialist corps had its own rank system ("cadet engineer," etc.) and operated under a separate chain of command from the rest of the navy. Such a segregated system in a peacetime organization naturally produced significant friction over authority and rights to promotion. To resolve this conflict, the US government and the navy bureaucracy first merged cadets of all types into a single Naval Academy curriculum in 1882.

When friction continued, the engineering corps was abolished, and the ranks were formally unified in 1899.[4]

Not only did this long-standing animosity contribute to the well-known rivalry between topside and belowdecks enlisted personnel (known to each other as "apes" and "snipes," respectively), but this prolonged period of internal conflict between the executive and engineer officers also created a deep-rooted and lasting rift in the officer corps. This was not limited to officers whose commissioning predated the unification of the ranks; even officers coming through the Naval Academy *after* unification were forced to grapple with the prejudices of their teachers, mentors, and fellow officers who had preceded them. This collective experience clearly developed into an institutional aversion to overspecialization and a poorly concealed contempt for career engineers by less specialized individuals. This is readily apparent in the oft-cited memoirs of Admiral Bowen (who graduated from the Naval Academy in 1905) and is also clear in the debate surrounding the creation of specialist designations in the decades that followed.[5]

After 1899, *all* regular officers received their initial training at the Naval Academy in Annapolis. Admission to the academy was contingent upon passing a competitive entrance exam. Once accepted, the new midshipmen received a standardized, four-year education directed toward their transformation into a "general line officer." In the tradition of the age of sail, this type of officer was expected to have a wide range of professional knowledge; familiarization with gunnery, engineering, and navigation were considered the basis for the effective assertion of command.[6] As such, the academy curriculum focused on indoctrination (leadership, drill, naval history), the sciences (navigation, mathematics, practical engineering, chemistry, and physics), and a limited amount of general seamanship. However, no great depth was reached on any particular subject.[7]

As a supplement to the academy, the Naval Reserve Officer Training Corps (NROTC) was created at six college campuses across the United States in 1926. The intent was to provide a pool of candidates from which additional officers could be drawn in a time of emergency expansion. These individuals were encouraged to major in engineering or the sciences and were instructed in basic drill on weekends. During the summers, reserve officers were sent on fifteen-day training cruises to provide a limited amount of practical experience. Outside of these basic guidelines, there was little standardization of the curriculum. As the only navy officer reserve in existence by 1939, the NROTC was underutilized as a supply of regular officers prior to World War II due to the restricted authorized strength of the officer corps.[8]

An Annapolis education was therefore generally the prelude to an officer's first posting to sea duty. As in the age of sail, newly promoted ensigns were expected to rotate through nearly every junior officer position available aboard their first vessels. This would theoretically allow them to absorb a large quantity of practical knowledge and ultimately qualify them to stand as a deck watch officer in any department after up to one year at each particular task.[9] The concept did not always function precisely in the intended manner, but it always formed the basis of an officer's early experience. It also typically resulted in the discovery of a favored area of command, even if official specialization was out of the question. In Admiral Bowen's case, the later portion of his initial time afloat found him posted aboard USS *Hopkins* (DD-8), an early destroyer suffering from perpetual boiler problems. "Like all passed Midshipmen," Bowen wrote, "I performed the duties of a junior officer on deck and in the engine room."[10] In the case of the *Hopkins*, much of his time as one of the two officers aboard was spent in the latter. His later passion for engineering should therefore come as little surprise.

The first sea posting itself represented only the initial step in an extensive career-long training process. All regular officers alternated between shore and sea duties after their initial postgraduation posting. This was interspersed with shore leave for more extensive education in the basic subjects covered at the Naval Academy. Officers received this gradual accretion of experience until they were considered qualified for increasingly important commands. In line with this policy of continuous professional development, the navy organized the US Naval Postgraduate School as a division of the US Naval Academy in 1909. Designed to serve as an adjunct to sea experience, it was intended that 9 percent of the navy's officers would be in postgraduate training at all times, most of them in the "general line" leadership course offered at the school.[11]

In principle, this system was not intended to favor any particular skills or interests. As is so often the case with good intentions, reality played out differently. A premium was often placed on seaborne command over the command of shore installations, and individual ships had a wide variety of unique requirements and challenges. Most significantly, the introduction of various technologies such as the turbine, centralized fire-control, and advanced armor between 1900 and 1915 rapidly complicated the design and maintenance of newer warships beyond the basic understanding of the line officer. The navy responded by grudgingly creating a single subclassification for general line officers in 1917: EDO, or engineering duty only.[12]

From our modern perspective, the choice of the blatantly pejorative label "engineering duty only" for mission-critical personnel is a clear act of petty vengeance by those opposed to specialization of the officer corps. This was not lost on Bowen's contemporaries; Admiral Robert S. Griffin, a former chief of BuEng himself, commented soon after EDO's creation that "the EDO is like a mule, no pride of ancestry and no hope of posterity."[13] For his own part, Admiral Bowen wrote in his autobiography that the term was "not a particularly happy choice, appearing to represent animus or lack of acquaintance with the unusual opportunities presented by the English language for exact and gracious expression."[14] Yet, despite the negative connotation, officers who chose to accept the EDO label were highly qualified individuals. These men were generally around thirty years old at the time of designation, had demonstrated exceptional performance in engineering duties at sea, and were either enrolled in or had passed the limited engineering course offered at the Naval Postgraduate School.[15]

EDO officers were intended for highly placed advisory or design posts (either on a fleet staff or at a major navy-owned shipyard). Yet, the number of such positions was extremely limited. Additionally, as the "engineering duty *only*" title might indicate, EDO officers were disqualified from holding the seaborne command or high command positions of the general line (they were not "qualified" by seaborne experience). Accepting the EDO title thus represented a calculated risk that was more likely than the general line to result in career stagnation. For those who had not (or could not) reach the highest positions, an alternative eventually developed. In keeping with the traditions of the rest of the navy, the less experienced of these men were given command of the engineering spaces of major combatants, thereby concentrating shipboard engineering duties in the hands of the best-educated (and least numerous) officers in the navy. Between 1917 and 1940, these over-qualified men played the role of mentors, capable of imparting the intricacies of early steam-turbine propulsion to the navy's youngest officers. Such was the structure of naval education and training at the dawn of the high-steam era.[16]

During the rise of high steam, it is important to note that while BuEng was staffed by EDO personnel with a specialty in propulsion engineering like Bowen, BuC&R and INSURV (as the chief opposition) were much more heterogeneous. The Bureau of Construction and Repair naturally had a number of highly trained engineers, but Admiral DuBose and his staff were focused on overall hull design, not technological systems. They were naval *architects*, much closer to the "generalist" category than Bowen's "techno-centric" cadre of *engineers*.[17] For its part, Admiral Brinser's Board of Inspection and Survey was staffed by officers with a far more general background. Brinser himself was the epitome of this, having commanded the battleship USS *Mississippi* (BB-41) and, most recently, Cruiser Division 4 before becoming president of INSURV. The general board hearing over high steam thus represents a major clash between specialists and generalists for ultimate control of naval design. It is clear evidence that the unification of the ranks had not systematically eliminated the navy's aversion to specialization or specialist control, even by 1938 (figure 5.1).

FIGURE 5.1. No time for interruptions. From left to right in the front row: Chief of Naval Operations William D. Leahy, Secretary of the Navy Claude Swanson, Judge Advocate General Walter B. Woodson, Chief of the Bureau of Construction and Repair William G. DuBose, and Chief of the Bureau of Engineering Harold G. Bowen open bids for the *South Dakota*-class battleships on November 2, 1938. This photograph was taken a few days after Bowen testified to the General Board on the subject of high steam and well before a formal decision had been made. The individuals in the back row are unidentified. Image NH 54603 courtesy of the Naval History and Heritage Command.

RADICALS, REACTIONARIES, AND THE
GENERAL BOARD OF THE NAVY

It is within this dubious design environment that Admirals Robinson and Bowen had spent the 1930s forcing high-steam propulsion on BuC&R and the "Big Three" shipyards. Perhaps the real question is what took so long for the general board to step in!

While the unrest generated by this friction within the bureau system simmered throughout the decade, it had finally burst into open flame in 1938 following the negative publicity generated by three specific events. That year, a number of newly completed high-steam destroyers received scathing reviews from Brinser's Board of Inspection and Survey. These reports cast considerable doubt on the durability of high-steam machinery, the practicality of using complex propulsion systems in destroyers due to the limited available space, and the overall stability of numerous warships under construction. The bureaucratic finger-pointing that ensued between Bowen, DuBose, and Brinser was then amplified by "Big Three" shipbuilder Bethlehem's renewed lobbying for a return to lower-pressure Parsons turbines.[18] To make matters worse, by this stage the navy's internal dissension over steam conditions was relatively well-known with Congress and was beginning to reach the ears of the general public. Any deficiencies of design that might be attributed to this inability of the navy bureaucracy to cooperate, whether real or imagined, could be a PR nightmare in the making for Secretary Swanson. It was therefore ultimately to avert this looming crisis that Admiral Hart received the secretary's request for the general board to study "steam conditions of pressure" in the closing months of 1938.[19]

During Thomas Hart's time as chairman, the General Board of the Navy was usually composed of seven general line officers, the majority of whom were admirals either fresh from seaborne command or expected to assume such a role in the near future. In late 1938, the board's ranks included Admirals Frederick J. Horne (former commander of Aircraft, Battle Force), Julius C. Townsend (former commander of Cruiser Division 2), Frank H. Sadler (former commander of Cruiser Division 6), and Andrew C. Pickens (former aide to the secretary of the navy). The junior members of the board were Captain William R. Purnell (board secretary and former commander of the tanker USS *Cuyama* [AO-3]), and Commander Charles A. Baker (former commander of the *Clemson*-class destroyer USS *Edsall* [DD-219]).[20] These men met daily in a series of rooms in the rear of the seventh wing of the Navy Department. These meetings were either "open" or "closed" depending on the agenda. "Open" meetings were generally when experts were interviewed for their knowledge and views on topics assigned to the board for study. On the other hand, "closed" meetings were usually attended only by the members of the board and often took the form of informal discussions of which little or no record was kept. General board studies commonly included a number of both types of meetings. After a consensus had been reached on the topic in question, a report would be composed for submission to the secretary of the navy. This "Judgement of the Board," which would carry Hart's signature, was what Swanson was after to put an end to the high-steam controversy in a Supreme Court decision–like manner.[21]

As mentioned in the last chapter, Thomas C. Hart was an opponent of high steam (figure 5.2). And as might be expected from such a remark and his role on the board, Hart was a nontechnical officer, albeit one with a record of various submarine commands in addition to his recent command

FIGURE 5.2. Admiral Thomas C. Hart, chairman of the General Board of the Navy from 1937 to 1939. Image NH 95164 courtesy of the Naval History and Heritage Command.

of Cruiser Division 6 from 1934 to 1936. He reported to the general board in 1936 to assume the role of chairman, and by October 1938 his tenure had been characterized by advocacy for advanced submarine, destroyer, and cruiser building projects.[22]

The conflict between Hart's own progressivism and his suspicion of Bowen's motives put him in an awkward position for the high-steam study—particularly as there were no EDOs on the board. While the chairman of the board would often delegate the facilitator role for the "open" meetings (often also referred to as "hearings") to a more junior member, the tension in the officer corps surrounding this particular study left Hart open to potential claims of bias.[23] He therefore took the laudable step of summoning the closest thing he could find to an expert, *outside* mediator: Rear Admiral Ormond L. Cox, the director of the navy's Engineering Experiment Station in Annapolis. Rather than question expert witnesses directly, as was commonly the board's practice, Hart placed Cox, an engineer himself, "somewhat in the position of a Judge Advocate." It was primarily Cox who did the questioning of witnesses, with Board members speaking up only for purposes of clarification.[24]

With Cox in hand as a facilitator, requests were sent out beginning on October 20, 1938, for a variety of witnesses to provide testimony over the following six weeks. It was ultimately Hart's decision to rely not only on the opposing arguments of the claimants involved in this particular dispute (BuEng, BuC&R, and INSURV) but also on the knowledge of the increasingly broad base of companies now contracting for the navy. This included engineers from the "Big Three" shipyards, boiler manufacturer Babcock & Wilcox, turbine manufacturers like General Electric, and William Francis Gibbs himself. However, while the technical information from all these parties was clearly valued and carefully considered, it was surprisingly not the defining feature of the board's overall report. Instead, that honor was accorded to the testimony provided by Lieutenants Charles J. Hardesty Jr. and Carl M. Dalton, the engineering officers of USS *Somers* (DD-381) and USS *Warrington* (DD-383).[25]

There are a number of possible reasons why Hardesty and Dalton's testimony was so heavily quoted in the board's records while that of other witnesses was not. The men themselves appear to have been fairly typical junior members of the interwar officer corps, working in the engineering spaces of their destroyers as a standard part of their early career rotation.[26] They were therefore about as unbiased as could possibly be expected for a general line officer at that time (and as we shall see, while understandably defensive about their own handling of their ships' equipment in front of a panel of admirals, these men were willing to openly weigh the positives and negatives of their machinery). Additionally, Hardesty and Dalton were the first witnesses the board interviewed, reporting the same day (Thursday, October 20) that the requests for interviews went out. Finally, these men had some of the *only* firsthand experiences with the most advanced machinery then in service with the fleet.

Ultimately, as board secretary, it was Captain Purnell's responsibility to keep transcripts and file reports (although anything written by *any* member of the board was naturally subject to the scrutiny of all other members before filing). It is therefore reasonable for us to assume that it was ultimately his decision to feature Hardesty and Dalton so prominently (figure 5.3).[27] *Why* he chose to do so is another matter entirely; but given the nature of the board's closed-meeting process, it is likely that the lieutenants' testimony was repeatedly brought up and heavily debated among the board members once behind closed doors. While we cannot be completely certain of this,

FIGURE 5.3. Captain William R. Purnell. Pictured here as a rear admiral in 1943, Purnell was a captain while he was secretary of the General Board of the Navy in 1938. Image NH 47252 courtesy of the Naval History and Heritage Command.

what we *can* clearly see in Purnell's report is the use of Hardesty and Dalton's testimony as a point of departure for the examination of evidence provided by other sources (and particularly that of Admiral Bowen).

A close reading of Purnell's report reveals that five major topics came to form the core of the debate over high steam: operational range, fuel, production/maintenance, cost, and manpower. The first of these is fairly well-known to us and formed the basis of Bowen and BuEng's justification for high steam's adoption. However, the rest of these subjects reveal substantially more about the complexity of Brinser and the other so-called reactionaries' motivations than has been previously recognized through relying on Bowen's account in *Ships, Machinery, and Mossbacks*. A review of this report therefore makes it quite clear that even in the late 1930s, there was enough cause for concern to discourage the general board from fully endorsing the transition to a complex high-steam system.

OPERATIONAL RANGE

As described previously, by the 1930s fleet exercises had generated substantial concern surrounding the operational ranges of many US Navy warship classes, particularly when considered in the context of Pacific war planning. The need for increased range is therefore easily identifiable as the primary motivating factor for the development of the navy's high-steam system in the 1930s. Consequently, when Admiral Bowen appeared before the board on Tuesday, October 25, 1938, the anchor of his testimony was that trial data indicated a marked increase of the calculated operating radii of all vessels so equipped.[28]

As fast, multirole escort vessels, the unique design problems of destroyers were partly responsible for the commonality of their range limitations across international boundaries. While the development of underway refueling had begun to remedy some of these problems, destroyers remained the weak link in the US fleet's power projection capability (see chapter 4). This was because these vessels had by this point fully assumed the role of fleet escorts. No naval operation was possible without a screen of fast destroyers to both protect capital ships from torpedo attacks and serve as the eyes and ears of the fleet. Speed was essential for this role, and its desirability was a major factor in the persistence of range deficiencies in ships like destroyers that had limited space for fuel. The interwar Fleet Problems had made all of this quite clear, so the need for increased range was a consistently remarked upon fact in the contract orders for the various US destroyer classes of the 1930s.[29] Admiral Bowen therefore argued that high steam was a necessary and purely beneficial move to remedy this deficiency.

Fortunately for Bowen, this was also broadly similar to the opening statements given by Hardesty and Dalton five days earlier. Unfortunately for him, the statements all had a similar weakness: they relied upon data gathered in specific, ideal conditions, a fact that did not escape Admiral Cox's attention:

> ADMIRAL COX: Will you please state approximate fuel consumption at different operating speeds?
> LIEUTENANT HARDESTY: Taking the normal standard speed of 15 knots as used on destroyers, the old destroyers with 275 pounds pressure would use about 38 gallons per mile, 1400 tons displacement. The later 1500-ton boats under 1800 tons load displacement use about 31 gallons per mile. The SOMERS at around 2600 tons at 15 knots uses only about 23 to 24 gallons per mile. These figures I am quoting from memory. These two ships, the SOMERS and the WARRINGTON, on heavier tonnage, are far more economical than the 1500-ton class equipped with lower steam temperature.
> ADMIRAL COX: At 15 knots speed you are using the cruising turbine?
> LIEUTENANT HARDESTY: Yes, sir. The limit of operation is about 18.5 knots at the heavy tonnage; under the lightest possible tonnage, about 2150, it is 19.8.[30]

The majority of the evidence provided to the board was calculated based on the best possible ranges obtained with new ships like *Somers* while making use of their cruising turbines. The reader may recall that these were additional turbines that would be utilized only at moderate speeds in order to make the best possible use of steam characteristics at that particular RPM. Other nations had occasionally experimented with full-size cruising turbines, but they had been standardized only in the US system by 1938 thanks to the increased effectiveness they promised when paired with double-reduction gearing. In *Somers* and *Warrington*, these turbines were directly attached at the head of the high-pressure turbine, and as Lieutenant Hardesty indicated, they would be bypassed with a series of valve changes when operating above 18–20 knots (depending on load). While the high-steam system as a whole was superior in power and efficiency to older propulsion systems, the cruising turbine was at the heart of the incredible reductions in fuel consumption so often cited by the high-steam "radicals."[31]

Although this trial data presented to the general board—representing up to a 25 percent decrease in fuel consumption at cruising speeds—was remarkable at a glance, the board's members repeatedly remarked throughout the high-steam study that *trial* data was not representative of true performance in all weather and conditions. While high steam did indeed *appear* to radically improve the operational range of those ships fitted with it, actual steaming data from newer vessels was lacking due to the limited numbers of comparable ships in service. Further, the step-by-step addition of components and pressure/temperature increases meant that only a small amount of experience existed with the "latest and greatest" configuration in *Somers* (600 PSI / 850°F), which itself was substantially less than the more radical numbers Bowen had proposed for the *North Carolina*-class battleships (1,200 PSI and 950°F).[32] Put simply, while high steam *appeared* to deliver on the promise of substantial increases in operating range, there was as of 1938 no *experience* to prove that it was a necessary modification for the rest of the fleet—let alone its largest, most expensive, and most important units. While some range improvement appeared likely, it remained an open question whether the additional complications to the system (discussed below) would outweigh the benefits.

FUEL

While the terms "operational range" and "fuel consumption" are often used interchangeably, fuel consumption is usually tied much more closely to boiler operation than to the functioning of the entire propulsion system. This seemingly minor difference was a point of telling confusion for Lieutenant Hardesty. During his cross-examination by Admiral Cox, Lieutenant Hardesty was specifically questioned about unique variables with the high-steam system that might affect fuel usage. He responded that his own vessel's efficiency seemed to depend on the quality of the installation's maintenance, the skill of the individual crew, and the quality of the fuel oil being used. This was due in part to the particular demands of his Babcock & Wilcox boilers, which required alterations to the burners in use for various speeds, and the touchy nature of the closed-feedwater system upon which the *Somers*-class vessels depended. This, ultimately, led to the following exchange:

ADMIRAL COX: There is no ship built that operates at a lower temperature and pressure that has the same economic installations as you have, such as economizers in the boilers, double-reduction gears, and cruising turbines. Is that right?

LIEUTENANT HARDESTY: As I remember, that is right. We are anywhere from 10 to 15 percent more economical per mile at normal cruising speeds than any of the previous low-pressure ships, and about 10 percent more economical than the PORTER, which is also an 1850-tonner with low-pressure installation.

ADMIRAL COX: The PORTER has single-reduction gear, no economizers in the boilers, so that we really have no fair comparison of one ship with high-pressure and high-temperature against an identical installation using a lower-pressure lower-temperature installation.

LIEUTENANT HARDESTY: Yes, sir, that is right. I was comparing actual performances of the ships as built.[33]

As a specialist himself, Cox was able to recognize the fact that while Lieutenant Hardesty was cognizant of the relative superiority of his ship's (that is, *Somers's*) capabilities with regard to other vessels, he may not have been entirely aware of where those advantages were coming from. After all, high steam was a *system*—one made up of a number of significant changes even from contemporary low-steam destroyers like *Porter*. This had to raise some complicated questions about the rest of the evidence being provided to the board that appeared to favor high steam. It is also likely why Hardesty's acknowledgement of Cox's correction is the last line from his testimony provided by Captain Purnell in the board's report.[34]

PRODUCTION, MAINTENANCE, AND SUPPLY

One of the major arguments against high steam presented by Admiral Brinser and the Board of Inspection and Survey was the perceived difficulties with the production and maintenance of the high-steam system (figure 5.4). Along with the debate over operational range, this subject (and the related topics of reliability and service life) became one of the focal points of the investigation.[35]

As covered in previous chapters, one of the primary issues with the transfer of high-steam technology from the electrical utility industry was the attendant shift in developmental emphasis. Power plants, civilian vessels, and warships all exist in substantially different environments. As a result, each brings a variety of concerns to prominence that may not be of issue elsewhere. For example, while damage might be a minor concern for a power plant, battle damage was a fact of life for a warship. Similarly, each entity that adopted high steam during the first three decades of the twentieth century had a different reason for doing so. This meant that "successful" use of high steam for one purpose did not necessarily guarantee it would work well for another. Brinser sought to weaponize this logic for use against Bowen.

When directly questioned on these matters on October 25, Admiral Bowen responded by explaining the principal differences between older steam propulsion turbines and the new type used with high steam.

FIGURE 5.4. Rear Admiral Harry L. Brinser, head of the Board of Inspection and Survey (INSURV) in 1938. Image NH 56246 courtesy of the Naval History and Heritage Command.

96 / CHAPTER 5

Specifically, smaller machinery is possible with high pressure and temperature steam because best utilization of the energy of "heat drop" requires expansion of steam from small to large volumes. This lends itself to smaller turbines for increased pressure of the same amount of steam. Similarly, high-pressure steam is preferable to use with an accordingly high starting temperature in order to prevent excessive saturation from major pressure changes, which would cause excessive corrosion. Thus, a high starting pressure *and* temperature are desirable. Additionally, decreases in the size of machinery and the addition of double-reduction gearing results in shorter and stiffer turbines that, according to Bowen, are "free from torsional vibration troubles, subject to less distortion under changing temperature conditions and permit a space saving in machinery arrangement." In short, the move to high steam should have decreased the size, weight, and complexity of many individual propulsion components, particularly the turbines, and therefore represented a long-term savings in maintenance costs.[36]

Testimony and data provided by William Gibbs on November 9 also contributed considerable detail about the additional machinery required to accommodate high-pressure and high-temperature steam. This was, in turn, accompanied by a sharp increase in the amount of piping in the engineering spaces in early iterations of the system's design (such as in the destroyer *Mahan*), though in *Somers* and *Warrington* this characteristic was not as pronounced.[37] Nevertheless, engineering congestion and inaccessibility had been one of the major charges brought repeatedly by Brinser and INSURV against Bowen and BuEng over the last several years and had become widely enough known that Admiral Hart felt the need to question Lieutenant Dalton on the matter directly:

> ADMIRAL HART: Lieutenant Dalton, keeping in mind only the hot steam feature of your installation, what is the comparison in ease and certainty of maintenance and preservation as compared to older installations?
> LIEUTENANT DALTON: It has been my experience that the plant is a little more inaccessible due to the increased temperature than has been the case with the lower pressure ships. The boilers are of such a nature that thorough cleaning in many spaces is rather difficult. So far as the arrangement is concerned in the engine room that is fairly accessible. The plant I believe will require slightly more time devoted to

opening up, but the process of cleaning and replacing parts is the item requiring extra time.[38]

The ease of accessibility for general maintenance and cleaning was critical for determining long-term reliability. For example, while boilers that were difficult to clean properly may not seem like a major issue in peacetime, a wartime environment would likely not provide enough time to complete routine maintenance on *easily* accessible machinery. As a result, dangerous complications could develop at the most critical times.

While this was a particular concern of Hart's, it formed a part of a broader discussion about general reliability in which other members of the board spoke up. As was the case with operational range, at the time of the hearing, there was no substantive data on whether high-steam systems would actually prove as reliable over their entire service life as older systems—and the board zeroed in on this fact:

> ADMIRAL HORNE: Mr. Hardesty, have any inspections been made to determine the condition of the metals that come into contact with high temperature in the plant?
> LIEUTENANT HARDESTY: No, sir, no metallurgical examinations.
> ADMIRAL HORNE: Have any inspections been made that indicate any change?
> LIEUTENANT HARDESTY: No, sir.[39]

The best reliability information available to the board was the commercial and experimental data provided by Gibbs and a detailed list of all propulsion casualties experienced by destroyers from the *Farragut* through *Somers* classes. The latter of these was fairly substantial despite the limited amount of time involved. However, no new vessel is ever without teething problems, and all of the vessels contained on the list had been in service for fewer than five years, making the data difficult to interpret. While Hardesty and Dalton made it known that they believed their systems would prove at *least* as reliable as those of previous vessels, the board as a whole was openly skeptical of these claims. Unfortunately, not much could be proven on the subject without additional operational experience at sea.[40]

Finally, discussion of these topics eventually turned to the related subject of production. As junior officers brought in for their experience *operating* high-steam systems, Hardesty and Dalton had nothing to contribute on this matter. This was instead Admiral Bowen's time to shine, as he was *the* relevant subject matter expert in uniform. Production changes therefore formed a major component of Bowen's justification for adopting high steam.

On October 25, Bowen described at length his enforcement of the Espionage Act that by 1938 had forced all major shipyards to purchase propulsion machinery from American (rather than British) companies. This transition, he argued, had pushed General Electric and Westinghouse into "unprecedented" efforts to ensure that the US Navy was provided with the "best turbines in the world" (see chapter 4).[41] Implied within this testimony was an assurance that the supply of rugged and efficient propulsion machinery had, in no manner, been endangered by the adoption of high steam and that the equipment being provided to the navy was at least as reliable and easily available as it had ever been. This explanation was corroborated by the November testimony of William Gibbs, who provided background on his company's relationship with shipyards and equipment manufacturers prior to the arrival of navy contracts earlier in the decade.[42]

However, as was the case with the concerns surrounding reliability, there was simply a lack of cooperative experience between the US Navy and companies like General Electric, Westinghouse, and other high-steam contractors such as DeLaval (which produced double-reduction gears). Hart and the rest of the general board understood that war could dramatically upset the status quo that had been tentatively achieved by Bowen's BuEng in its relationship with the "Big Three" and smaller shipyards and threaten quality control at the very least. Such a problem could easily upend the advantages that Bowen sought in range and reliability. Unfortunately, these concerns would prove to be well-founded, as we shall see later.

Throughout this discussion, the critical questions relating to production, maintenance, and reliability of the American high-steam system remained unanswered. It was made clear from the direction of his argument that Bowen was aware of potential difficulties attached to the transition of high steam from shore to warship. In fact, he even repeatedly cited ruggedness and reliability as the second objective of high steam's adoption, followed by the perceived weight savings that high-steam turbines promised. However, it was simultaneously demonstrated that Bowen was making more of a leap of faith than he was willing to openly admit.[43]

FINANCIAL CHANGES

Surprisingly, the financial changes that accompanied high steam were downplayed throughout the course of the general board hearings. It likely comes as no shock to the reader in our modern era of astronomical defense budgets that pushing the technological envelope often entails a hefty price tag. While naval high steam did not represent what we might consider state-of-the-art steam technology in 1938, we can safely assume that its adaption to the unique requirements of marine and combat use came at a huge price.

The significant cost of high-steam propulsion quickly became clear in the course of Hardesty's interview with the board. When questioned about maintenance, the lieutenant offered the following statement:

> LIEUTENANT HARDESTY: So far we have experienced no difference in amount of personnel necessary for upkeep due to high-pressure high-temperature steam. However, the cost of upkeep has considerably increased. This is necessarily due to the expensive fittings such as machine steel gaskets. A ¼-inch gasket costs 90 cents and a 5-inch gasket as much as 6 dollars; under the low-pressure, low-temperature type an ordinary gasket costs about 5 cents. The same holds true for all other fittings that go with high-pressure, high-temperature steam.[44]

While this information had to be important on some level if Hardesty was so quick to offer it, the point was not pressed by Cox or any member of the board.

For his part, Bowen himself testified that a particular alloy—carbon molybdenum steel—was required for many components in direct contact with superheated steam. Traditional carbon steel underwent a chemical transformation as it heated up, making it not only expand excessively but develop critical weaknesses when approaching the temperatures used in the navy's modern destroyers. Carbon molybdenum steel was capable of handling up to 950°F before deforming, but this advantage came at a considerable cost in both monetary amounts and casting complexity. Similarly, 4–6 percent chrome alloy steel was required in the superheater itself due to the consistency of the heat and the potential for temperatures to rise even higher than desired. Similar requirements were represented by every part of the high-steam system that came in contact with the steam itself, particularly the turbines.[45]

None of these changes inherent with high steam were inexpensive. While specific amounts were not defined by the board's final report at the end of 1938, it is safe to assume that its members were well aware of the escalating costs directly associated with it. In fact, less than a year later, the Bureau of Supplies and Accounts reported an increase in machinery costs from $1.867 million in the *Farragut* class (which had British-designed Parsons machinery) to $2.823 million with *Somers*, an exercise necessary due to the close monitoring of defense spending by Congress of the interwar period (table 5.1). Nevertheless, Bowen and BuEng believed that the costs were justified for the advantages they offered, particularly the gains in operational range. For Hart and the rest of the general board in 1938, the high costs associated with high steam must have ultimately been understood and thereby regarded as a necessary evil to be suffered only if high steam was justified by other means.[46]

EDUCATION AND MANPOWER

The final major topic to be addressed during the high-steam study was the educational and manpower requirements of the new system. As was the case with funding, this was a particular concern during the interwar period when the navy was short on both cash and manpower. Unlike the cost

Table 5.1. Comparative Costs of Destroyer Construction

Year Completed	Ship (Class)	Tonnage (Standard)	S.H.P.	Hull and Machinery Cost	Average Machinery Cost	Cost per H.P.	Cost Per Ton
1921	Perry (Clemson)	1,215	24,975	$1,444,000	$947,000	37.92	$1,175
1935	Worden (Farragut)	1,365	40,127	$2,721,000	$1,867,000	46.52	$1,965
1939	Sampson (Somers)	1,840	51,200	$3,745,000	$2,823,000	55.14	$2,393

A comparison of expenses associated with three classes of destroyers constructed in the interwar period reveals the rapidly escalating costs that can be directly attributed to high-steam machinery. While *Perry* and *Worden* were constructed with British-designed Parsons machinery (the latter capable of 400 PSI, 650°F operation), *Sampson*'s home-grown machinery represented a substantial increase in overhead.

Source: Chief of the Bureau of Supplies and Accounts to Secretary of the Navy, "Cost of Naval Vessels," September 21, 1939, General Board File 420 1938-1939, General Board Subject File 1900–1947, Box 55, RG 80, NAB, 14.

factor, however, there was considerable effort expended by the board to investigate during its study the issue of manpower changes brought by high steam.

Both Admiral Bowen and William F. Gibbs asserted unconditionally that high steam required no more manpower than the system it replaced. Using evidence provided by Gibbs & Cox, their claim was primarily based on the day-to-day activities observed by commercial vessels using high-pressure and high-temperature steam rather than warships.[47] However, Lieutenant Dalton of *Warrington*, one of the few military men with direct experience operating a high-steam system, specifically testified that the new air-encased Babcock & Wilcox boilers in his ship required "very good water tending" and "necessitate at least one extra [enlisted] man in the fire room."[48]

While the addition of one extra man or increased attention to one ship's equipment might not sound significant, Dalton's testimony played into another accusation from Brinser and INSURV: that high-steam installations would require significantly better-*educated* officers and men as well as increased overall manpower to operate. It was for this reason that Admiral Hart intervened to question Lieutenant Dalton further on this matter:

> ADMIRAL HART: Lieutenant Dalton, will you give us an estimate of the comparative demands on the personnel in operating the old-time destroyer plants or, say, the more recent plants at lower pressure, and your own plant?
>
> LIEUTENANT DALTON: I feel that higher-type men and men better qualified are necessary in view of the fact that there is the possibility of damaging the boilers unless operated in accordance with instructions and unless the people are well-trained. Likewise, I feel that in the engine room well qualified men are necessary in order to operate the machinery properly and in order to keep it up in the best of condition because everything is a new design and a complete change from that machinery which the men have normally operated; therefore I believe that the men should be of a higher type in so far as to their ability to grasp a knowledge of machinery.[49]

Responses from both Hardesty and Dalton up to this point appear to have been clear, concise, and to the point. That is not the case with this explanation; instead, Hart's question appears to have caught Dalton off guard and resulted in a hesitant, meandering answer. This is likely due to a combination of it being the first time Captain Purnell records Admiral Hart as speaking up during the hearing and Lieutenant Dalton's own surprise at an admiral asking a junior officer such a high-level question. Regardless, while Dalton's answer was given primarily in terms of enlisted men rather than officers, he gave voice to the unique situation that the navy's officer *and* enlisted corps found itself in by 1938.

As discussed earlier in this chapter, the late-interwar navy represented a highly trained cadre of career men who had learned their trade through a considerable amount of time and experience in the lower ranks. This held true for both the officers and the enlisted corps, who were just as likely to be long-service professionals as their leaders were. While *this* group of men was likely capable of making the transition to high-steam propulsion without great difficulty, Admiral Hart (and, it appears, Lieutenant Dalton) perceived that any changes to that core of men *could* potentially cause significant operating problems for the fleet. Dalton's confusing use of the term "better qualified men" in his response to Hart's question underscores his uncertainty on this subject. While both Admiral Bowen and William Gibbs argued to the contrary in the weeks after this interview, they were very specific in that they considered only *experienced* engineers in a severely limited set of data.[50] Considering what was already published regarding the importance of operator proficiency with older propulsion systems, it is unlikely that Bowen and Gibbs failed to perceive the same potential issues should conflict require the rapid expansion of the navy.[51]

VICTORY BY NO DECISION

Having reviewed the major points of contention, the dreams and fears of the US Navy's venture into high steam should be clear. Bowen, Gibbs, and the "radicals" who supported them desired high steam for what they saw as its overwhelming advantages in operating range, fuel efficiency, and power-to-weight ratio. They also asserted that the new system was likely to be *at least* as reliable as the old and that in future designs it would probably occupy less hull space.[52] The "reactionary" opposition headed by Brinser believed that these advantages were too expensive to manufacture and maintain, took up too much space *now*, substantially increased the educational requirements for new recruits, and were potentially prone to dangerous failure from improper maintenance.[53]

The lack of data on which to base an unequivocal judgment on this matter clearly troubled Admiral Hart and the rest of the general board throughout their study of the subject in the final three months of 1938. This shortcoming was so acute that from the evidence presented, it would not have been surprising if the board had decided to rule against any increases beyond 400 PSI as the "reactionaries" desired. There was, however, one wild card that we have not touched upon. Submitted to the general board on October 26, 1938, was an extensive memorandum from Admiral William R. Munroe, director of the Office of Naval Intelligence (ONI). This was a compilation of what the US Navy perceived as the experience with high steam of the British, Japanese, German, French, and Italian navies according to their best sources. The document describes both the Japanese and Germans as potentially far exceeding US efforts in high-pressure steam usage, with suspicions that many of their known technical difficulties had by 1938 been resolved. While we know today (and discussed previously) that this assessment was far from accurate, it likely had the effect of strongly reinforcing Admiral Bowen's assertions the day before that the United States was in danger of falling behind the world standard in marine propulsion. This appears to have overcome the general board's reservations about continuing the adoption of high steam.[54]

The Hart board ultimately determined that it did not feel justified in issuing an "opinion based on opinions" on the subject of high-steam propulsion. Instead, its position statement, "An Estimate on Temperature and Pressure," which was signed and submitted to Secretary Swanson by Admiral Hart in December 1938, was highly critical of the radicals' methods but deferred to Bowen's expertise:

> Commitments have now been made involving huge sums appropriated for National Defense; by those commitments the Navy Department, not heretofore given to following the advanced ideas or whims entertained by particular sets [sic], has declared itself an ardent proponent of high pressure and of temperature approaching but not exceeding 850 degrees. . . . The lower pressure plant could never realize the economies of the higher and if it did afterwards develop that the theorists [supporting high steam] had been able to make good on their theory in practice the new ships would be old by a small percentage. The Navy Department has gone too far on a whim to walk back on a hunch. There must be a well-established fact to show that the decision to follow the advanced thought is wrong and there is no such fact known to this board.[55]

The General Board of the Navy decided it could not rule against high steam. However, the growing belief that additional testing was needed—which the board additionally cited in its final statement—influenced the subsequent decision to maintain pressures and temperatures at 600 PSI, 850°F rather than going any further.[56] Bowen's high-steam system was, as a result, the propulsion system of the bulk of the US Navy's modern warships during World War II. This was Bowen's victory—such as it was.

Chapter 6

FULL STEAM AHEAD

At the end of 1938, the General Board of the Navy concluded its study of the high-steam question with a refusal to recommend that BuEng back down from its progressive agenda. In doing so, Admiral Hart and his fellows effectively endorsed the course upon which Admiral Bowen had placed the navy: toward spreading the newly developed high-steam system throughout all new warship designs. However, the controversy that had accompanied Bowen's actions resulted in a number of repercussions the admiral had not anticipated. The most significant of these were a freeze placed on further modifications of the high-steam system and the merger of the Bureau of Engineering and Bureau of Construction and Repair (which eliminated Bowen's de facto position of engineer in chief). These changes effectively locked in 600 PSI, 850°F high steam as the propulsion system with which the US Navy would fight World War II.

FALLOUT FROM THE HART BOARD'S DECISION

Lacking any hard evidence for or against high steam, the General Board of the Navy allowed development to continue after 1938. Circumstantial evidence in the form of design specifications, trial data, and performance in shore-based electric utility systems indicated that high steam would be useful in BuEng's ultimate mission of extending warship operating range. However, the board was ever mindful of the fact that, despite appearances, the navy had markedly different requirements and operating conditions from existing uses of high steam. The judgment of the board clearly reflected this sentiment that experience held the potential to shift the balance of advantage and disadvantage against the new system: "It is only in service tests that true experience is obtained and, as concerns materials and machinery for shipboard use, comparisons end at water's edge. Shore establishments are of little value in obtaining directives for sea operation and even at sea commercial practices and problems differ so widely from the Navy that they offer unsound guidance in a consideration of the power plants of combatant ships. Even the men who operate the plants are different, with different objectives and different controlling laws."[1]

Yet it was with those ominous words that the US Navy committed itself to the use of the high-steam system for the foreseeable future! In refusing to become the definitive voice against high steam, the general board was in effect endorsing Bowen and permitting his organization to move forward. This, by extension, guaranteed that all warship types designed and built after 1938 would be equipped with a high-steam system, just as BuEng had planned before the hearings.

Also clear from the general board study was that Bowen and DuBose—and by extension, their organizations BuEng and BuC&R—were incapable of working together on design matters. On this subject, high steam was simply the straw that broke the camel's back.[2] In 1939, both Admiral Bowen and Admiral DuBose were replaced as chiefs of their respective bureaus, the former by a recalled Admiral Robinson, who as the reader might recall, had initiated the high-steam transition with the *Farragut* design earlier in the decade. Under Robinson's supervision, the bureaus were then combined into BuShips in 1940. As a direct result, the navy would not have an engineer-in-chief during World War II.[3]

The simultaneous adoption of these two courses of action—the adoption of the high-steam system as it stood at the end of 1938 and the dissolution of the engineering organization responsible for bringing that system about—placed the navy at a crossroads. Continued development of high steam was not off the table, particularly since Admiral Robinson was familiar with the concept. But it was naturally disrupted by the merger of the navy's two primary design organizations, a fact quickly made apparent during the first substantial building program authorized by Congress in 1939. Rather than allowing more time for the combined BuEng-BuC&R to draft and issue contracts—and given the lack of performance data available—contracts issued for the destroyer program were effectively repeats of those authorized in the previous fiscal year. This would be a recurring trend as orders continued to pile up. During World War II, design changes on all types of American military equipment were kept to a minimum in order to avoid production losses due to retooling.

The technical development of the American high-steam system was effectively stopped at the point it had reached at the end of the general board

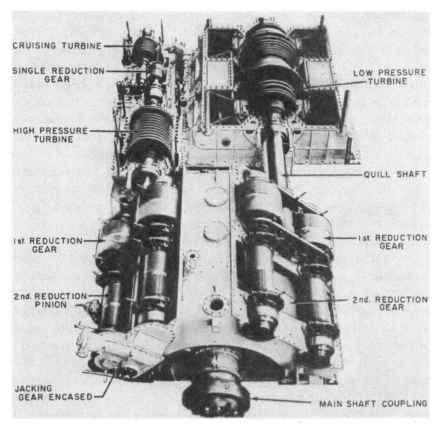

FIGURE 6.1. Cross-compounded turbine "set" for an *Allen M. Sumner*-class destroyer. Representing one propeller shaft's worth of turbines and gears, this machinery is changed only in size from that installed in the later destroyers of the 1930s. The casings have been lifted here to expose the rotors. Source: Bureau of Naval Personnel, *Principles of Naval Engineering*, 101.

hearings—not due to any specific order, but out of necessity. High steam as embodied in the *Gleaves*-class destroyers would be repeated, essentially unchanged, in all US warship designs throughout World War II (figure 6.1).

CHANGES TO THE CAST

The Hart board's ruling marked a watershed moment not only for US naval design but also for many of the individuals who were vital characters in the high-steam crisis.

Admiral Thomas C. Hart, chairman of the General Board of the Navy in 1938, was appointed commander in chief, US Asiatic Fleet in July 1939. When the Japanese attacked American forces in late 1941, Hart's handful of PT boats, old "S-boat" submarines, and *Clemson*-class destroyers and his single *Omaha*-class cruiser were all that he had to oppose Japanese operations in the Philippines. As a result, he was forced to move his headquarters from Manila to Java in January 1942, where he was appointed naval commander of the short-lived American-British-Dutch-Australian Command (ADBACOM). That, too, was overwhelmed just over a month later, after which Hart returned to the United States politically tainted by defeat. After a brief retirement, Hart was recalled to serve out the war as a member of a much-diminished General Board of the Navy. He then retired for good in early 1945 to serve out a single-year appointment as a US senator for Connecticut.

After Hart left the general board for the Asiatic Fleet, Board Secretary William R. Purnell was briefly transferred to command of the cruiser USS *New Orleans* (CA-32) before being summoned to Manila in January 1940 to serve as Hart's chief of staff. Unlike his patron, Purnell politically survived the destruction of both the Asiatic Fleet and ABDACOM. Promoted to rear admiral just before the outbreak of war, he found himself assigned the job of deputy chief of naval operations for material in late 1942—a role that landed him on the Military Policy Committee, the three-man panel that oversaw the Manhattan Project. As the navy's primary liaison to the program, Purnell was a central figure in the deployment and use of the "Little Boy" and "Fat Man" weapons against Japan. Purnell retired from the navy in October 1946.[4]

Admiral Harry L. Brinser, who acted as Bowen's chief antagonist during the general board study of high steam, briefly took over the role of chairman of the General Board of the Navy on an interim basis following Hart's departure in 1939. He continued to serve as president of INSURV until 1940, when he retired. After the Japanese attack on Pearl Harbor, Brinser was recalled to active duty to command the New York Navy Yard, where he remained until his death in December 1945.[5]

After being removed from BuC&R in 1939, Admiral William G. DuBose was appointed director of the David W. Taylor Model Basin in Carderock, Maryland. The following year, DuBose retired from the navy to assume the role of director for a resurgent Cramp Shipbuilding, which the US Navy was reopening to aid its buildup efforts. The company encountered significant problems with the refurbishment of its facilities—the original yard on the site, which had built Gibbs's *Malolo*, had closed in 1927—and never lived up to the hopes the navy pinned upon it. Cramp closed again in 1947.[6]

Admiral Harold G. Bowen Sr. initially seemed to weather the high-steam controversy well. The admiral was elated with the outcome of the general board hearing and, given this "success," fully expected to be named chief of the new Bureau of Ships. To his disappointment, instead the admiral was appointed the director of the Naval Research Laboratory (NRL) in Washington, DC, with the opportunity to lead that organization through one of the critical moments in modern US history. Unfortunately, Bowen's tenure at the NRL was brief. Continuing personality conflicts between the admiral and Frank Knox, Swanson's successor as secretary of the navy, led to Bowen's removal in 1941 after only two years on the job.[7]

It is a testament to Admiral Bowen's dogged determination that even this was not yet the end of his naval career. Instead of leading naval scientific development into new fields like radar, 1942 found Bowen in the good graces of Undersecretary of the Navy James V. Forrestal. Although the admiral was politically radioactive elsewhere, Forrestal nevertheless named Bowen special assistant to the undersecretary. In this role, Bowen was charged with seizing and operating companies working defense contracts who underwent major strikes or were otherwise perceived to suffer from severe mismanagement. He appears to have been highly successful in this role—enough that Forrestal, now secretary of the navy, rewarded him in 1946 with control of the newly created Office of Research and Invention (ORI). This was effectively a second chance for Bowen to make a play for control of the navy's stake in nuclear technology, one that he is widely perceived to have squandered with the NRL in 1941. In the end, this effort would also conclude with failure. Instead of Bowen and the ORI, control over nuclear technology in the navy went to the successor of Bowen's old bureau: a division of the Bureau of Ships led by Hyman G. Rickover.[8]

Bowen retired from the navy in 1947 and wrote his memoir, *Ships, Machinery, and Mossbacks*, in the immediate aftermath of these events.

PREPARING FOR WAR PLAN ORANGE

Ideally, national naval strategy should dictate the parameters of warship designs. In reality, financial, political, or logistical considerations often place limits on the imagination of naval architects. While this held true for the Treaty-era US Navy, the longevity of War Plan Orange as a focal point of American naval strategy resulted in an unusually consistent drive to satisfy many of the plan's prerequisites. By 1939, Orange prescribed a long campaign across the Pacific to relieve the Philippines, expected to be taken under siege by the Japanese soon after the outbreak of hostilities. Whether American forces were able to hold out or not, their relief remained the priority of US planning right up until the attack on Pearl Harbor.[9]

Such a campaign as that depicted in War Plan Orange demanded the development of warships with the longest-possible operational range and with provisions for long cruising intervals between engagements. It is clear, at least, that the US Navy (and particularly Bowen and BuEng) had come to believe that high-steam technology would satisfy this need and also offer decreased machinery weight, ease of maintenance, and a leg-up on rival navies. When combined with the navy's development of underway refueling, this technological combination would in theory open up new operational possibilities for any conflict in the Pacific Ocean and beyond.

However, like the majority of the US Navy's building programs in the first half of the twentieth century, many ship classes were being designed before adequate test data existed from previous designs. As of 1938, there was no absolute proof that high steam would deliver on its promise in wartime. The navy, including even high-steam proponents in BuEng, had no illusions about this. They were also aware of other critical obstacles, such as required increases in capital investment, changes and disruption to production practices (and the existing problems with production due to the Depression and lack of previous production), and the shortage in overall funding and manpower available to the navy. What they did not foresee was the full extent of the education or production disruptions associated with implementing high steam. Worse, navy experts failed to recognize that the wartime environment for which this propulsion system had been designed was rapidly changing. All of these would place severe constraints on the operational capability of the US Navy during the first two years of its participation in World War II.

PART II

High Steam at War, 1939–1945

After Japan's withdrawal from the Naval Treaty system in 1936, Congress proceeded to authorize a number of modest increases in the total tonnage of the US Navy, concluding with an 11 percent increase in the beginning of June 1940. The same month, France surrendered to Germany, and aggressive Japanese activity in Asia intensified. As a result, the largest naval expansion bill in the history of the US Navy was passed in July 1940. The Two-Ocean Navy Act authorized a 70 percent increase in the size of the navy, an addition of 1.325 million tons that included 115 new destroyers.

This was the beginning of the crucial test for high steam. Large-scale production would place unprecedented demands on the new methods of warship construction by networks of subcontractors. Once completed, these ships had to be capably operated by officers trained by the "general line" officer education and recruiting system. Unfortunately, both of these would prove startlingly inadequate, significantly inhibiting the ability of the United States to rapidly field new warships.

The Japanese attack on Pearl Harbor in December 1941 not only brought the United States formally into World War II, but that strike—using carriers and aircraft to stretch thousands of miles across ocean considered safe—symbolically eliminated the very spaces in which the 15-knot cruising efficiency standard of high steam was to be employed. Making matters worse was the simultaneous discovery that theoretical methods used to calculate warship cruising radii over the previous thirty years were not keeping pace with high-steam development and could no longer be relied upon. The result was an immediate need for fast fleet oilers that simply could not be provided in adequate numbers. This proved catastrophic for US early-war operational planning in the Pacific theater. It also represents the forgotten legacy of high steam.

Chapter 7

THE SHIPYARD REVOLUTION

The adoption of high steam pushed the US Navy to award contracts to smaller shipyards that were more amenable to its engineering ideas than the traditional "Big Three." Unlike large yards, these companies often relied on networks of specialized subcontractors for the majority of their equipment. In the late 1930s, this network included General Electric, Westinghouse, and Allis-Chalmers—the very same companies that had developed high-steam machinery for the electrical utility industry. Their ability to supply this machinery without substantial retooling or redesign overhead instantly made reliance upon them the cheapest option for *all* shipyards after Admiral Bowen's enforcement of the Espionage Act against Parsons in 1935, and thereafter normalized this practice.

While GE and its fellows were well-placed to transfer high-steam technology to the navy, they were not prepared for a dramatic acceleration of the pace of warship construction that began in 1940. Such an extreme increase in demand was unprecedented for companies previously working only for (recently depressed) civilian industries, and many of them proved unable to meet such a challenge. The result was a confusing tangle of production delays requiring considerable time for the navy to remedy. This severely limited the resources available for additional construction programs and posed a serious risk to the overall US war effort in the opening stages of World War II.

STORM ON THE HORIZON, 1938–1940

Following the general board study, turbine and gear manufacturers General Electric, Westinghouse, Allis-Chalmers, and DeLaval became the primary providers of propulsion machinery for the US Navy. However, despite this additional demand, there is no evidence prior to the beginning of

World War II that any of these companies substantially increased production capacity in anticipation of a heavier load of navy orders. In retrospect (knowing what we do about the navy's massive buildup during World War II), this was a significant misstep.

Inaction on the part of turbine and gear manufacturers was largely dictated by common sense. The Hart board's indecision over whether to press forward, stand fast, or retreat on high steam hardly guaranteed future naval contracts to the companies in question. Rather than providing a definitive ruling, the study gave the impression that it was just as likely that the major shipyards would again begin building their own turbines following changes within the Navy Department.[1] Additionally, with the Treaty system still in effect until 1938, it appeared highly unlikely that any *major* contract orders would materialize in the near future. Existing capacity was adequate to manufacture turbines for the small numbers of destroyers and other warships then under construction.

A general lack of interest in supply mobilization planning on the part of the US Navy prior to World War II exacerbated the unknowns surrounding production. Unlike the US Army, the navy had no single agency monitoring the service's current and future needs, nor did it have any sort of contracting oversight. The navy's supply system was highly decentralized and had been ever since its apparent success during World War I. As a result, no fewer than six separate bureaus were charged with procurement during the interwar period: Engineering, Construction and Repair, Supplies and Accounts, Aeronautics, Ordnance, and Yards and Docks. These organizations were nominally supervised in this capacity by the secretary of the navy and the chief of naval operations, but neither used this power before 1941. As already observed at length with BuEng and BuC&R, the individual navy bureaus had thus become set in their ways and highly territorial by 1939, and disagreements were common. The navy had no means of coordination and no will or ability to accurately predict future needs. In this environment, it is no surprise that naval contractors were unwilling to take the risk on expansion.[2]

The end of the Treaty system, the rising threat posed by Japan in the Pacific, and the rearmament of Germany combined to change this situation entirely after 1938. Beginning with the *Benson* and *Gleaves* classes that year, destroyers were the first warship class to be ordered in rapidly escalating quantities in an attempt to provide adequate numbers of escorts to a fleet facing the prospect of war on two oceans. While the US Navy had ordered 106 vessels of this type between 1932 and 1940, 412 destroyer contracts would be issued between January 1941 and December 1945—four times as many ships in half the time (table 7.1).[3]

Complicating matters further was the dramatic administrative change to the bureau system that resulted in large part from the high-steam controversy. The reader will recall that in June 1940, BuEng and BuC&R were merged. Admiral Robinson—the head of BuEng from 1931 to 1935 and Bowen's replacement the previous year—became head of this new organization, while Admiral DuBose's replacement as head of BuC&R, Rear Admiral Alexander Van Keuren, became Robinson's deputy. Robinson and Van Keuren were therefore charged with managing an increasingly complex and unwieldy network of contractors newly converted to the "shipyard as assembly yard" process while simultaneously attempting to integrate the staff of two mutually antagonistic bureaus. This would prove to be a gargantuan task.[4]

The same month that BuShips came into being, the rapid collapse and surrender of the French Third Republic to Nazi Germany upended what

Table 7.1. US Destroyer Production, 1932–1945

Year	Laid Down	Launched	Commissioned
1932	3	0	0
1933	8	0	0
1934	21	6	2
1935	13	13	6
1936	9	17	22
1937	12	9	15
1938	14	16	5
1939	15	15	17
1940	11	18	18
1941	87	24	23
1942	101	119	81
1943	89	101	130
1944	87	85	86
1945	48	72	72

As one of the largest ship types constructed in substantial numbers, the destroyers entering service are an excellent portrait of the sudden materiel and manpower problems the navy faced in 1941–1942.

Source: Friedman, *U.S. Destroyers*, 488–513.

remained of US congressional antipathy toward the navy. Four weeks later, on July 19, the Two-Ocean Navy (or Vinson-Walsh) Act was passed in an attempt to prepare the United States for the potential of fighting simultaneous wars in the Atlantic and Pacific Oceans. The 257 ships authorized by this legislation included 18 aircraft carriers, 7 battleships, 33 cruisers, 115 destroyers, and 43 submarines. *All* of these ships had to be drawn up, contracted, designed, supplied, and built as rapidly as possible, and the *entirety* of this task landed squarely in the lap of Admiral Robinson.[5]

The initial results of this effort were predictable. As an individual bureau chief, Robinson had total control over his domain—and thanks to the recent merger, BuShips was relatively well-positioned to dictate the terms of warship design. But the combination of recent organizational upheaval and the raw quantity of contracts in need of creation and issuance limited the options available to the diplomatic admiral. He and Van Keuren therefore issued contracts for warships that were generally repeats or iterations of previous orders. As discussed in chapter 6, this resulted in the *Gleaves*-type high-steam system being propagated throughout the navy. Unfortunately, the massive increase in orders of this type also revealed the primary weakness of Robinson's position—he had no control over the allocation of strategic materiel for his priority contracts.

As part of the existing navy procurement system, shipyards awarded building contracts were expected to hire their own subcontractors to satisfy their needs for raw steel, power-plant components, or any other necessary materials. While the Bureau of Ships directly controlled the allocation of work to upper-level contractors like Bethlehem Steel, it had no immediate influence over the successive lower tiers of material production. Yards were thus free to set delivery dates and priorities for their subcontractors (like General Electric) based on their own internal schedules, and raw material producers who supplied them weren't coordinated either. Naturally, such a situation resulted in direct competition between companies for basic supplies, creating order pileups with turbine manufacturers in particular as demand skyrocketed.[6]

The resulting delays in warship construction were both immediate and obvious. As early as late 1940, it was clear to Robinson and Van Keuren that the navy's interwar disregard for supply oversight and Admiral Bowen's platitudes on the subject in 1938 had resulted in the fundamental changes to the shipbuilding process being completely overlooked.[7]

As discussed previously, the transition to high steam was not merely a change in temperatures and boiler pressures but a radical shift incorporating numerous innovations in a uniquely American *system*. Although many within the Bureau of Ships understood this as it related to machinery (boilers, superheat control, high-pressure turbines, reduction gears, etc.), they failed to grasp fully the extent of this transformation as it affected material requirements. High-pressure and high-temperature steam propulsion was made possible only with the commercial development of high-tensile alloys, particularly the aforementioned carbon molybdenum steel, which was able to withstand the enormous stresses caused by prolonged exposure to superheated steam.[8] These materials were not available in adequate amounts during World War II due to limited production capacity combined with competing orders from the navy, the rest of the US military, and the civilian economy. Although this shortage was eventually recognized and eased, the initial damage was severe. Surprisingly, this lack of oversight was also problematic in the areas of more common steel and bronze casting. Unforeseen and conflicting demands, exacerbated by a lack of even expansion of production capacity, caused widespread shortages both real and perceived. Such an issue demonstrates both a lack of familiarity with long chains of industrial production on the part of the Bureau of Ships and the shortcomings of the navy's decentralized supply structure.[9]

While BuShips was able to quickly identify this major failure, it was compounded by another factor that has only more recently begun to be fully appreciated: shortages in critical machine tools. This may sound somewhat disingenuous; special- and general-purpose machine tools are vital and well-recognized components of any major production line and this fact was understood by the leadership of BuShips in 1940. However, it is important to note that while general-purpose machine tools can perform many roles in different industries, special-purpose tools are designed with a very specific task in mind and cannot easily be put to other uses. In the United States, both before and during World War II, special-purpose machine tools were produced via a lengthy cooperative process between the tool producers and product manufacturers. As one might expect, this practice was not well-suited to rapid expansion.[10]

Unfortunately for the US Navy, the use of special high-tensile steel alloys and the need for precision manufacturing meant that high-steam turbines and reduction gears required special-purpose machine tools for their manufacture. The length of time required for new tools to be produced meant that, despite early orders, it was not until late in the war that the turbine industry could expect to meet demand.[11] At the same time, areas of warship production that could get by with general-purpose tools were able to expand with relative ease to accommodate navy contracts. This included the shipyards themselves, which were no longer required to manufacture their own turbines. Such a capacity mismatch between the yards and their turbine suppliers—still principally General Electric, Westinghouse, and Allis-Chalmers during this time—made the shortage of raw materials necessary for turbines and high-steam valves much more visible. This was where BuShips and its predecessors had badly missed the mark.[12]

The perfect storm was brewing for the navy. A dependence on private shipyards utilizing independent subcontractors, combined with a total lack of bureau oversight of warship component production, limited capacity of turbine manufacturers, and a shortage of machine tools, set the navy's expansion plans on a course for disaster with the onset of war.

THE SNOWBALL EFFECT, 1940–1943

Although wartime problems associated with high-steam component production were manifest well before the outbreak of war, the recognition of their existence by the navy only came gradually as conflict approached and orders for spares and new ships rapidly increased.

By May 1941, turbine and gear shortages were most clearly apparent in delays surrounding new destroyers under construction. That month, "Big Three" builder Bethlehem reported to Robinson that turbine components for twenty-four destroyers were encountering significant delays that would substantially extend the build time of these vessels. While schedules for deliveries for four of these ships had been made, the production delays were such that the company was unable to promise individual turbine delivery for the rest of the hulls in question by a specifiable date. Instead, engines would be assigned "according to when they are needed most" with hopes of preventing any significant delays.[13] Considering the fact that most shipyards (including Bethlehem at this time) installed propulsion machinery while a ship's hull was taking shape, this was a serious problem. Such a bottleneck in construction risked setting off a "domino effect," delaying the completion not only of that specific vessel but also of all those scheduled to be subsequently built on the same slipway.

Large private shipyards such as Bethlehem were not alone in their problems with turbine contractors in mid-1941. By June, Robinson was receiving reports that an additional forty-three destroyers were facing delays due to the failure of turbine manufacturers General Electric and Allis-Chalmers to meet their respective yard delivery dates. The estimated delays in question for these yards—Consolidated of Orange, Texas, Gulf S.B. Company, and various US navy yards—ranged from one to sixteen months (table 7.2). It is worth noting that BuShips personnel collectively recognized there was the tendency of some yards—in this case Consolidated—to request components "much earlier than [actually] required."[14] However, while the bureau did not believe pushing back or simply ignoring the requested turbine delivery dates would result in the on-time delivery of Consolidated's twelve destroyers, it would theoretically reduce the delay to two to six months rather than the claimed twelve to sixteen. BuShips acknowledged, however, that there was a bottleneck in turbine production that had resulted from both the lack of overall capacity and the low availability of machine tools for the creation of turbine blading. It added that delays caused by this problem tended to be underestimated and were likely to be more severe than predicted.[15]

These two reports precipitated Robinson's initial attempts to mitigate the turbine production problem by reassigning the responsibility for

Table 7.2. Destroyer Delays Reported to BuShips, June 11, 1941, and February 2, 1942

Destroyer Delays Reported to BuShips, June 11, 1941

Number of Destroyers	Shipyard	Machinery Contractor	Reported Delay (Months)
10	Navy	Allis-Chalmers	4 to 5.5
4	Gulf S.B.	General Electric	2 to 6
12	Consolidated	General Electric	12 to 16
17	Navy	Allis-Chalmers	1.5 to 4

Destroyer Delays Reported to BuShips, February 2, 1942

Number of Destroyers	Shipyard	Machinery Contractor	Reported Delay (Months)
23	Bath Iron Works	Westinghouse	1 to 8
25	Bethlehem	Westinghouse	3 to 8
2	Seattle-Tacoma	Westinghouse	3 to 4

Sources: G. B. Ogle, "Main Turbine Delivery & Requirement Dates for Navy Destroyers," 1–2; Correspondence, W. J. Kastor, Westinghouse Electric & Manufacturing Co. to Inspector of Machinery, USN, "Propulsion Equipment—2150 Ton Destroyers," February 2, 1942, Bureau of Ships General Correspondence S41-1 (Main Propulsion, Turbines), RG 19, NACP.

a handful of turbine contracts to the Charleston and Norfolk Navy Yards. Although this action resulted in these units being six months late, the bureau collectively expressed hope that it would reduce the delay in subsequent vessels. Reassignment orders such as this, which were guaranteed to result in *some* sort of delay, make clear the severity of turbine- and gear-production bottlenecks at the end of 1941.[16]

As the production crisis deepened further through November 1941, Robinson issued a directive to all supervisors of shipbuilding and navy yard commandants to cease the manufacture of shore spares for all new warships. The capacity freed up by this action was to be devoted entirely to the completion of turbines and reduction gears for immediate installation in new warships. Shore spares, essentially duplicate steam plants delivered in tandem with components intended for immediate use, were critical in both war and peace for keeping engines well maintained and minimizing repair time. Thus, suspending production of shore spares was an extremely risky expedient considering that tensions with Japan were at an all-time high *and* an undeclared battle for the Atlantic had been raging with Germany for months.[17]

Unfortunately, even this drastic measure was not enough to significantly alleviate production delays. Additionally, giving production priority to new shipping over maintenance was not a viable wartime solution. Such an act would virtually ensure the rapid degradation of the fleet's combat power due to battle damage and heavy wear. As a result, by April 1942, a 30 percent reduction in the *entire* naval construction program was considered a definite possibility unless solutions could be found.[18] As we shall see, the ultimate solution would require not only a complete transformation of how the navy issued and managed production resources but also a heavy reliance on alternative propulsion for the majority of future orders. This would dramatically impact America's ability to fight Japan for the entirety of World War II.

BOTTLENECKS AS PART OF THE BIG PICTURE

Part of Admiral Bowen's justification for the adoption of high steam was the elimination of any reliance on foreign designs or contracts. In theory, builders of US Navy warships could entirely depend on materials and components supplied by other American companies. Additionally, such a move had allowed smaller shipyards to compete with the likes of Bethlehem on the grounds that *nobody* possessed the full capability to build all of the new components of a high-steam system on-site. This resulted in the transformation of the shipyard into more of an assembly site where various components were brought together from disparate manufacturers. Bowen was particularly proud of this transformation and believed it to be nothing but beneficial to the navy.[19]

As naval expansion took hold in 1940 and 1941, the vision of a more efficient production system failed to materialize. Instead, the navy was rapidly confronted with an increasing series of complex delays for the propulsion machinery of its warships that were under construction. This was due to the very reliance on subcontractors that Bowen had championed. American producers of turbines and gears by the late 1930s consisted almost entirely of companies that had relied on either the electric utility industry or civilian shipbuilding for their orders during the interwar period. Given the limited availability of navy contracts until the 1940s and the depressed economy before then, there was little, if any, incentive to increase production capacity from the bare minimum. The result was a massive increase in demand that simply could not be met by the suppliers available to US shipyards. This put the navy in a seemingly no-win situation of having to decide between the production of new machinery and that of spare equipment used to repair ships already in commission and provided no capacity for additional construction orders.

A pause here is necessary to assess the full implications of the position the US Navy found itself in at the beginning of 1942. The threat of a significant slowdown in the completion of modern destroyers that resulted from high steam's adoption now risked lengthening the time it would take to bring the United States' superior industrial capacity to bear on the Imperial Japanese Navy. Such a delay would extend the time available for the IJN to strengthen its position or even cause irreparable damage to Allied morale. Additionally, these production delays of existing warships were simultaneously impacting seemingly unrelated (but no less important) construction programs. As we shall see, this specifically interfered with the navy's ability to produce "destroyer escorts" and an adequate number of fast fleet oilers—the latter of which had rapidly grown in importance due to related problems associated with high steam. While the navy would find a way to mitigate many of these production issues by 1943–1944, unfortunately, by this time, much of the damage had already been done.

Chapter 8

RIDING THE WILDCAT

While the US Navy was attempting to mitigate the impact of turbine and gear shortages caused by the adoption of high steam, the rapid expansion of the fleet that began in 1940 simultaneously demonstrated the distressing inadequacy of engineering education in the officer corps. While it was the Bureau of Navigation (BuNav) that held ultimate responsibility for officer education through the 1930s, it was the obligation of Bowen's Bureau of Engineering to keep the navy abreast of any changes in requirements within its field of expertise. Bowen did not abide by this directive.

The reader might recall that one of the arguments posed against the wholesale adoption of the high-steam system revolved around its potentially higher-educational requirements for efficient operation. This was both distasteful and impractical for a navy that had long avoided large-scale specialized education for its officers, instead relying upon hands-on learning to develop expertise. During the 1930s, the highly experienced and veteran officers of the Treaty navy were capable of using the resources available to them to grasp the particulars of the new technology gradually introduced with high steam. Unfortunately, neither time nor the oversight of experienced peers was available to new recruits after 1940. The war gave lie to the assumption that understanding high-steam propulsion systems required no additional specialized training. As a result, a shortage of highly educated engineering officers would plague the navy throughout World War II.

STAYING THE COURSE, 1935–1940

The Bureau of Navigation's total responsibility for training and education in the US Navy had been acquired gradually but was consolidated by 1889. The fact that this date coincides with the initial efforts to integrate and standardize engineering and general officer education discussed in chapter 5 is no coincidence; BuNav's reorganization was a major component of that effort.[1] Throughout the early twentieth century, it was therefore this bureau that had ultimately guided the development of the "general line" concept while simultaneously promoting specialized education for the bluejackets—the enlisted corps.[2]

As discussed in chapter 5, through 1938 all US naval officers received a standardized education at the Naval Academy in Annapolis. This had already proven to be an inadequate means of developing the specialized engineering force required for both ship and shore duties. As a result, the navy had introduced EDO (engineering duty only) status earlier in the century. While this practice produced a trickle of highly experienced engineering officers adequate for the Treaty era, it was not a solution suitable for employment on a large or accelerated scale. Additionally, the 1938 general board study had underlined a fear within the navy that the high-steam transition had resulted in a dangerous increase in the complexity of propulsion systems throughout the fleet.[3] Though Admiral Bowen claimed otherwise, we have already seen for ourselves that there were *many* more complex components of a high-steam propulsion system than there were in the system it replaced. While each individual component of high-steam technology might have been comprehensible to the average line officer, the problem was that these components had proliferated.

Despite these worries, Admiral Bowen and BuEng had been so focused on pushing for high steam's adoption that they had completely neglected to study high steam's more demanding support requirements.[4] As a result, there had been no significant alterations to the navy's training programs aside from the gradual expansion of the NROTC prior to 1939. Understanding how and why Admiral Bowen was easily taken on his word that no changes were needed requires a brief detour. During the Treaty period, the navy's preexisting aversion to overspecialization combined with four factors—treaty constraints, political-financial limitations, public antipathy, and directional uncertainty—to ensure that educational reform appeared neither palatable nor necessary to the Bureau of Navigation.

Between 1922 and 1937, the US Navy was limited in size by the terms of the Treaty system. The existence of tonnage restrictions was significant in and of itself, but for the navy's officer corps what was more significant was that the United States was already *well* over its tonnage allotment for battleships when the Washington Naval Treaty was signed. Therefore, implementation of the Treaty system quickly resulted in the decommissioning and disposal of all active pre-dreadnought battleships in the US Navy. In addition, it led to the cancellation and destruction of the *South Dakota*-class battleships and all but two of the *Lexington*-class battlecruisers under construction.[5] This placed a significant limit on the number of available posts for higher-ranking officers. If the navy were to have grown *at all* during the Treaty period, it would have to have been through smaller ship classes such as cruisers and destroyers.

Amplifying the navy's international constraints was the political climate of the United States during this period. Since the implementation of the Treaty system, the US armed forces had labored under dual handicaps. The American public, increasingly dominated by the view that World War I (and war in general) had been a huge mistake, became preponderantly isolationist and thus indifferent to the condition of its armed forces. For its part, the US administration prior to Franklin Roosevelt's taking office in 1933 had been largely responsible for initiating the Treaty system and favored its maintenance over any increase in military spending. The Great Depression reinforced this position. Focus was placed on efficiency, economy, and disarmament talks as government spending across the board was severely curtailed. This not only held back new naval construction but actually kept the US Navy from even *reaching* its allowed limits (under congressional authorization) for officer personnel throughout the 1930s.[6] Instead, the navy was forced to siphon off officers for sea duty who would ordinarily be sent to the Postgraduate School, mortgaging the future for the sake of the present—a dangerous precedent for the later years of the decade.[7] The atmosphere of frugality for the navy began to change only in 1934 through the legislation pushed by Congressman Carl Vinson, chairman of the House Naval Affairs Committee from 1931 to 1946, that allowed for the replacement of "obsolescent" vessels. However, no substantial expansion of the officer corps was authorized until 1938–1940.[8]

This unfavorable political and financial climate prior to 1938 was compounded by an atmosphere of uncertainty surrounding the navy's personnel system. This had several facets: a "hump" of junior officers, the uncertainty surrounding high steam, and (later) the uncertainty of the ultimate manpower requirements of the national emergency that became World War II.

Despite an overall insufficiency of manpower, there was a glut of officers at the rank of lieutenant commander and below by the mid-1930s. This had its roots in the demobilization after World War I. That event was paradoxically accompanied by the resumption of naval construction authorized by the Naval Act of 1916, which had previously been suspended due to a change in construction priorities during the war. The result was a serious officer shortage. In an attempt to remedy this situation, the navy decided in 1920 to take up twelve hundred wartime reserve officers into the regular navy's junior ranks.[9] Coupled with several rapidly graduated Naval Academy classes during World War I, this theoretically would have enabled the navy to adequately man its new warships due for completion by the mid-1920s. Unfortunately, these men suddenly found their prospects limited after the sharp downsizing of the navy to meet the requirements of the Washington Naval Treaty of 1922. As the navy thereafter possessed a limited number of seagoing commands (a vital prerequisite for promotion at the time) and an even more limited number of high-command positions (there was no permanent rank above rear admiral in the US Navy until 1934), this group of junior officers created a logjam in the ranks. Though not "qualified" for command, these long-service individuals possessed significant experience in all aspects of naval officer duties, including pre-high-steam engineering. An environment with ample time to learn in the lower ranks was not conducive to reform of the navy's education and training system.[10]

To this we must add that there was no assurance that high steam would prevail in the navy until the general board study took place in 1938. The limited number of high-steam ships entering service prior to that time was a drop in the proverbial bucket considering the navy's total inventory. Thus, there was little reason to educate *all* naval officers on the nature and intricacies of high-steam systems until very late in the 1930s.

Conversely, by the time it *was* apparent that high steam was to become a permanent feature of a naval officer's responsibilities, massive naval expansion had been authorized under the Naval Acts of 1938–1940. The navy's small, undermanned officer corps was thus required to balloon in size to meet expanded manpower requirements. This was *further* complicated by the lack of a defined target size for the navy prior to 1943. As an organization already dealing with a long-term officer shortage, BuNav responded by employing tools it was familiar with: abbreviation of academy education and a reduction in postgraduate training. The lack of a clear manpower ceiling would thus become a severe limitation on long-range planning for that bureau and would continue to be a problem into 1944.[11]

Treaty constraints, political and financial limitations, public antipathy, and directional uncertainty combined with a naval culture averse to overspecialization to create conditions unfavorable to training reform in the US Navy between 1935 and 1940. There were no significant educational changes, and even engineering reference material (when it was made available) was significantly outdated. Among these was BuEng's nearly wholly obsolete *Manual of Engineering Instructions* of 1921.[12] For its part, *The Bluejacket's Manual* of 1940, a universal reference guide given to every man who joined the navy, had no mention of steam propulsion whatsoever.[13] Instead, the best way for any officer to learn about propulsion machinery continued to be through actual service in the engineering spaces. The result was that, despite entering the decade with a relative surplus of knowledgeable junior officers, by the end of the 1930s the navy found itself with a shortage of personnel knowledgeable in high-steam systems.

THE WILDCAT EXPEDIENT, 1940–1943

In 1940, the US Navy was poised for war. The Battle Fleet was dispatched to a "forward position" at Pearl Harbor, US Atlantic convoy escorts were engaged by German U-boats, and massive naval expansion commenced with the passage of the Two-Ocean Navy Act. During this early war period (1940–1943), events would lead to a disintegration of BuNav's officer education program, a disjointed attempt to remedy the situation through the introduction of several unsuccessful reserve programs, and the rapid propagation of so-called wildcat field-expedient training outside of BuNav's administrative control.

Prior to 1940, it had been common practice to staff new ships with a high percentage of experienced men—as much as 90 to 95 percent. This was due to the surplus of long-service junior officers and also because it provided the best opportunity for training. In this environment, the few "green" members of the crew would have been immersed in a veritable sea of experience and officers provided with the opportunity to take extended educational leave. Though difficult, it had been possible to maintain this policy, as the officer corps had more than doubled in size to thirty thousand men by the end of the 1930s. However, by the early 1940s, very few experienced hands were available, and the shortage would only worsen as nearly 380,000 *more* officers would be added by the end of 1945. Crews assembled to man new ships between 1940 and 1943 on average contained an experienced complement of 20 percent or less. While bluejacket training directed toward the creation of enlisted specialists was able to muddle through, these catastrophically low numbers rendered the "general line" officer training system completely ineffective.[14]

BuNav—under the command of the soon-to-be-famous Admiral Chester W. Nimitz from mid-1939 until the end of 1941—did not react to this problem in a coordinated fashion. The initial response to the shortage was a deeper, even more severe curtailing of academy training to the "bare minimum necessary." This was accompanied by a near-complete termination of the policy of sending officers to the Postgraduate School and the expansion of NROTC units from nine in 1938 to twenty-seven by 1941. Though BuNav may not have foreseen its engineering deficiencies, it was not ignorant of the danger that the complete elimination of postgraduate education presented to the quality of its officer corps. NROTC expansion provided some relief, but it was still a small operation (around three thousand students), had little centralized control prior to 1944, and, as it was a four-year college program, expediting it posed the same critical problems as regular academy training.[15]

In an attempt to help rectify the dire overall shortage of highly educated officers, Nimitz's BuNav also implemented the V-1 and V-7 college training programs in the middle of 1940. The V-1 program was targeted at seventeen-to-nineteen-year-olds able and willing to attend college at their own expense. They remained inactive in the navy while in school, preferably majoring in engineering for two academic years. These individuals would then be tested and advanced into the V-7 program (officer candidates) or the V-5 program (flight training) or directly called up as an apprentice seaman (enlisted personnel) depending on their scores. The V-7 program, which was actually introduced slightly earlier than V-1, immediately enlisted academically qualified individuals as apprentice seamen for one month's training at sea. They would subsequently be appointed reserve midshipmen and given a ninety-day crash-course version of Annapolis training before being formally commissioned as a reserve ensign.[16]

Unfortunately for BuNav, neither program was a success. Their primary shortcomings lay not in the methods of training but in the uneven quality of education available at each college, a lack of civilian interest (due to the need for navy approval of each individual course of study), and the high washout rate of the V-7 program in its first year of operation (it added only a few thousand officers). Two years of college simply did not provide an adequate foundation in science and engineering for the modern naval officer. There were further attempts to remedy this through raising the academic prerequisite for V-7 to four years of college education and the elimination of any sort of quotas on each major (*especially* engineering). But, neither of these actions did much to increase the trickle of officers entering the navy by early 1942.[17]

Making matters worse was the manner in which V-1, V-7, and other measures were implemented by BuNav; they were without any recourse to centralized planning. This saddled the bureau with a large number of programs that varied significantly in both difficulty and *length*. Such a system created logjams at various stages where the programs were required to intermingle or exchange personnel. In other words, officer candidates who had completed one of the programs often discovered that they were then left idle for weeks or even *months* as they awaited an open space in the next required course. The voluminous *Administrative History of the Bureau of Naval Personnel in World War II*, a wonderful resource on the operations of BuNav and its successor organization throughout the conflict, identifies this particular problem as the most critical mistake made by the bureau during the entire decade. This disruption would remain, later in diminished form, throughout World War II.[18]

The increasingly rapid construction of ships and the inadequacy of existing training programs led to the rise of field-expedient training from a hodgepodge of different sources. Referred to by BuNav as wildcat training, some of these programs were sponsored by other bureaus. However, the most common form of this phenomenon was one-off operational training by small groups from individual ships.[19]

By 1942, it had become nearly impossible to train officers at sea not only because of a lack of experienced hands but also because of a lack of *time* before a new ship was sent into combat. As a result, crews began to take advantage of the period between their assembly and the completion of their ship (formerly a period of months, now usually only weeks). As long as the men were ashore and in the presence of experienced design engineers employed at the various naval yards, the crews—that is, officers *and* enlisted together—could simulate self-contained operational training under the guidance of EDO officers or other experts. Such a system was utterly impossible to either standardize or track and was often initiated entirely without the knowledge of BuNav itself.[20]

In the end, the administrative morass of wildcat training was vital to getting engineering crews functional enough to keep the navy moving. Although never grasping the entirety of this phenomenon, BuNav by the end of 1942 was quite aware of the existence of wildcat training as well as its own shortcomings in response to personnel shortages. It was at this stage that the navy would finally come to terms with its aversion to specialization and overhaul its approach to the training of new officers.[21]

EMBRACING THE INEVITABLE, 1943–1945

In late 1942, the Bureau of Navigation was reorganized into the Bureau of Naval Personnel (BuPers). Now under the direction of Nimitz's successor as bureau chief, Rear Admiral Randall Jacobs (1941–1945), this action spurred a fresh look at the reference material and courses available to the fleet in 1943. Ultimately, it resulted in a new strategy for approaching knowledge standardization and the creation of a specialized, standardized college education and training program.

By 1943, improvised wildcat training outside the control of BuPers was widespread. This rendered ineffective the ongoing efforts of the bureau to standardize knowledge through a universal curriculum. Therefore, in 1943, the bureau primarily elected to pursue an indirect, two-pronged approach to addressing this problem. The first angle was fairly simple: the rapid expansion of available "specialty" courses that could be taken during what was previously officer candidate downtime. Although there were initial difficulties procuring enough qualified teachers, the approach seems to have been effective in correcting the uneven flow of candidates between each level of their initial education and training. Second, in the interest of making standardized information readily available to the fleet (and better standardizing the V-7 program curriculum), the bureau set out in mid-1943 to produce a definitive manual for each major aspect of naval warfare.[22]

In recognition of the shortcomings of the V-1 and V-7 programs, BuPers held a conference with participating universities in May 1943 aimed at standardizing their curricula. Here, it was decided to put Columbia University's syllabi to use in the creation of the Introduction series of manuals for the fleet, beginning with *Introduction to Seamanship* and *Introduction to Ordnance and Gunnery* later that year.[23] One of the primary companions to these was *Introduction to Engineering and Damage Control with Notes on Ship Construction and Installations* (hereafter, *Introduction to Engineering and Damage Control*), intended for widespread publication at the earliest possible date in 1943. However, BuPers—operating independently within its own bureaucratic fief—failed to compare much of Columbia's information with the contemporary state of naval technology. The unfortunate result was that the first edition of *Introduction to Engineering and Damage Control*, already late when it was finally printed in February 1944, proved almost as outdated as the 1921 *Manual of Engineering Instructions* that it was meant to replace.[24]

This was the last straw in the exclusion of engineering considerations from the education and training of US Navy officers. By early 1944, knowledge of at least the *changes* wrought by high-steam technology had become quite widespread. After the distribution of the first edition of *Introduction to Engineering and Damage Control* in the middle of that year, these deficiencies were immediately detected, the manual withdrawn from service, and BuPers sent back to the drawing board. Primarily in the interest of time, the bureau was compelled to look outside its previous sources for help—and that help was provided by EDO personnel present in BuEng's successor organization, the Bureau of Ships.

Utilizing the knowledge of this group of individuals who had been deeply immersed in the adoption process of high-steam technology, BuPers circulated the second edition of *Introduction to Engineering and Damage Control* in April 1945. Deceptively simple in appearance, this work managed to cover steam engineering from its most basic thermodynamic properties to its extremely complex manifestation in state-of-the-art boiler and turbine systems present in the fleet. All of this was accomplished in a detailed manner that was easily understood by the more advanced reserve officer candidates in the V-7 program. Ultimately, this manual and its successors were so highly regarded that they were formally adopted by the postwar NROTC and the Naval Academy as required reading. Although this was not an instant solution to the uneven education offered through wildcat training, the programs that arose after the publication of the Introduction series now had a standardized base of knowledge at their core.[25]

In July 1943, NROTC, V-1, and V-7 were all amalgamated into the V-12 college training program. It consisted of four to eight semesters—sixteen weeks each—throughout which students were considered to be on active duty. The first two semesters followed a universal curriculum intended to provide a basic background in science, mathematics, and very basic naval indoctrination. In recognition of the rapid advance of technology and the extreme difficulty of quickly providing a line officer-style education to all candidates, the second semester played host to the screening of candidates into various categories. Depending on the academic strengths of the individual candidate, each would be sent through a relevant part of the V-12 program from the third semester onward. Individuals intended for deck or ordnance duty, for example, would remain for two additional semesters before being dispatched to their next assignment. Individuals designated for engineering duties would remain for up to *six* additional terms, far exceeding the average engineering education of the prewar general line officer. In the end, all individuals would qualify for an officer's commission, but they would be trained to undertake a very specific duty. Of course, the caveat on all of this was that BuPers planned to provide V-12 officers with "full" line-officer educations after the war, should they choose to remain in the regular navy.[26]

Driven by necessity, from V-12's genesis in late 1943 and onward, the navy had begun to pay much closer attention to the pre-naval education of its incoming officers with the goal of quickly assigning specializations. Although this paralleled the navy's activities with its enlisted training since 1902, for officers it represented a monumental about-face. Although its hand had been forced by time constraints, the navy could no longer pretend that formal officer specializations were unnecessary or even undesirable. In 1944, the specialization trend was taken to the next level, as choosing a preferred area of expertise was openly encouraged in the regular navy beyond V-12. In 1944 and 1945, BuPers even went so far as to begin issuing the *Journal of Officer Classification and Selection*, detailing the possible areas that a naval officer could specialize in and the combination of education and training that would most help him perform that job.[27]

By 1944, the navy had made major changes to the manner in which it trained its officers, and also to the concept of the officer itself. No longer intended to immediately become a "jack of all trades," the officer candidate entering the navy after the middle of 1943 was provided with a specific specialization for which he was extensively educated and trained. This was particularly true for individuals with engineering backgrounds who through V-12 received a far more substantial educational foundation than the prewar general line. Even though the navy began to make up lost ground with its overall officer corps through these changes, it did not fully meet demand before the end of World War II. With the defeat of Germany in May 1945, the various training programs began to be consolidated and closed down as projected demand for new officers peaked and began to dwindle. However, shortages of engineers, who were some of the most difficult-to-train officers in the navy, would persist after the end of the war.[28]

By late 1941, the navy had become aware of two significant shortcomings accompanying the adoption of its high-steam system. These were the production complications and increased officer educational requirements just discussed, and they were both proving highly disruptive to naval expansion efforts. However, following the attack on Pearl Harbor, the increasing administrative focus on these issues proved to be a case of missing the forest for the trees. For, as the navy moved to remedy these problems, it became distracted from the far more ominous failure of high steam to live up to its promised gains in operational range.

Chapter 9

The "Battle of the Fuel Oil," 1941–1945

After the Japanese attack on Pearl Harbor, the US Navy found itself confronted by global conflict for which it was ill-prepared. Nevertheless, much of the United States' strategic position in the Pacific had been accurately predicted by War Plan Orange. While American and Filipino forces would fail to hold against the Japanese long enough for relief forces to arrive, the US Navy would fight a long campaign across the Pacific to reach the Philippines. Unfortunately, one of the prime tools that the US Navy developed throughout the 1930s for such a situation—high-steam propulsion—quickly proved to be operationally troublesome.

At its most basic level, the American high-steam system was designed for an ocean environment that included "safe" areas. In the age of carrier aviation and long-range submarines, these areas no longer existed.[1] This was not recognized prior to World War II in part because of a broad lack of understanding at the highest levels within the navy that high steam *needed* these spaces to produce its best fuel efficiency. Making matters worse was an increasing awareness within the fleet of widespread engineering inexperience and long-standing inadequacies of range calculation that combined to distract naval leaders once the war began.[2] Ultimately, this inability to employ cruising turbines and other special fuel-saving configurations of the high-steam system meant that the commanders of ships so-equipped had significantly less range than expected and little idea of how much fuel they might actually consume in the course of operations. The navy was thus forced to plan and fight a Pacific conflict without reliable knowledge of the operational reach of its own ships.

THE PROBLEM OF *RANGE* IN WARTIME

The US Navy entered World War II completely unaware that the data and methods it used to calculate the range of its ships under war conditions that were to prevail after 1941 were unsound. The root of this problem lay in the vastly different operational requirements under which naval vessels operated in times of war and peace. While large military exercises—the Fleet Problems—were carried out during the interwar years, they were rarely extended activities. The conditions they featured made it impossible to properly simulate an extended period of combat operations from which range data might be drawn. As a result, the calculation of modern warships' combat ranges between 1918 and 1940 was a purely theoretical exercise.[3] This led to severe overestimation of the operational range of the most modern (high-steam) vessels in the fleet.

While exact ranges were unknown, it was no secret before World War II began that no warship ever performed quite the same under war conditions as it did in peacetime.[4] This was due to the emphasis that different practices received in each environment. For example, in peacetime conditions, US warships were generally kept in good repair and had their bottoms cleaned in dry dock frequently to reduce drag produced by marine growth. They were also generally manned by a highly experienced and professional crew capable of getting the best out of their machinery. Most importantly, peacetime warships were loaded only with what they needed for a given trip (as they were more often in port) and were capable of traveling directly to their destinations utilizing the most economical speeds, weather conditions, and routes. Accordingly, crews were conscientious of how much fuel they typically had on board since strict allowances were provided and based on the ship's past performance. Performance was scored regularly and was passed up the chain of command monthly as "engineering efficiency scores," a form of competition that was at least partly intended to help train engineers to get the best possible range and reliability out of their machinery.[5]

Conversely, wartime ships were more heavily loaded in an attempt to prepare them for any conceivable encounter. These vessels might spend long periods of time at sea and could go many months without servicing in a dry dock. They also rarely sailed directly from origin to destination and would not typically travel at a wholly economical speed or configuration. Additionally, any prolonged war was likely to see sizable naval expansion requiring the dispersal of experienced officers and men throughout the fleet and their augmentation with large numbers of inexperienced reservists or draftees. Since all of these factors could compromise fuel economy, it was abundantly clear that warship ranges *must* be more conservative in a wartime setting. How much was a matter for the Bureau of Engineering to determine.[6]

While BuEng recognized all of the above factors, the extent of their impact on operational range could not be determined purely on the basis of tests during the interwar period. Instead, they depended on small-scale experiments (particularly in the case of antifouling paint), observations from the United States' limited naval experience in World War I, and mathematical guesswork. These three inputs were paired with peacetime observations on the influence of operator efficiency (the efficiency scores mentioned previously) to estimate the largest influences on modern warship range in wartime. Under Admirals Robinson and Bowen, BuEng concluded that the biggest factor was likely to be operator experience and efficiency. This was followed by fouling, formation station keeping, the shutting down of unneeded machinery, and smokeless operation, respectively.

We know that BuEng came to these conclusions from the surviving range calculations housed in the National Archives and their inclusion in two primary fleet resources. These were known alternately as "Fleet Tactical Publications" and "Fleet Technical Publications" (FTPs), books distributed by the Office of the Chief of Naval Operations to every warship in the US Navy. The first was the navy's *FTP 143: War Instructions*, a compendium of basic doctrine for naval operations in a time of war issued to all vessels. This handbook contained various procedures and watch patterns to be employed under combat conditions and also general information on *why* such practices were required. By 1944, revisions of this manual (referred to as *FTP 143(A)*) contained a particular emphasis on the influence of inexperienced personnel on operations, a change likely influenced by the educational growing pains traced in the previous chapter.[7]

The second major resource that detailed how combat conditions might influence operational range was known as *FTP 136: Cruising Radii of U.S. Naval Vessels from Actual Steaming Data*. As its name would indicate, *FTP 136* was intended to be *the* definitive collection of operational ranges of all US warships. This handbook was a comprehensive review of how *much* certain factors were believed to impact fuel economy and, by extension, which factors were believed to have the largest influence on warship range (table 9.1). This publication was intended for use in operational planning. As such, *FTP 136* represents a snapshot of precisely what kind of reach the navy as a whole believed it had leading into World War II.[8]

Table 9.1. *FTP 136* Fuel Consumption Variables (1940)

Type	Fuel Consumption Increase
Fouling	Up to 5.0% per month*
Efficiency	10–15%
Smokeless Operation	5–8%
Extra Boilers/Auxiliaries Standing by	5–10%
Station Keeping in Column	4%
Change per 100 Tons Displacement	4–6% for Destroyers, 0.8–1% for Cruisers

*Highly variable based upon weather conditions and paint type used.
Source: Office of the Chief of Naval Operations, *FTP 136, Change No. 2 (1940)*, v–vii.

The range tables in *FTP 136* were compiled from a combination of the data produced during a given ship's trials and the average fuel economy achieved by that same class over its lifetime prior to the date of publication. This was displayed in a table adjusted for intervals of 1 knot from 5 knots up to maximum achievable speed. Each entry contained expected engine RPM, gallons of fuel consumed per hour, gallons of fuel consumed per mile, barrels of fuel per mile, and expected cruising radius in "miles." All were calculated for "average" conditions of weather, displacement, and fouling but were considered to be the best possible performance of the class in question (table 9.2). A specific ship's range for a given constant speed in knots was then calculated by dividing the recent average range of a specific ship by that of the entire class of ships provided by *FTP 136*. This percentage was that particular vessel's "engineering economy score," which we touched on above. The range of that ship was then calculated by adding the difference produced by the ship's economy score (say, 11 percent for a vessel with an economy of 89 percent) on top of the values provided in *FTP 136*. This was projected to take into account the impact of crew performance. Additional percentage points were then added to that difference for other less critical factors previously mentioned (table 9.3).[9]

Throughout *FTP 136*, the US Navy considered crew performance to be the single largest variable in the ability of a ship to achieve high fuel efficiency in wartime prior to World War II.[10] Accordingly, maintaining a high degree of engineering efficiency became a paramount concern throughout the fleet. Evidence for this priority is everywhere in the archival sources.

Table 9.2. 1,850-ton DDs from *FTP 136*

Somers (381), Warrington (383), Sampson (394), Davis (395), Jouett (396)

RPM	Knots	Gallons per Hour	Gallons per Mile	Barrels per Mile	Clean-Bottom Cruising Radius in Miles
47	5	124	25	0.6	7,040
56	6	132	22	0.52	8,000
65	7	143	20	0.48	8,800
74	8	154	19	0.45	9,263
84	9	167	19	0.45	9,263
93	10	181	18	0.43	9,778
103	11	197	18	0.43	9,778
113	12	212	18	0.43	9,778
123	13	233	18	0.43	9,778
133	14	267	19	0.45	9,263
143	15	300	20	0.48	8,800
153	16	334	21	0.5	8,381
163	17	377	22	0.52	8,000
173	18	444	25	0.6	7,040
183	19	511	27	0.64	6,519
194	20	585	29	0.69	6,069
204	21	659	31	0.74	5,677
215	22	751	34	0.81	5,176
226	23	843	37	0.88	4,757
237	24	974	41	0.98	4,293
249	25	1,139	46	1.1	3,826
261	26	1,305	50	1.19	3,520
275	27	1,529	57	1.36	3,088
289	28	1,807	65	1.55	2,708
303	29	2,102	72	1.71	2,444
314	30	2,380	79	1.88	2,228
325	31	2,657	86	2.05	2,047
336	32	2,935	92	2.19	1,913
347	33	3,348	101	2.4	1,743
359	34	3,882	114	2.71	1,544
371	35	4,416	126	3	1,397
383	36	4,952	138	3.29	1,275
				Gallons	Barrels
	Total Fuel Capacity (95%)			179,000	4.26
	Total Fuel Available			176,000	4.19
	Port Consumption per Hour			49	1.17

Note that while this is the entirety of the data provided for each class, *FTP 218* contains considerably more detail.

Source: Office of the Chief of Naval Operations, *FTP 136, Change No. 2 (1940)*, 87.

Table 9.3. Example Use of *FTP 136* Tables.

Determine radius of Farragut (DD 348) for following conditions: Speed 15 knots. Out of dock 3 months. Navy standard shipbottom paint (5.0%). Fueled to capacity (170,561 gallons). Average wind and sea. Smokeless operation. Steaming singly. Current engineering economy score 96%.

(A): Fuel consumption is increased by:

Fouling (5% per month out of dock)	15%
Smokeless Operation	8%
Engineering Economy Score of 96%	4%
Total Increase	27%

(B): Tabulated fuel consumption is based on displacement corresponding to 119,393 gallons of fuel on board (70% of 170,561 gallons capacity), but during this run (assuming all available fuel is burned) the mean fuel on board will be 86,346 gallons (50% of 168,430 gallons available plus 2,131 gallons, which remain in tank bottoms below pump suctions). For a 1,500-ton destroyer, the fuel consumption decreases 4.5% for every 100-ton decrease in displacement or 28,000-gallon expenditure of fuel.

Decrease in fuel consumption =

$$(119{,}393 - 86{,}346) / 28{,}000 \times 4.5\% = 5.3\%$$

(C): The net change in fuel consumption (27.0% increase less 5.3% decrease) is an increase of 21.7%

(D): Radius =

Fuel available/Gal. per mile

168,430/28 = **6,015 miles**

Source: Office of the Chief of Naval Operations, *FTP 136, Change No. 2 (1940)*, vii–viii.

For example, the reader might recall similar words from the analysis of officer training shortcomings in the previous chapter. Additionally, this idea seems to have only grown in prominence following the general board study on high steam, as it is particularly evident in fleet-wide communications after that time. "An officer's knowledge of the engineering equipment installed," wrote Admiral Charles P. Snyder to the Battle Force in 1940, "should be such that he never need place dependence on the assistance of others under any circumstances... The qualification of an officer as a watch stander cannot be considered to terminate the necessity for further training in all marine engineering subjects."[11]

It is with this in mind that we transition from theory to application. Fewer than ten days after the Japanese attack on Pearl Harbor, in a memorandum dated December 16, 1941 (the day before he was removed from his post as commander in chief of the Pacific Fleet), Admiral Husband E. Kimmel warned his subordinates:

> Reports reaching the Commander-in-Chief indicate excessive and alarming rates of fuel consumption in the various types of ships. In some instances a cruising radius of about half of that to be expected has been indicated. This is a matter of the gravest concern. Our theater of activity covers vast ocean areas. The logistic problems are difficult of solution at best. Improvement in engineering performance is essential, in order that this fleet may not suffer serious handicap in planning and in execution of operations of the greatest importance.[12]

After a little more than one week of wartime operations, the commander of the Pacific Fleet had a logistical crisis on his hands with dire implications. Much higher than anticipated rates of fuel consumption would mean not only that vastly more fuel would have to be supplied but also that the cruising radii Kimmel's forces used for operational planning were horribly inaccurate. Such consumption, were it to continue, would severely restrict operational planning for the foreseeable future and demand drastic changes in tactical behavior. Identifying and solving this problem therefore quickly became a major objective of the Office of the Chief of Naval Operations and the Bureau of Ships.[13]

THE PERCEPTION: "GREEN" MEN AND COMPLEX MACHINES

Rather than question the methodology that had produced the data, Kimmel and his subordinates logically believed that fuel overconsumption was due to the impact of inexperienced engineering crews exceeding what had been anticipated by *FTP 143* and *FTP 136*. As previously noted, by late 1941, the navy had already increased the size of its officer corps by several orders of magnitude and in the process had encountered a number of educational and training dilemmas. These men would not yet have had time to fully adjust and learn the intricacies of high-steam propulsion through the on-the-job training schemes that the US Navy continued to operate during this period.[14]

The shortcomings of a system in which engineers train through shared experience were assessed from an educational perspective in the previous chapter. It bears repeating here, however, that we know at this stage that the US Navy recognized the need not just for operational capability with its engineers but for high operational *efficiency* in order to achieve the fuel economy necessary for a Pacific conflict. High-steam systems consisted of complex and sensitive machines. What we have not discussed is exactly *how* sensitive they were and what this meant for less-experienced crews.

While the implementation of high steam did not add any new jobs to the engine spaces of warships, it did complicate the long list of tasks that each man was required to carry out. For example, the superheater had to be closely regulated, as too little heat and pressure at the outlet would dramatically reduce the power output of the turbines, while too much could irreparably damage them in mere seconds. Feedwater had to be monitored for tiny amounts of excess air or salinity, as either could cause rapid corrosion of the entire system. Burner operators had to understand and ensure the proper fuel/air mixture in the boilers for various temperatures and pressures, and each individual boiler often had its own quirks that needed to be learned. Finally, the turbines had to be run at the most efficient RPM settings at all times, and operators had to be constantly on the lookout for errant vibrations that could be the first warnings of internal damage. These tasks were critical to the efficient operation of a World War II steam propulsion system. Yet they represent only a fraction of what was expected of engineering crews on a daily basis. An individual may have been capable of learning the general operation of a high-steam system fairly quickly, but retaining the proper degree of knowledge to maintain the entire plant in various sea or operating conditions, at different pressures, with various turbine and boiler configurations, through repeatedly and possibly dramatically changing conditions, and knowing it all well enough to *teach* it is another matter entirely.[15]

Then, add to the equation the discipline and memory to do all of the above *quickly* and under tremendous pressure. The early stages of the Pacific War were an extremely stressful time for the majority of US military forces, but especially for the US Navy. After all, it had just been figuratively caught with its pants down at Pearl Harbor. Commanders from the smallest patrol craft to the surviving capital ships understood that the Japanese were capable of striking the US Navy from virtually anywhere. Combined with the fact that many of their subordinates likely did not yet have a full grasp of the engineering plants on their ships, it logically follows that most commanders would err on the side of caution. They would limit the demand on their engineers while simultaneously keeping their ships in a maximum state of readiness. This meant a continuously high reserve of steam pressure and a system configuration best suited to producing maximum power at a moment's notice—not a setup expected to achieve high fuel economy.

This was the perspective of Admiral Kimmel and his staff. Only days into the Pacific War, it made perfect sense to believe that this edginess (which was highly apparent at the time) was producing a negative synergy with relative inexperience.[16]

By this logic, then, Kimmel responded to the fuel-efficiency crisis by pressing home the need for practice—practice using the equipment, practice getting the best out of the equipment, and practice maintaining the equipment in the manner prescribed. "Force, Type, Task Force, Unit and Ship Commanders," Kimmel wrote, "each bear a heavy individual responsibility in bringing about prompt and marked improvement. The operating seniors in prescribing speed, boiler power, and reserve requirements must do so in accordance with the situation existing at the time. The type and ship commanders must make every effort to insure efficient plant operation in meeting the prescribed requirements."[17]

Kimmel's actions were in accordance with long-standing assumptions in the US Navy, and his words parroted those of his predecessors and subordinates as commanders of the Battle Force. However, they also reveal that, for whatever reason, poor engineering performance threatened to badly disrupt operational planning. Over the next several months, the subject of Kimmel's memorandum proved to be more than an isolated or short-term aberration. Although Kimmel was relieved of his command on December 17, 1941, the fuel problem would continue to loom large with his eventual successor, Admiral Chester W. Nimitz, throughout the Pacific War.[18]

THE COMPLICATION: THE CHANGING MEANING OF "FUEL ECONOMY"

The persistence of high rates of fuel consumption by naval task forces throughout the first months of the Pacific War, despite strongly worded command circulars, amplified US weaknesses in that theater. Operational planners from Chief of Naval Operations Admiral Ernest J. King on down were forced to cope with uncertainty surrounding the actual ranges of their most modern warships. This, in turn, forced a much higher degree of reliance on the availability of fast tankers, whose numbers were severely limited. King's office declared postwar that this predicament "slowed down and restricted offensive operations" and referred to the entirety of the early war as the "Battle of the Fuel Oil."[19]

Fortunately for the US Navy, the new commander of the Pacific Fleet was intimately familiar with the challenges that such an environment posed.

Admiral Nimitz had been involved in the development of underway refueling procedures almost from their very beginning in the second decade of the twentieth century.[20] As recognition of a larger systemic problem with the fleet began to spread through the chain of command, King and Nimitz tasked Admiral Robinson's Bureau of Ships with reviewing the situation in early 1942. Their mission was to survey *everything* that went into the determination of a warship's range, from crew training to mechanical advantage. While this review contributed to the eventual production of *Introduction to Engineering and Damage Control*, which became an integral part of crew training very late in the war, its greatest gift to the navy was the long-term collection of revised performance statistics for every major warship. It quickly became apparent to BuShips that a lack of engineering training was not the only (or potentially even the primary) reason for the fleet's fuel issues.[21]

The BuShips investigation discovered that high steam had created a fatal flaw in the concept of engineering efficiency scores. *FTP 136* had been developed by the same means as its predecessors had: through data collected during peacetime operations, with relatively minor adjustments expected in a time of war. This was predicated in part on the use of two traditional engineering expedients that saved fuel—reduced boiler and reduced speed operation. By World War II, these methods had been joined (and in some cases supplanted) by high steam's far more numerous engineering conditions resulting from myriad configurations of staged turbines, superheaters, double-reduction gears, and other integral systems. When run together in consistent patterns as they could be in peacetime, these devices produced a far greater economy; but in reality, this was usually done only when crews were actively striving to achieve a high economy score. In short, high steam's adoption had resulted in a variety of engineering conditions that *FTP 136* simply did not account for, creating huge margins of error in the manual's estimations. Complicating matters was the realization that, by adjusting the data provided to absolute values for intervals of knots in the age of the double-reduction gear, *FTP 136* had dangerously oversimplified the entire process of calculating range. This practice also badly underrepresented the influence of sea states, fouling, and mechanical wear on operational range, which were found to have a much greater influence than previously thought.[22]

The bottom line was that the navy was left with little choice but to completely revisit how to calculate the expected ranges of its warships. This process relied heavily on the collection of fuel and machinery usage statistics from vessels already active in the Pacific War, forcing the navy to press on while blind to the full extent of its own capabilities. It was only in these operational logs that BuShips could identify where the problem lay with *FTP 136*, and the information gleaned would serve as the foundation for a new range manual. Until then, these observations were made available, upon request, to commanders at sea. The lack of reliable range information for much of the war mandated, in turn, an increased reliance on fleet oilers capable of keeping up with the pace of task force operations. The effects of this dependence were enormous, virtually dictating the terms of all American activity in the Pacific.[23]

THE REALITY: *FTP 218* AND THE CRUISING TURBINE

The efforts of the Bureau of Ships to modernize the methods used to determine the operational range of US Navy warships ultimately produced *FTP 218, War Service Fuel Consumption of US Naval Surface Vessels*. This manual not only fundamentally altered the way the navy thought about range but served as a damning review of high steam's wartime effectiveness. First distributed to the fleet in 1945, *FTP 218* represents the fruits of several years of research by BuShips and claims to be the final authority in wartime range calculation. The bureau's studies, as detailed within this publication, determined that inexperienced manpower was *not* solely responsible for the dramatic increase in US naval fuel consumption. Instead, the actual range of all warships (but particularly destroyers and some cruisers) was "appreciably less than originally expected" or even in some cases "inadequate."[24] These pronouncements do not just challenge the data contained within *FTP 136* but fundamentally alter the terms of the entire discussion.

In *FTP 218*, range is presented first as *endurance*. Instead of knots, each ship class has a primary table that is adjusted for propeller RPM as related to gallons of fuel consumed per hour. These values remain much more consistent across the board, regardless of outside influences. Calculated in this manner, the total time that the engine can be run at a given propeller RPM is thus a ship's overall endurance—a more accurate measurement of a warship's possible reach. *FTP 218* avoids making any direct declaration about a given warship's range in *navigational* miles, as was detailed in *FTP 136*. It is instead calculated by multiplying the endurance figure provided for a ship at a given propeller RPM by the "corresponding ship speed found by navigational means" when actually at sea.[25] What *is* provided in addition to RPM/fuel rates is an approximate range of ship speeds (in knots) and *engine* miles traveled. Accordingly, a healthy margin of error is built into all of

Table 9.4. *Somers*-class Data from *FTP 218*

DD 381 Class
1,850-Ton Class
Table I. War Logistics Data for Steady Steaming
Data Period: 1942–1943, Based on Radius Oil

Prop Speed	Mean	Fuel Rate Normal Range	Daily	Endurance Mean displacement 2,750 tons	
1	2	3	4	5	6
R.P.M.	Gal./hr.	Gal./hr.	Bbl./day	Hours	Days
100	256	217–299	146 ± 9	699 ± 11	29.1
110	288	244–337	165 ± 10	622 ± 10	25.9
120	325	275–380	186 ± 11	551 ± 10	23
130	367	311–429	210 ± 13	488 ± 9	20.3
140	414	351–484	237 ± 14	432 ± 9	18
150	467	396–546	267 ± 16	383 ± 8	16
160	527	446–616	301 ± 18	340 ± 8	14.2
170	595	504–696	340 ± 20	301 ± 7	12.5
180	671	568–785	383 ± 23	267 ± 7	11.1
190	757	641–885	433 ± 26	236 ± 7	9.8
200	854	723–999	488 ± 29	210 ± 6	8.8
210	964	816–1,127	551 ± 33	186 ± 6	7.8
220	1,088	921–1,272	622 ± 37	165 ± 6	6.9
230	1,227	1,039–1,435	701 ± 42	146 ± 5	6.1
240	1,385	1,173–1,620	791 ± 48	129 ± 5	5.4
250	1,562	1,323–1,827	893 ± 54	115 ± 5	4.8
260	1,763	1,493–2,062	1,007 ± 61	102 ± 4	4.2
270	1,989	1,685–2,326	1,137 ± 68	90 ± 4	3.8
280	2,244	1,901–2,624	1,282 ± 77	80 ± 4	3.3
290	2,532	2,144–2,961	1,447 ± 87	71 ± 4	3
300	2,857	2,420–3,341	1,633 ± 98	63 ± 4	2.6
310	3,224	2,731–3,770	1,842 ± 111	56 ± 3	2.3
320	3,638	3,081–4,254	2,079 ± 125	49 ± 3	2
330	4,105	3,477–4,801	2,346 ± 141	44 ± 3	1.8
340	4,632	3,923–5,417	2,647 ± 159	39 ± 3	1.6
350	5,226	4,426–6,111	2,986 ± 179	34 ± 3	1.4
357	5,688	4,817–6,652	3,250 ± 195	31 ± 3	1.3

By this time, the class consisted only of *Somers, Sampson, Davis,* and *Jouett*. This is merely the first of several pages of data dedicated to this class alone.

Speed	Radius	Speed	Radius	Fuel Rate
Mean displacement 2,250 tons		Mean displacement 2,750 tons		
7	8	9	10	11
Knots	Engine miles	Knots	Engine miles	Gal./eng mi.
10.5 ± .1	7,800 ± 230	10.4 ± .1	7,270 ± 220	24.6
11.6 ± .1	7,630 ± 230	11.5 ± .1	7,150 ± 220	25
12.6 ± .1	7,370 ± 230	12.5 ± .1	6,890 ± 220	26
13.6 ± .1	7,030 ± 230	13.5 ± .1	6,590 ± 220	27.2
14.6 ± .2	6,790 ± 230	14.4 ± .2	6,220 ± 220	28.8
15.6 ± .2	6,490 ± 230	15.4 ± .2	5,900 ± 210	30.3
16.6 ± .2	6,130 ± 210	16.4 ± .2	5,580 ± 210	32.1
17.6 ± .2	5,760 ± 210	17.4 ± .2	5,240 ± 190	34.2
18.6 ± .2	5,390 ± 190	18.3 ± .2	4,890 ± 190	36.7
19.5 ± .2	5,010 ± 190	19.2 ± .2	4,530 ± 190	39.4
20.5 ± .2	4,670 ± 190	20.1 ± .2	4,220 ± 190	42.5
21.4 ± .2	4,320 ± 190	21 ± .2	3,910 ± 190	45.9
22.4 ± .3	4,010 ± 190	22 ± .3	3,630 ± 190	49.5
23.3 ± .3	3,700 ± 170	22.9 ± .3	3,340 ± 160	53.6
24.2 ± .3	3,410 ± 170	23.7 ± .3	3,060 ± 160	58.4
25.1 ± .3	3,140 ± 170	24.6 ± .3	2,830 ± 160	63.5
25.9 ± .3	2,850 ± 170	25.3 ± .3	2,580 ± 140	69.7
26.7 ± .3	2,620 ± 150	26.1 ± .3	2,350 ± 140	76.2
27.4 ± .3	2,380 ± 150	26.8 ± .3	2,140 ± 140	83.7
28.1 ± .4	2,160 ± 150	27.5 ± .4	1,950 ± 140	92.1
28.8 ± .4	1,960 ± 150	28.2 ± .4	1,780 ± 140	101.3
29.5 ± .4	1,770 ± 150	28.8 ± .4	1,610 ± 130	111.9
30.3 ± .5	1,640 ± 130	29.5 ± .5	1,450 ± 130	123.3
31.2 ± .5	1,500 ± 130	30.3 ± .5	1,330 ± 130	135.5
32 ± .6	1,380 ± 130	31 ± .6	1,210 ± 130	149.4
32.9 ± .6	1,250 ± 130	31.8 ± .6	1,080 ± 130	164.3
33.5 ± .7	1,170 ± 130	32.4 ± .7	1,000 ± 130	175.6

Source: Office of the Chief of Naval Operations, *FTP 218 Change No. 1 (1946)*, 235.

Table 9.5. CL-49 Data from *FTP 218*

CL 49
Table I. War Logistics Data For Steady Steaming
Data Period: 1942–1943, Based on Radius Oil
Excerpt: 150–250 R.P.M.

Prop Speed	Mean	Fuel Rate Normal Range	Daily	Endurance Mean displacement 13,500 tons	
1	2	3	4	5	6
R.P.M.	Gal./hr.	Gal./hr.	Bbl./day	Hours	Days
150	1,149	940–1,385	657 ± 47	495 ± 11	20.6
160	1,294	1,059–1,560	739 ± 53	440 ± 10	18.3
170	1,457	1,192–1,756	833 ± 60	391 ± 10	16.3
180	1,641	1,343–1,978	938 ± 68	347 ± 9	14.5
190	1,848	1,512–2,227	1,056 ± 76	308 ± 9	12.8
200	2,082	1,704–2,509	1,190 ± 86	273 ± 8	11.4
210	2,344	1,918–2,825	1,339 ± 97	243 ± 8	10.1
220	2,640	2,160–3,182	1,509 ± 109	216 ± 7	9
230	2,973	2,433–3,583	1,699 ± 122	191 ± 7	8
240	3,349	2,741–4,036	1,914 ± 138	170 ± 7	7.1
250	3,771	3,086–4,545	2,155 ± 155	151 ± 6	6.3

Source: Office of the Chief of Naval Operations, *FTP 218, Change No. 1 (1946)*, 5.

Speed	Radius	Speed	Radius	Fuel Rate
Mean displacement 11,500 tons		Mean displacement 13,500 tons		
7	8	9	10	11
Knots	Engine miles	Knots	Engine miles	Gal./eng mi.
15.5 ± .1	8,650 ± 250	15.3 ± .1	7,570 ± 220	75.1
16.5 ± .1	8,280 ± 240	16.3 ± .1	7,170 ± 220	79.4
17.5 ± .1	7,880 ± 240	17.3 ± .1	6,760 ± 220	84.2
18.5 ± .1	7,490 ± 240	18.3 ± .1	6,350 ± 210	89.7
19.4 ± .1	7,060 ± 240	19.2 ± .1	5,910 ± 210	96.2
20.4 ± .1	6,670 ± 240	20.2 ± .1	5,510 ± 210	103.1
21.3 ± .1	6,260 ± 240	21.1 ± .1	5,130 ± 210	111.1
22.3 ± .2	5,820 ± 240	22 ± .2	4,750 ± 210	120
23.2 ± .2	5,430 ± 240	22.9 ± .2	4,370 ± 210	129.8
24.1 ± .2	5,010 ± 220	23.8 ± .2	4,050 ± 210	140.7
25.1 ± .2	4,690 ± 220	24.8 ± .2	3,740 ± 190	152

Table 9.6. Sample calculations from *FTP 218*

(A). Find the quantity of fuel consumed by CL 49 in 4 days of steady steaming at 200 RPM.

$$\text{Bbl./day} \times 4 \text{ days} = 1190 \times 4 \pm 86 \sqrt{4}$$
$$4760 \pm 172 \text{ Bbl}$$

(B). Find the endurance and radius that CL 49 will have at 200 RPM. if she fuels to radius oil capacity and holds 25% of her fuel in reserve.

$$\text{Radius oil} - 25\% \text{ reserve} = 75\%$$
$$\text{Endurance (hours)} = 0.75 \times 273 \pm 8 \sqrt{0.75}$$
$$205 \pm 7 \text{ hours}$$
$$\text{Endurance (days)} = 0.75 \times 11.4 = 8.6 \text{ days}$$
$$\text{Radius} = 0.75 \times 5510 \pm 210 \sqrt{0.75}$$
$$4130 \pm 190 \text{ engine miles}$$

(C). Find the radius of CL 49 in navigational miles at 200 RPM.

Let S = actual ship speed at 200 RPM, as determined by navigational means.

$$\text{Radius} = S \times \text{Endurance (hours)}$$
$$S \times 273 \text{ navigational miles}$$

Source: Office of the Chief of Naval Operations, *FTP 218, Change No. 1 (1946)*, 5.

these values to emphasize their estimated nature and provide a higher degree of accuracy for operational planning. This accounts for different sea states, time out of dry dock, or crew inexperience. The data even goes so far as to include additional data for fuel oil capacities, varying displacements, and other factors in an attempt to be as comprehensive as possible (tables 9.4, 9.5, and 9.6).[26]

While part of the blame for the range conundrum was laid at the feet of the unpredictable and antiquated RPM-knot relationship, it was never intended to be a precisely accurate representation and was not the chief culprit. Instead, BuShips identified the practice of relying on peacetime "engineering efficiency scores" as the largest single reason for the navy's woes. However, what the wartime study had revealed was not simply that there was a need for a metric that better accounted for the variety of engineering conditions introduced by high steam. Instead, the near-complete disregard for economical propulsion operation, which had earlier been assumed by Kimmel and others to be the result of inexperienced and cautious crews, was revealed to have become the norm rather than the exception. "In time of war," declares *FTP 218*'s introduction, "task force speeds and other operations are dictated by the strategical and tactical situation, and individual ships must maintain maximum safety and readiness to meet sudden heavy demands while operating under relatively unfavorable conditions. Single or reduced boiler operation, cruising turbines and other fuel-saving arrangements can rarely be utilized."[27]

At the heart of the issue was nothing less than one of the primary components of the high-steam system: the modern cruising turbine. The reader might recall that this was a "declutchable" turbine intended for use during travel at moderate speeds over long distances. Proper employment of this device produced significantly improved fuel economy. Unfortunately, the procedure required to shut this turbine down and reroute steam in preparation for full power could take several minutes or even *longer* with an inexperienced crew.[28] This was far too dangerous in the combat environment of World War II. Particularly in the early days, aerial or torpedo attacks could develop suddenly and without warning anywhere in-theater, leaving a ship and its crew only moments to react. The time needed to declutch a cruising turbine could prove to be the difference between a narrow escape and a watery grave. Kimmel's memo indicates that this was quickly realized by the vast majority of the navy following Pearl Harbor.[29]

For most of the war, cruising turbines were used so sparingly that the data from *FTP 218* reflects a modern US Navy with only about two-thirds the range it had been promised at best.[30] Largely aware of this situation by 1943–1944, BuShips seriously entertained the prospect of eliminating cruising turbines entirely from new warships to save parts, labor, money, and time, thereby easing the production backup. Although this was not actually carried out, that it was considered at all makes a major statement about what the navy thought about its high-tech propulsion system by the middle of the war.[31]

WHAT IT ALL MEANS

BuEng, and by extension the US Navy, had long believed that range would be a significant hurdle to overcome in any conflict against the Imperial Japanese Navy. The adoption of high steam was thus carried out in large part due to the belief that it promised unprecedented range that would ease the burden of supplying fuel to any forces operating in the Pacific. This was predicated upon a number of operational assumptions about conflict in that theater. Among these was that combat would be largely localized to specific areas closer to the Japanese Home Islands.[32]

As the US Navy began to expand and war seemed more imminent with each passing day, the issues of production and education discussed in the previous chapters increasingly interfered with established plans. Educational difficulties were particularly troubling to a navy that had come to rely on its highly trained interwar officer corps. Fleet manuals and circulars from the final years of peace reveal an acute sensitivity to the importance of engineering expertise in getting the most out of high-steam propulsion, and "engineering efficiency" reports led commanders to believe that the technology in question was delivering on its promises of long range.

Contrary to what the US Navy initially assumed, the abrupt and extreme increases in fuel consumption that accompanied the outbreak of war were *not* due to the fact either that the high-steam system had failed to live up to its promises or that engineering crews were lazy. Instead, the combat environment for which the system was designed had changed. There were several components of high steam that proved very successful: properly regulated superheat, double-reduction gears, feedwater preheating, and numerous others. But assumptions about range had been made based on the expectation that the next war would be fought in a manner similar to the last: close to primary objectives like the Philippines or the Japanese Home Islands. If this had held true, vast areas of the Pacific between the US West Coast and Japan would have been relatively safe and provided the opportunity to use a warship's optimum cruising configuration. Air power in particular had heavily contributed to eliminating this safety area. In the same way that the Imperial Japanese Navy continually pushed the area of their planned "decisive battle" east during the interwar period, air power and submarines slowly shrunk any area that could be considered immune from enemy attack. By the attack on Pearl Harbor, this imagined safe cruising zone had virtually ceased to exist.[33]

After belatedly recognizing this, the US Navy was forced to reassess how it determined the operating range of its warships while simultaneously attempting to first halt and then roll back Japanese advances in the Pacific. Particularly in the early days of the war, commanders were forced to rely significantly more on the limited number of fast tankers available to sustain operations. Logistical concerns thereby became far more critical of a bottleneck than had been anticipated in prewar planning and resulted in a period of improvisation that was subsequently dubbed "The Battle of the Fuel Oil."[34]

It is a tempting but ultimately fruitless endeavor to indulge in speculation at this stage about how things might have turned out if any one of the factors just reviewed had changed. Instead, it is critical that we now consider how the US Navy handled itself in World War II once these problems were discovered. While an in-depth look at the day-to-day impact of high steam is beyond the scope of this study, a foundational assessment of the problem can be assembled from the production, training, and planning problems discussed previously. This will provide a fresh perspective on the operational problems the navy confronted in the Pacific.

Chapter 10

THE IMPACT OF HIGH STEAM ON THE PACIFIC WAR

Throughout World War II, modern high-steam-equipped vessels were preferred over older warships for operational purposes. This was due to a number of different factors, some related to propulsion and some not. High-steam vessels were all significantly younger than low-steam designs, and thus generally boasted better weaponry, electronics, and survivability. Worn-out machinery in older ships also contributed to breakdowns and reduced range. High steam *did* offer improved range and power over its predecessors in general, although the extent of this advantage was uncertain after the United States joined World War II and eventually proved to be far less than expected. Finally, the deficiencies of high steam's design did not become clear throughout the fleet until well after the war was underway.[1]

While the full extent of high steam's effects on the US Navy's thinking might be impossible to determine without dedicating another thousand pages to a day-by-day operational study, we can discern the outlines of the limiting influence it exerted over the operational tempo of the Pacific War with the evidence we have already reviewed here. Specifically, changes we can observe in fuel requirements, refueling practices, and the dramatic expansion of the use of alternative means of propulsion (such as turbo-electric or diesel) were signals that all was not well with high steam. Together, these factors had a significant but obscured influence on the war effort.

FUEL, OILERS, AND THE PACE OF US OPERATIONS IN THE PACIFIC WAR

Perhaps one of the best ways to trace the navy's thinking on operational matters is to examine the gradual changes in the composition of its fuels and its methods of getting that fuel to the fleet. While fuel was discussed during the general board study of 1938, the reader might recall that it was a matter quickly dismissed as inconsequential. This was due in part to the extensive research that the navy had been putting into its fuel supply and resulted in Admiral Bowen asserting that no high-steam vessel would have different fuel requirements from any other.[2] Naturally, this did not mean that fuel requirements would never change. One of the known factors regarding mechanical efficiency during World War II was that increases in fuel quality directly led to increases in power and efficiency. However, there are more factors involved than simply these. Some types of fuel might burn more easily when exposed to a brief flame or might freeze at a lower temperature than other types. During the interwar period, which featured constrained budgets, the navy tended to burn the cheapest fuel possible.[3]

Throughout the interwar period and World War II, the US Navy used "heavy" fuel oils for propulsion defined by the Bureau of Engineering as "a hydrocarbon oil, free from grit, acid, and fibrous and other foreign matter."[4] Diesel was a separate categorization within fuel oil, as it was utilized only for submarine propulsion and for secondary generators on surface vessels (although by 1945 it had made the transition to use in some destroyer escorts, which we will discuss shortly). In the mid-1930s, navy fuel oil was divided into four primary classifications by the Bureau of Engineering: Grade "A," "B," "C," and "D" (also referred to as "Bunker A, B, C, and A Special"). These were defined by three primary characteristics: viscosity, water content, and sediment content. While the latter two categories are self-explanatory, it is important to note that the former was measured in Seconds, Saybolt Furol (SSF) at a given temperature. The higher the numeric SSF value, the thicker and stickier the oil. While Grade D fuel oil was intended only for "metallurgical purposes," A, B, and C were considered to be viable marine bunker fuel in descending order of quality. Grade A in 1933, for example, had a viscosity rating of 100 SSF at 77 degrees Fahrenheit with a sediment content of less than 1 percent. Grade B only had a requirement of 100 SSF at 122 degrees with a similar sediment content, while Grade C required only 300 SSF at 122 degrees but with a sediment content of 0.25 percent or less.[5]

Generally, Grade C was issued only to noncombatant vessels and shore-based facilities for power generation, while Grades A and B were issued to power combatant ships. Grade B is where the navy sought to save money, by reducing the requirements for its fuel contractors in peacetime. Grade A was considered to be high-quality wartime fuel. Unfortunately, the higher viscosity of Grade B meant that there was a resulting lower efficiency rate (and higher number of breakdowns) in pumps, suction lines, and oil sprayers of warship boilers if the oil was used as is. Grade B was thus, by necessity, only issued to vessels capable of adequately preheating their oil to achieve the required viscosity (or to ships expected to operate in temperate zones).[6]

As early as 1936, BuEng under Bowen was already moving to revise navy fuel standards. This does not appear to be a direct *result* of the move to high steam but rather an awareness that more stringent fuel requirements could very well lead to better results. These specifications were initially submitted for approval in August 1938 and eliminated Grades A *and* B fuel while redesignating Grades D and C as I and II, respectively. While Grade II was largely left alone, Grade I was given a minimum viscosity to go with its maximum, as well as flash and fire point minimums for increased safety. The justification for the substitution of a "special" metallurgical fuel for the best fuel available to warships was the reduction of its ash and carbon residual content. In theory, this should have increased the amount of time between required boiler cleanings for the navy's warships should they be supplied with Grade I fuel. The former Grade B fuel continued to be issued as long as stocks remained until the outbreak of war.[7]

At first glance, this appears to be the end of major fuel revisions until 1944, at which point BuShips, which had inherited the responsibility of maintaining fuel specifications from BuEng, made changes to the required fire points of Grade I fuel in an attempt to increase efficiency.[8] However, in that revision, Grade I fuel is referred to by the alternative name of "Navy Special," a nonexistent category in the 1938 specifications. This can be traced back to early 1942, when there was a stir among navy fuel suppliers as new contracts suddenly began specifying "Navy Special." This represented one very specific change: a reduction in the maximum acceptable viscosity rating by 40 SSF.[9] Preheating Navy Special fuel was thus required so that no significant alterations to sprayers or other shipboard equipment would be needed. While one might suspect that this change was made to increase the navy's fuel sources, it in fact served to make the requirements for warship fuel more difficult to meet and more challenging to monitor on the part of the Bureau of Supplies and Accounts. The switch to lower-viscosity fuel directly served the purpose of expediting its transport and transfer to warships.[10] While this is an obvious benefit, why would the navy choose to increase the difficulty of fuel acquisition just as this strategic resource was needed in the maximum possible quantity?

The answer to this question lies at the intersection of high steam's effects and the gradual development of the navy's national defense tanker program. Just as the navy was beginning to discover in late 1941 and early 1942 that its modern ships consumed far more fuel than anticipated, it was realizing just how badly prewar orders for "fast fleet oilers" had undershot the mark. This is the other half of *FTP 218*'s "Battle of the Fuel Oil."[11]

The concept of "underway refueling" has been mentioned several times in this study in reference to the development of the capability to refuel warships at sea. Though sometimes accomplished in the age of coal, it was only the wide-scale adoption of oil that made such an operation truly practical. While such a process could and was sometimes accomplished between combatant ships, the "fleet oiler" (AO) was developed as a specialized vessel to carry out this task. Unlike tankers that are simply outfitted to carry oil between major ports, oilers are equipped with the unique machinery required to refuel at sea. This equipment went through numerous iterations in the interwar period as the technique developed but always included some sort of crane, davit, or king-post arrangement for suspending fuel hoses between ships.[12]

The US Navy was one of the earliest experimenters with this process, beginning in 1916–1917, owing to being one of the first large-scale adopters of oil-fired boilers. Though it may sound relatively simple, transferring large quantities of heavy fuel oil through small hoses between two dangerously close steel warships in anything other than dead-calm seas was a formidable technical challenge that naval officers wrestled with for decades. Collision was not the only danger in such an operation. During at-sea refueling, hoses had to be kept out of the water to prevent excessive cooling of the fuel but simultaneously could not be overstressed lest the hoses part—often violently. Numerous tactics were tried throughout the 1910s and 1920s, with the navy eventually settling on what has been referred to as the "broadside" method. In this practice, the vessel to be refueled and the vessel to do the fueling would maneuver alongside each other before passing over steel tension lines fore and aft, and then one or more rubber fuel hoses that contained considerable slack to account for wave action. Speeds during this early period never exceeded 6 knots. While a fleet oiler was usually the primary source for this procedure, larger ships such as battleships and aircraft carriers were rigged to be capable of transferring some of their considerable fuel stores to their smaller consorts (usually destroyers). Naturally, the problem with such a procedure was the reduction in fuel available for the larger ships themselves. Additionally, it was exceedingly rare for the navy to attempt to refuel larger ships during the 1920s and 1930s, as it was believed that the danger inherent in having an oiler and a large combatant within such close proximity outweighed the potential benefits of extended operational range.[13]

By the middle of the 1930s, the US Navy possessed eighteen ships with the "AO" designation, although two were laid up and only a handful were equipped as fleet oilers. Among these, the most capable were also the oldest: the six vessels of the *Kanawaha* class, which rated at 14,500 tons full load and were designed for a maximum speed of 14 knots. Commissioned between 1915 and 1921, these vessels were twenty years old by the 1930s and were hard-pressed to sustain anything approaching their declared top speed. Like the combat ships of the navy, the fleet's supporting forces had been subject to the strict budget limitations of much of the Treaty period and had not yet been either significantly upgraded or replaced.[14]

As the navy began to replace its obsolescent combat ships, renewed attention was directed to the need for sufficient support vessels to carry out War Plan Orange. As discussed previously, throughout the interwar period, the US Navy conducted a series of Fleet Problems intended to assess various components of wartime plans, as well as operational procedures and tactics. It had been these exercises that had driven home the need for increased range among the fleet's destroyers in particular. However, what had also been made abundantly clear was the lack of truly effective at-sea refueling practices and the need to keep escort vessels "topped off" before entering a potential combat zone.[15] This meant that fleet oilers needed to be capable of accompanying the gradual 10-knot procession across the Pacific with the main fleet as well as faster strike forces dispatched to secure the main fleet's passage. This (and the threat of submarine attack at low speeds) was part of the reason for the 15-knot standard cruising speed adopted for the fleet during the 1930s and meant that all existing navy tankers were too slow to accomplish the mission envisioned for them by Orange.

This dilemma eventually led to the general board proposing a large new support force of fleet oilers capable of a sustained speed of 15 knots in late 1933. A serious problem resulted: while the navy had always planned to have a handful of its own fleet oilers in commission, War Plan Orange depended on the availability of significant numbers of suitable *civilian* tankers to help meet requirements in a time of war. By the 1930s, the standard speed of commercial vessels serving in this capacity topped-out at 12 or 13 knots, making them unsuitable for this purpose.[16]

The solution eventually adopted was the creation of the national defense tanker program. It provided government subsidies for the construction of commercial vessels that exceeded their then-standard economical requirements, particularly in the area of speed. An agreement was finally reached with the Standard Oil Company in January 1938 to build the first twelve of these "high speed tankers" (i.e., tankers capable of sustaining 15 or greater knots). They would become known as the *Cimarron*-class oilers, "T3" standard-type vessels that would prove critical to US operations in the Pacific War.[17]

Though not representative of the *entire* force of oilers at the navy's disposal during World War II, the *Cimarron* T3 fast fleet oilers exemplified everything demanded of the type by War Plan Orange and served with distinction in nearly every major operation in the Pacific theater. These ships displaced 24,600 tons at full load and utilized steam at 450 PSI and 750°F. Equipped with the double-reduction gearing then making its way into the navy's warships, USS *Cimarron* (AO-22) was capable of over 19 knots in ideal conditions.[18] This meant that these oilers were perfectly suited for accompanying both the main fleet and the higher speed skirmish forces that the navy planned to employ.

Unfortunately for the navy (and as was the case with high steam), circumstances interfered to prevent the timely acquisition and employment of these oilers where they were needed most. The high speed and large capacity of the *Cimarrons* meant that, as the first twelve were gradually turned over to and then commissioned by the navy between 1939 and 1941, they were immediately employed as *tankers* rather than refitted for use in their intended role as *oilers*.[19] This was the result of a decision in the middle of 1940 for the main fleet to remain forward deployed at Pearl Harbor rather than to return to the West Coast. While intended to serve as a deterrent to further Japanese aggression in East Asia, this decision also placed a tremendous strain on the logistical forces of the US Navy. Whereas previously the fleet was essentially based where its fuel supply was, fuel would now have to be brought forward to the fleet. *Cimarron* itself, as well as a number of its siblings, would end up engaged in this laborious operation throughout the majority of 1940, 1941, and 1942.[20]

This combination of circumstances—the age and low speed of the interwar oiler fleet, the late start on fast-fleet-oiler acquisition, and the forward deployment of the fleet at Pearl Harbor—meant that when the Japanese attacked in December 1941, the navy was still almost entirely reliant on its limited interwar force of twenty-plus-year-old slow oilers for combat operations (table 10.1).[21] When paired with the overall "Europe First" policy, the losses suffered on December 7, and the unknowns surrounding operational range that quickly manifested themselves thereafter, the result was a significant delay in the implementation of any kind of aggressive westward advance as had been envisioned for most of the interwar period by War Plan Orange. Instead, the bulk of the navy's capital ships remained tethered to existing US bases for all of 1942 and much of 1943, relying on fleet oilers only as a means to effectively extend a given task force's cruising radius from the Hawaiian Islands for relatively brief operations.[22] This, by extension, reinforced command preference for the utilization of only the most fuel-efficient vessels in what combat operations *were* possible with Pearl's limited supply capacity, sidelining the remainder until the situation could be properly addressed.[23] In this first phase of the war, a specific style of raid quickly became the calling card of US operations.

The "carrier raid" consisted of the movement of a carrier task force (usually a single aircraft carrier plus a screen of a handful of destroyers and one or two cruisers) in the company of an oiler from Pearl Harbor to a point just beyond the edge of the range of a target location's land-based aircraft. Once there, the task force would refuel all of its destroyers from the oiler before proceeding at high speed (25 knots or greater) toward the target with the plan of attacking at dawn. Once the task was completed and all aircraft recovered, the force would withdraw the way it came, rendezvous with the oiler and refuel again, and then return to Pearl Harbor.[24] This type of operation was neither new in 1941–1942 nor a direct substitution of carriers for battleships as has sometimes been claimed. Instead, these raids and the related tactic of carrier "ambushes" exemplified by the battles of Coral Sea and Midway were the employment of existing carrier doctrine originally meant to compliment the westward movement of the battle line as envisioned in War Plan Orange. This component of the original US playbook was simply all that the navy was capable of carrying out at the time.[25]

While a carrier raid of this style sounds relatively straightforward, the reality quickly proved to be anything but. For example, a similar operation to relieve Wake Island in the first weeks of the war was aborted due to difficulties that developed while refueling Task Force 14's destroyers from the old fleet oiler USS *Neches* (AO-5).[26] This operation and the subsequent attempt to strike Wake Island that was recalled following that same oiler's sinking by a Japanese submarine made it abundantly clear that the older oilers couldn't be depended on for fleet operations. The limited capacity and low speed of these vessels made them both inefficient tenders and highly vulnerable to torpedo attack. Additionally, despite interwar practice with the broadside refueling method, the need to refuel task force vessels in *all* kinds of weather rather than simply when conditions were ideal meant

Table 10.1. Fleet Oilers Available to the US Navy in Late 1941

Name	Displacement (Full Load)	Speed (Knots)	Commissioned
Kanawha	14,500	14	1915
Maumee	14,500	14	1916
Cuyama	14,500	14	1917
Brazos	14,800	14	1919
Neches	14,800	14	1920
Pecos	14,800	14	1921
Patoka	16,800	10.5	1919
Sapelo	16,800	10.5	1921
Ramapo	16,800	10.5	1919
Trinity	16,800	10.5	1920
Kaweah	14,450	10.5	1921
Laramie	14,450	10.5	1921
Mattole	14,450	10.5	1940*
Rapidan	16,800	10.5	1921
Salinas	16,800	10.5	1921
Sepulga	16,800	10.5	1922
Tippecanoe	16,800	10.5	1940*
Cimarron	24,800	18	1939
Neosho	24,800	18	1939
Platte	24,800	18	1939
Sabine	24,800	18	1940
Salamonie	24,800	18	1941
Kaskaskia	24,800	18	1940
Sangamon	24,800	18	1940**
Santee	24,800	18	1940**
Chemung	24,800	18	1941
Chenango	24,800	18	1941**
Guadalupe	24,800	18	1941
Suwannee	24,800	18	1941**

At the time of the attack on Pearl Harbor, the United States was still largely reliant on a very old force of slow fleet oilers that themselves would have been a detriment to operations. The difficulties introduced by the problems with calculating range and other shortcomings of the American high-steam system significantly amplified this problem. Additionally, the 18-knot *Cimarron*-class oilers that were commissioned at this time were mostly either not yet equipped with their refueling equipment, engaged in tanker duty hauling oil to Pearl Harbor and other bases, or both.

* Those ships marked with a single asterisk were purchased in 1922 but laid up until 1940.

**Those ships marked with two asterisks were converted to escort carriers (CVEs) in 1942 and were therefore not available to the fleet.

Source: Wildenberg, *Gray Steel and Black Oil*, 272–74.

that the first months of the war in particular represented a harsh logistical learning experience for the US Navy.[27]

Compounding the problems with older fleet oilers was the uncertainty surrounding fuel consumption with high steam. The twin interests of maximum speed and fuel efficiency for these raids meant that there was an immediate and heavy reliance on high-steam-equipped vessels after 1941.[28] The obsolescence of the navy's range tables as provided in *FTP 136* and the inability of the fleet to utilize its cruising turbines meant that it was even more important for a given task force commander to ensure the maximum amount of available fuel before his run to strike a target. If this was not done, unexpected maneuvering could deplete the reserves of his escorts and reduce his maximum available speed. Such a mistake could prove fatal.

In light of these experiences, it was very clear by early 1942 that keeping a capable oiler close at hand was critically important to operational success. This message was received so strongly that, following the loss of *Neches* in January 1942, carrier task forces operated almost exclusively in conjunction with modern fast fleet oilers, becoming largely dependent on the navy's ability to make them available at need. In 1942 and 1943, this reliance dictated the pace of offensive operations, a situation that King's office had subsequently bemoaned in *FTP 218*.[29]

"In a war of maximum effort," Navy Secretary Swanson had written in March 1937, "the Navy will have a need upon mobilization for twenty fast tankers to accompany the fleet. To assemble those twenty fast tankers in a reasonably short time, there will, of necessity, have to be a greater number of such vessels under American registry at the time."[30] While Swanson and others such as Admiral Emory S. Land were aware of the need for an increased number of modern oilers before America's entry into World War II, it would take the crisis just detailed to finally get the message through to the navy at large. Most of the resulting vessels that were on-order by the beginning of 1942 were only delivered in 1943 or later. Four were converted to badly needed escort carriers for the Atlantic in 1942 before the range and oiler crises were fully understood.[31]

By the fall of 1943, some thirty fast-fleet oilers of various types had become available to the navy and substantially more similar fast tankers were under construction for civilian use. This, in conjunction with a marked increase in available warships, permitted the shift to a general offensive style more akin to that prescribed by War Plan Orange. Rather than the close attachment of one or two oilers to a single task force as "range extenders," oilers after this time were grouped together with their own dedicated escorts and other auxiliaries as independent task units known as "replenishment groups." These units conveniently dealt not only with the critical issue of getting fuel forward to the fleet but also conveyed ammunition and provided light repair capabilities. Replenishment groups were stationed at predesignated locations where warships could rendezvous with them to top-off as desired. When the ships of a group ran low on fuel or other supplies, they were simply relieved by a new group fresh from Pearl Harbor. In this manner, warships could remain on-station nearly indefinitely (independent of maintenance or significant repairs) by relying on resupply from these replenishment task groups, enabling much larger, longer, and more distant offensive operations.[32]

As US forces advanced further west through the south-central Pacific, the logistics effort was further aided by the seizure of forward anchorages such as that at Kwajalein Atoll. These staging areas served both as repair stations for ships that were damaged or in need of maintenance and as forward oil depots, shortening the return time for resupply groups working directly with the fleet. For their part, the number of fast civilian tankers had grown significantly enough that they could be relied upon to transfer fuel oil from the West Coast to navy depot locations such as Pearl Harbor, freeing the fleet oilers previously engaged in this task. By the war's end, the navy had some seventy fast fleet oilers of various types available to assist operations, a far cry from the lone member of the type, USS *Neosho* (AO-23), that had been in the Pacific at the war's outbreak.[33]

HIGH-STEAM PRODUCTION PROBLEMS AFTER PEARL HARBOR

The dramatic need for fast oilers resulting from high steam's adoption also served to put additional strain on the already-overloaded collection of turbine and gear manufacturers after 1941. As previously discussed, the supply of turbines and gears suitable for high-steam systems was a major bottleneck in the early stages of World War II. Because of the shortage, strict limits had been placed on the production of spare parts as early as 1940 in the interest of expediting new construction.[34] This problem had grown to serious proportions by the beginning of 1942—even before the desperate need for fast tankers was readily apparent. Overall, the most significant noncombat result of this situation was a substantial improvement in the navy's understanding of and involvement in the operations of its contractors.

The attack on Pearl Harbor on December 7, 1941, presented the navy with its first large-scale emergency need for spares and posed the certain prospect of further spikes in demand in the near future. It was at this point that maintenance of the navy's existing warships took priority over new construction. Fortunately, while maintaining the American high-steam system was not easy or inexpensive, it appears that it largely lived up to expectations in the area of durability. The primary difficulty on this front instead lay with a relatively high rate of production defects that held overall supply down once it resumed.[35] With this limitation plaguing turbine and gear suppliers, these companies had continued to fall behind in their contracts by 1942. It was at this point that the navy finally moved in earnest to deal with the production shortfalls.

In January 1942, the diplomatically minded Rear Admiral Samuel M. Robinson, two-time former chief of BuEng and current chief of BuShips, was promoted to vice admiral and placed in charge of the newly created Office of Procurement and Material (OP&M). Succeeding Robinson as chief of the Bureau of Ships was first his deputy, Rear Admiral Alexander Van Keuren (January 1942–November 1942), and finally Rear Admiral Edward L. Cochrane (November 1942–1946). Cochrane was a naval architect (rather than an engineer like Bowen and Robinson), with a master of science degree from the Massachusetts Institute of Technology.[36] Unlike the tenures of his predecessors in BuShips and BuEng, Cochrane had no interest or time to particularly concern himself with advancing the state of naval propulsion in the navy. Instead, the long list of problems with high steam and general procurement during World War II that we have been detailing saddled the admiral with a management crisis that he and Robinson have been best remembered for mitigating.

Conceived by Secretary of the Navy Frank Knox, Robinson's OP&M was charged with supervising and coordinating procurement efforts for every bureau in the navy. The office served to both centralize control over the "shore establishment" of the bureaus as well as provide a means by which accurate supply statistics and projections might finally be calculated and utilized. It was under Robinson's watch that OP&M handled the rationing of critical raw materials and conflicting demands with other branches of the military.[37] Although bureaucratic infighting would continue to cause production ripples, the period of direct competition between the bureaus for raw materials was finally over. Centralized control by a mostly civilian, business-savvy OP&M ultimately pressured BuShips to take a much more directed approach to counteracting the turbine and gear shortages plaguing the navy. What followed was the implementation of three policies, elements of which had already been tried experimentally during Robinson's tenure. All three included direct and unprecedented intervention by the bureau in the affairs of both contractors and subcontractors.[38]

With the wartime stresses on the economy, BuShips's ability to counter the turbine and gear shortages was largely limited to resources already available. Minimizing the downtime any individual contractor had was thus the first method relied upon to reduce turbine production delays. After 1942, it became common for Admiral Cochrane's BuShips to shuffle partially completed turbines and turbine components from one manufacturer to another depending on their workload. This reduced the load on more heavily committed companies but resulted in some additional delays due to transport time and paperwork concerns. Instances of confusion regarding exchanges are apparent in the records of the Bureau of Ships as well, particularly in the early days of this practice.[39] In several instances entire contracts were mistakenly dropped due to simple miscommunication between the various companies involved in an exchange. Fortunately, it seems that this problem was usually quickly discovered, and in general, these efforts helped decrease some of the worst turbine-related delays.[40]

The second method that BuShips employed to reduce delays was, ironically, to have navy and private yards act as subcontractors for turbine manufacturers. This was initiated by Robinson in partnership with Allis-Chalmers in 1941. As might be expected, the use of navy yards for this type of subcontracting was far more commonplace than using private yards. Not only were the navy yards easier to supervise, but the navy typically had better access to the resources required for turbine blading, casings, and final assemblies. As a result, the various navy yards became a major source of turbine components (and even in numerous cases entire turbines) for the turbine manufacturers.[41] On the other hand, the use of private shipyards in this capacity was hampered by the fact that virtually no private yards retained the tools or expertise to produce turbines of any kind after 1938. Therefore, private yards that got involved often had to be provided with the necessary personnel and tools for this endeavor. Nevertheless, this was the most effective of the three methods employed by BuShips and OP&M to combat shortages.[42]

The third approach was to cultivate additional production sources from companies not yet involved in turbine production but in possession of the proper equipment and skilled labor to undertake such work. This involved contacting various owners of machinery similar to that used by the turbine suppliers, as they had the potential to be repurposed for producing turbines. With Westinghouse falling increasingly behind in its orders in early 1942, the bureau contacted DeLaval (a company that already produced reduction gears for the navy), the Elliott Company (an electrical utility manufacturer), and Murray Iron Works (a general machine tool manufacturer).[43] The response to this initiative was poor, however, as most companies lacked the capacity to take on any new types of work without significant retooling well into 1943. This was a formidable obstacle in light of the need for specialized precision machinery for turbine and gear manufacturing. This approach by the bureau was so unproductive that the navy was forced to rely largely on its other patchwork methods of subcontracting its own yards and component swapping between turbine suppliers to minimize effects of delays.[44]

As efforts to stabilize turbine production progressed, the navy was busy fighting a war that constantly required the Bureau of Ships to provide maintenance on vessels that had taken enough damage to require turbine or component replacements. Although this need for parts was previously met by the *parallel* manufacture of "shore spares," these were not regularly produced even after the middle of 1941. The sudden need for spare parts after Pearl Harbor caught the navy flat-footed. Initially, its response was to seize engines already completed for new vessels. As US industry began to hit its stride in 1943 and 1944, this transitioned first to the issue of "emergency priority" contracts before finally settling on the issue of "pre-emptive" contracts that could be escalated should circumstances demand it.[45]

At the onset of the war, spares could be obtained from engines already completed for new or existing warships. These were quick and effective options as far as repairs were concerned, but there were two problems with this course of action. First, if the navy chose to seize an engine from a ship nearing completion, that vessel was set back considerably in the contract queue. It would be useless to the navy until a new contract could be issued and filled, setting back ships already delayed by the wait for their turbines by an even larger margin. The second issue was that despite the relative standardization of engine specifications prior to World War II, turbines were not always interchangeable among different ship types and classes.[46] As a result, the options for this repair method were at times quite limited. Fortunately for the navy, the fleet opened the war in the Pacific with a large number of destroyers still in possession of their spares. It was primarily these units that were seized.[47]

As the war in the Pacific progressed, major battles and changing priorities caused contracts for spare turbine components to be regularly displaced from the order queues of the turbine manufacturers. This is evidenced by the manner in which Midway and the battles of the first half of 1942 pushed carrier turbines ahead of those for destroyers in Westinghouse's production orders. By and large, however, by the middle stages of the war, the navy was issuing contracts for spares primarily on an emergency basis only, immediately displacing all other orders. This policy was no less disruptive than seizing engines from nearly completed vessels. It, too, was dropped as quickly as was feasible.[48]

The final method for providing spare turbines and components for the US Navy's vessels, particularly its destroyers, was to issue contracts for components whenever possible far in advance of the expectation that they would be needed. The catch was these contracts were issued with the understanding that they could be escalated in size or priority should circumstances demand it. Unlike the issuance of emergency contracts on the spot, which displaced other orders significantly and worsened the overall turbine situation, this method ensured that the effects of sudden contract changes were minimal. By the latter half of the war, raw materials were significantly less of a problem for turbine manufacturers than manpower and capacity due to the efforts of OP&M. Issue of a contract in this manner therefore ensured that the contractor immediately began allocating the resources necessary to fulfill the conditions. Everything would be on hand were it to be abruptly needed, thereby minimizing the time required to retool and make other changes necessary to shift production. Instances of this method of contracting for spare parts are common in the records of BuShips after 1943.[49]

Despite these improvements, however, evidence suggests that turbine production capacity was still not at an acceptable level for the Bureau of Ships in 1944. The navy's displeasure is demonstrated in its contract negotiations with primary turbine suppliers for the production of replacement turbines and reduction gears for destroyers damaged in combat. These negotiations, conducted by the Bureau's Contract Negotiation Board, produced official transcripts covering precise content, nature, and proposed delivery dates of each job, as well as the navy's understanding and position for each. Common are deadpan statements such as, "We would like to have that equipment much earlier than March–April 1945, but we understand that it cannot be completed earlier without disturbing existing schedules."[50] BuShips appears by this point to have accepted that private turbine production would continue to be a bottleneck in warship construction despite the vast production increases elsewhere and its relatively successful attempts to counteract delays.

The navy never hit upon a perfect solution to the turbine production shortfall, but the Bureau of Ships' patchwork approach of subcontracting and disbursing available components to locations where they were most needed began to make turbine delivery dates ever closer to their yard requirements as 1943 drew to a close. Production orders after the middle of 1943 avoided significant delays as increasing machine tool availability finally brought up precision production capacity, and patchwork measures enacted by the bureau to meet deadlines became standard practice. Although production concerns persisted throughout the war, wide-scale disaster with prewar building plans due to the new technology and its associated production methods had been averted.

CHANGES TO SHIP DESIGN RESULTING FROM HIGH STEAM

While the problems of turbine and gear supply were somewhat mitigated by the navy's intervention in the affairs of its contractors, the shortages proved severe enough to affect the characteristics of additional types of ships designed and ordered during World War II. Uncertain that the requirements of existing orders could even be met, BuShips after Robinson's departure at the beginning of 1942 was understandably skeptical that additional orders could be filled. The result was the resurgence of alternative methods of propulsion that had been discarded for larger surface vessels in the 1930s. These developments, combined with a developing recognition of the high-steam system's increased susceptibility to crippling shock damage, would lay the foundations of propulsion development after World War II.

By late 1941, the difficulties encountered by US Navy turbine and gear contractors were serious enough to have prompted the proposal of radical solutions, such as reducing the number of warships on order by as much as 30 percent.[51] While this would not come to pass, even the vast number of vessels already on order by this time did not fully satisfy the needs of fighting a global conflict. As discussed earlier, fast-fleet oilers were a big part of this deficiency. As users of geared steam turbines, the navy's preferred class of oilers—the *Cimmaron* class—was a further burden on the United States' turbine and gear manufacturers, and attempts to increase their numbers therefore had to compete with both new warship production and the provision of spare parts. To make matters worse, this crowded and confusing situation was further complicated by the introduction of the "destroyer escort" (DE) program. This initiative was an effort characterized by the

Bureau of Ships after 1945 as simultaneously one of the greatest successes and the greatest failures of World War II.[52]

Displacing roughly half that of a fleet destroyer and carrying significantly less weaponry, destroyer escorts were envisioned as early as 1939–1940 as cheaper alternatives to their larger cousins that could be optimized for convoy escort duties. Ideally, this (originally British) proposal would minimize the resources required to properly protect groups of merchant ships, freeing up full-size destroyers for fleet-escort duties or other operations as needed. Unfortunately, such a role would require DEs, like their larger cousins, to operate at speeds significantly higher than those of their charges, allowing their proper employment against submarines while in escort service. Thus, under the initial proposals for the program, DEs were to have required the same or similar geared steam turbine propulsion machinery as destroyers.[53]

As a result of the projected propulsion requirements, the DE program was repeatedly put off and put down in 1940 and 1941 for fear of further aggravating the turbine and gear shortage, thereby only amplifying the destroyer shortage it was meant to alleviate.[54] However, the need for convoy escort vessels, particularly in the Atlantic, had become so acute by the end of 1941 that fully discarding the DE idea was politically untenable. The result was that, following the reorganization of procurement under Robinson's OP&M, many ships of the destroyer escort program were ultimately designed to employ propulsion methods that *were* available in sufficient numbers: lower-power diesel and turbo-electric drives.[55]

Although somewhat compromised from a design perspective (particularly compared to full-size destroyers), the speed that the alternatively powered DEs were able to achieve was judged sufficient for the protection of slower merchant convoys. Additionally, this decision allowed all ships of the initial order batch to be delivered to the navy by the end of 1943.[56] By the war's end, about 229 destroyer escorts had been completed with various diesel drives while another 124 were completed with steam turbo-electric drives that did not require reduction gears. The former category were limited to speeds between 19 and 21 knots. Eighty-three were equipped with traditional geared steam turbines that produced speeds of approximately 24 knots, all of which were available only after March 1944 (table 10.2).[57]

The rapid expansion of the navy's force of fleet oilers followed a similar course. While the number of large *Cimmaron*-type fast oilers capable of 18 knots was never able to grow beyond about thirty ships in service, these vessels were only required for direct action with the fleet itself. For support

Table 10.2. Destroyer Escort Classes of the US Navy, 1943–1945

Class Name	Propulsion Type	Number Built	Speed (Knots)	First Date Available
Evarts	Diesel-Electric	97	19	Apr-43
Buckley	Turbo-Electric	148	24	Apr-43
Cannon	Diesel-Electric	72	21	Sep-43
Edsall	Geared Diesel	85	21	Apr-43
Rudderow	Turbo-Electric	22	24	May-44
John C. Butler	Geared Turbines	83	24	Mar-44

The shortages of turbines and gears for existing production orders led the US Navy to search for alternative propulsion solutions for the Destroyer Escort Program. The result was a hodgepodge of different experiments.

Source: Friedman, *US Destroyers*, 137–61, 478–81, 518–37.

services such as the transport of oil to Pearl Harbor or other forward depots, ships that were *slightly* slower but easier to provide for served as a fallback. This was the initial impetus for the much more numerous types of AO-designated vessels in the navy during World War II, about half of which were equipped with varying types of turbo-electric drives. Additionally, as tactics and operational plans changed with the increasing availability of escorts, these slightly slower vessels were more easily protected than during the opening phases of the war and didn't *need* to keep up with warships, allowing for their participation in the replenishment groups of 1944 and 1945 (table 10.3).[58]

Together, these compromises in design forced BuShips to increase its investment in diesel engines and turbo-electric machinery as a means of primary propulsion for surface vessels. As discussed, this possibility was explored during the interwar period, particularly through the (unrealized) early designs of William Francis Gibbs. However, in the US Navy, diesel propulsion was almost exclusively reserved for submarines before World War II due to the inferior horsepower that even the best designs produced. Similarly, although turbo-electric propulsion had been experimented with in the last classes of "standard" battleships designed before the signing of the Washington Naval Treaty in 1922, it had also been discarded due to the apparent promise of higher power made through developments in high steam. In the end, investments in alternative propulsion that were required for the timely completion of the DE program and the provision of

Table 10.3. US Navy Oiler Classes Acquired During World War II

Class	Displacement (Full Load)	Machinery	Number Built	Speed (Knots)
Cimarron	24,800	Geared Turbines	30	18
Chicopee	21,800	Geared Turbines	2	16.5
Kennebec	21,000	Geared Turbines	6	16.5
Mattaponi	22,300	Geared Turbines	5	16.5
Suamico	21,300	Turbo-Electric	12	14
Chiwawa	21,500	Geared Turbines	5	15
Escambia	21,600	Turbo-Electric	15	15

Only the *Cimarron* class was large enough and capable enough to keep up the fleet in the manner originally practiced at the beginning of World War II. Fortunately, the increasing availability of escorts after 1943 allowed the US Navy to change up its tactics and make good use of its slower oilers.

Source: Wildenberg, *Gray Steel and Black Oil*, 274.

an adequate number of fleet oilers and tankers ultimately served to advance the field of diesel propulsion in particular, although at a cost of fielding a fleet of support ships with "inferior speed." This was the source of BuShips's postwar assessment of overlapping success and failure with the DE program.[59]

CHANGES TO SHIP SURVIVABILITY RESULTING FROM HIGH STEAM

Mixed use of high steam and alternative propulsion methods served another purpose apart from forcing investment in the latter: allowing for a direct comparison of the susceptibility of each to combat damage. The reader may recall that concern over the high-steam system's vulnerability to dangerous battle damage was evident during the general board study of 1938. At that time, there was no definitive way to demonstrate whether Admiral Bowen's assertions of the system's ruggedness would hold true in combat.[60] To this end, in 1944 and 1945, Cochrane's BuShips carried out a complete study of all warships that experienced propulsion damage of any kind in combat during World War II. The result is a complete handbook on what can go wrong in combat with high- (or low-) steam propulsion and how it might be addressed.[61]

BuShips's propulsion study details any kind of damage that affected the propulsion system of the vessel in question, including both ships that were lost and ships that managed to survive. Accordingly, some of the data is less complete for some ships than for others, often depending on who managed to escape the vessel or how quickly it sank. The most significant finding of the study is something of commonsense truth: that major damage to the propulsion system (and ensuing loss of power) is almost always fatal to a vessel if not immediately addressed.[62] In ships with high steam, a characteristic of its adoption was an alternating boiler-engine room arrangement that helped protect against single-hit elimination of power. This was previously only possible with turbo-electric systems, which did not require a direct mechanical linkage between the generators and motors turning the propeller shafts. The data seems to corroborate that such an arrangement likely saved a number of vessels by permitting them to keep moving and enabling their pumps to function long enough to either get assistance or stay on top of damage control by themselves.[63]

However, the report's evaluation of high steam is not all favorable. The large number of valves and additional sensitive equipment demonstrably increased the system's vulnerability to debilitating shock damage. While older propulsion systems had similar flaws, more modern systems merely magnified this weakness. In other words, hits that did not directly damage the engine or boiler rooms (or in some cases even actually hit the ship at all) held the potential to knock out power by tripping valves or breaking pipes, and high steam had introduced *many* more of these.[64]

This constituted a serious weakness, and accordingly, there is substantial evidence that BuShips acted aggressively in an attempt to compensate for it. Within BuShips's contract records of 1944 and 1945 are a number of experimental designs for valve and piping configurations designed to defeat (or at least minimize) the potential for disastrous shock damage.[65] While at this late stage the majority of these attempts did not reach the fleet before the war's end, the navy at least was made aware of the problem and was able to begin widespread dissemination of the danger through sources like *Introduction to Engineering and Damage Control*. Regardless, the mitigation of shock damage became yet another concern for the navy in the matter of the efficient manufacture and maintenance of a satisfactory propulsion system.[66]

All in all, it is clear that the adoption of American high steam dramatically impacted nearly every aspect of the United States' ability to make naval war for years afterward. Its effects—both positive and negative—can clearly be seen throughout World War II.

Conclusion

Bowen's Legacy

In late 1944, the US Navy began canceling contracts for ships that clearly weren't going to be completed before the war's end. This dramatically accelerated in the middle months of 1945, before eventually bringing new construction to a near standstill by the end of that year. Despite these mass cancelations, wartime production had left the US Navy with an incredible array of modern warships whose numbers utterly dwarfed the prewar fleet's greatest extent. As is often the nature of American military history, this high-steam-powered wartime force—Bowen's legacy—would continue in commission for decades in the relative peace that followed.

The reasons for high steam's persistence, like its performance record in World War II, are mixed. While the navy had certainly learned lessons from its experience with high steam in the war, no substantial new construction would be undertaken until the early 1950s. The combination of *massive* wartime construction, the lack of a peer competitor (after the destruction of the Imperial Japanese Navy), and traditional peacetime budget constraints created a congressional environment that was not conducive to funding new naval projects. Like the navy's reliance on pre-1916-funded warships in the interwar period, the US Navy after World War II would simply have to make do with what it already had.

These constraints largely defined the navy's approach to accommodating high steam's shortcomings in the immediate postwar period, which consisted of the transformation of engineering education and training inside and outside of Annapolis. *Introduction to Engineering and Damage Control* and subsequent works by the Naval Institute formed the core of this new curriculum, which for midshipmen included practical instruction in front of a full-size mock-up of a high-steam propulsion plant.[1] Once sent to sea, any officer assigned to the engineering spaces of a warship was, in a nod to wartime wildcat training, dispatched to an engineering school established and maintained by their type and theater command. Perhaps the most heavily utilized of these was that run by Cruisers/Destroyers Pacific Command (CRUDESPAC), which was set up as an intense, hands-on, six-week-long course. "For the first days, they had us take pencil and paper and trace steam lines through the entire ship," recalled one officer who attended this school in 1958. "Once we understood the system, we ran it—all of it—by ourselves."[2] By all accounts, these reforms clearly worked, and much of the knowledge stuck. However, they also did little to change the enduring perception by most officers of the engineering spaces as hot, dirty, and generally undesirable places to advance a career.[3]

Fortunately, postwar engineering officers, like their interwar predecessors, also had a considerable amount of help. This came in the form of veteran water tenders, throttlemen, machinist mates, and other enlisted sailors who could be found in engineering spaces throughout the navy. These highly competent individuals had learned how to operate high-steam warships during World War II. Like their own predecessors, they were long-service professionals. They represented a silent but invaluable educational resource—one that, ironically enough, enabled a return to the effectiveness of "learning on the job." This, at least, essentially guaranteed peacetime operator competence with the high-steam system.[4]

The apparent success of the navy's educational reforms aside, the experiences of 1950s-era naval officers with *Fletcher*-class destroyers and other vessels of World War II vintage additionally reveal the fallout of high steam's apparent transformation of American fuel economy—or rather, its failure to do so. While existing cruising turbines were left in situ, they were largely ignored. ("Cruising turbines?" responded one officer when queried on their use. "We only ever used those in rare, specific, and pre-scheduled circumstances on straight, predictable courses. Generally speaking, they were locked out.") Instead, the navy returned to reduced boiler operation to conserve fuel and omitted cruising turbines entirely from its "1200-pound" steam designs that began entering service aboard *Forrest Sherman*-class destroyers in 1953.[5] Similarly, the prewar "engineering economy scores," used by *FTP 136* to help calculate operational range, returned as "economy trials." Conducted once a year, these exercises were largely dedicated to ensuring that equipment was properly functioning and fuel was consumed at expected rates.[6]

From the preceding paragraphs, the reader can be forgiven for wondering why the navy might seem to have learned from its experiences, on the one hand, and doubled down on its mistakes, on the other. The return to prewar fuel economy practices can, however, be explained by the fundamental transformation of the navy's refueling mindset by the experience of the Pacific War. The late-war availability of independent replenishment groups (as well as the trauma of Typhoon Cobra in 1944) had resulted in a "top-off" mentality. In the words of one officer, destroyers operating in the Pacific in the immediate postwar period were expected to refuel, "by the time they had around 70% of their fuel remaining." As high-steam destroyers could burn up to 25 percent of their fuel in a single twenty-four-hour period of operating at or above 27 knots, this meant that "topping off" occurred nearly every day. As long as there were ships available to fuel *from*, "radius oil" was never again a concern.[7]

Therefore, while BuShips did eventually resume Bowen's quest with the aforementioned 1200-pound steam system that began entering service in the mid-1950s, by then the purpose and design of US naval propulsion had fundamentally changed. That system and its labor-saving automatic combustion control would develop its own laundry list of issues, but its relationship to the gas turbine's rise to prominence is a story for another time.

The idea of high-pressure and high-temperature steam as a singular American advantage had its origins in foreign experimentation with the same prior to World War II. The success of high steam in the pursuit of economies of scale by electric utility companies in the 1920s intrigued designers in nearly every major navy. The most exceptional cases were the French Marine Nationale and German Kriegsmarine, which employed pressures in excess of 500 PSI and 1,000 PSI, respectively. While each of these navies achieved their primary goals of exceptional speed and small machinery size, they were also equally disappointed with the inadequate operational range and poor maintenance record of their high-steam ships—the latter of which has become somewhat infamous among historians.[8]

In the 1930s, the US Navy, at the direction of Admirals Samuel M. Robinson and Harold G. Bowen Sr., began developing its own high-steam system. Characterized by its use of steam at 650 PSI and 800°F, this system also employed a number of innovations designed to increase operational range through the optimization of fuel efficiency at low-to-medium speeds. These included the unique development of controlled superheaters and double-reduction gears. This system, as it appeared in *Somers*-class destroyer leaders, set the standard for all US warship designs from 1938 through 1945.

While the employment of additional components was the primary characteristic that set American high-steam propulsion apart, the complicated nature of their design, interaction, and use has long relegated the system as a whole to a "black box" condition for historians. With this mindset, the inner workings of the system are not actually understood, being disregarded in favor of considering only the input (steam conditions) and output (range/endurance). From this point of view, high steam *did* improve the operational reach of American warships beyond what other nations accomplished. Unfortunately, such a perspective also completely overlooks the vast array of interrelated problems associated with this system. Our review of high steam and its internal issues to this point has thus been an exercise in *intent-based* history; an attempt to understand *what was actually predicted and expected* of high steam when it was adopted, rather than a raw comparison of range and pressure statistics between nations. It is only through this lens that we can grasp why high steam could simultaneously been seen to succeed *and* fail on such a grand scale.

Of course, part of why high steam has remained a black box until this point is due to the dearth of sources readily available on the subject other than Admiral Bowen's autobiography. *Ships, Machinery, and Mossbacks*—which remains a brilliant window into Bowen's professional life and mindset—is nevertheless undeniably a partisan source. Published in 1954 after Bowen's failure to secure the navy's nuclear portfolio for his short-lived time at the Office of Naval Research, the book is ultimately a recounting of injustices suffered by Bowen despite his career accomplishments. The admiral's sunny depiction of high steam contained within has therefore been long overdue for critical examination, particularly considering his disassociation with the system prior to its wide-scale use after 1939.

Ultimately, Admiral Bowen was what we would call today a *technocrat*—a highly skilled subject matter expert. As the head of the Bureau of Engineering in the late 1930s, Bowen was relied upon to be *the* guiding voice for the US Navy on matters of propulsion. As discussed throughout this book, the rapid evolution of steam technology in the first half of the twentieth century had made Bowen's position even more important to the navy than it had been when his bureau was established the better part of a century earlier. Propulsion technology had simply moved beyond the easy understanding of nonspecialists, resulting in the dramatic rise in power and influence of individuals like Bowen. Put simply, Bowen had the ability to change naval policy on a wide array of matters *related* to propulsion due to the fact that there simply was *no one else* in the navy who knew enough to countermand him. This was why the general board study on high steam was so critical at the time—it was the only available means to hold the navy's technocratic elite accountable. In the end, Bowen *was* held accountable; despite the supposed success of his high-steam project by a results-based analysis, the admiral did not find himself in an equally powerful position again.

This story should sound familiar. In our era of enormous defense budgets and the well-entrenched military-industrial economy, innumerable organizations are charged with regularly producing the next great technical breakthrough. In this context, the story of Bowen and high steam provides an eye-opening example of how far off the rails things can go if we lose sight of *why* innovations are pursued in the first place and instead pursue technological innovation for its own sake. Technocratic elites *must* be held accountable, or we may once again discover that we have gone too far on a whim.

Notes

INTRODUCTION

Epigraph. Alfred Thayer Mahan, *Naval Strategy: Compared and Contrasted with the Principles and Practice of Military Operations on Land* (Boston: Little, Brown, and Company, 1911).

1. Typos original. General Board of the Navy to the Secretary of the Navy, "An Estimate on Temperature and Pressure," 1938, General Board Study No. 420–13—December 1, 1938: Steam Conditions of Pressure, General Board Subject File 1900–1947, Box 104, Record Group (RG) 80, National Archives Building in Washington, DC (NAB).

2. Harold G. Bowen, *Ships, Machinery, and Mossbacks: The Autobiography of a Naval Engineer* (Princeton, NJ: Princeton University Press, 1954).

3. Bowen, *Ships, Machinery, and Mossbacks*.

4. A good sample of the effort involved in calculating even the simplest tasks can be seen in H. G. Donald, "Boiler Room Operation on Naval Vessels," *Journal of the American Society for Naval Engineers* 41, no. 4 (November 1929): 608–19. The math that went into these decisions is discussed in Rear Admiral Samuel M. Robinson, "The Stopping of Ships," *Journal of the American Society for Naval Engineers* 50, no. 3 (August 1938): 325–40. The actual process of maneuvering a ship from the point of view of the engineering spaces is outlined in general terms in a reprint of the Manual of Engineering Instructions titled "Instructions for the Operation and Maintenance of Main Propelling Machinery Section I.—Turbines" found in Navy Department Publications 1828–1947, Box N929, RG 287 Publications of the Federal Government, National Archives at College Park, MD (NACP). For brief information regarding engineering titles, see Theodore Roscoe, *United States Destroyer Operations in World War II* (Annapolis: Naval Institute Press, 1953), 12–14.

5. Frederick T. Wilson was a uniquely well-educated individual whose perspective we are incredibly lucky to have available today. While the time period his account covers ends long before the story of high steam begins in the US Navy, his perspective is nevertheless invaluable to us for the glimpse into recruiting and daily life outside officers' country that it provides. For its part, Frederick Harrod's work relies heavily on periodicals directed at enlisted personnel and administrative records prior to 1940. World War II records were not all readily available at the time that work was composed. James R. Reckner, ed., *A Sailor's Log: Water-Tender Frederick T. Wilson, USN, on Asiatic Station, 1899–1901* (Kent, OH: Kent State University Press, 2004); Frederick S. Harrod, *Manning the New Navy: The Development of a Modern Naval Enlisted Force, 1899–1940* (Westport, CT: Greenwood Press, 1978).

6. Designed and built when the destroyer was a brand-new concept, *Hopkins*'s machinery never worked as intended and was notorious for the number of engineering

"casualties" it reported. This notably included a boiler explosion while Bowen himself was fortunate enough to be ashore. Bowen, *Ships, Machinery, and Mossbacks*, 7–14.

7. Bowen, *Ships, Machinery, and Mossbacks*, 59–64.

8. Office of the Chief of Naval Operations, *FTP 218 War Service Fuel Consumption of U.S. Naval Surface Vessels* (Washington, DC: Government Printing Office, 1945), 1, as found in US Navy Technical Publications, Box 62, RG 38: Records of the Office of the Chief of Naval Operations, NACP.

9. In the lexicon of the US Navy, surface vessels are said to have "screws" rather than "propellers" (although the latter *is* used for submarines). While this work attempts to hold as closely to US Navy practices as possible, these terms are used somewhat interchangeably in the pursuit of maximum clarity for the reader.

10. This information is compiled from Bowen, *Ships, Machinery, and Mossbacks*, 47–125; Norman Friedman, *U.S. Destroyers: An Illustrated Design History* (Annapolis, MD: Naval Institute Press, 2004); and from General Board Study No. 420–13, General Board Subject File 1900–1947, Box 104, RG 80, NAB; Bureau of Engineering, *Special Specifications for Propelling Machinery with Boilers, Auxiliary Machinery, and Electric Plant for U.S. Destroyers DD 381 and DD 383* (Washington, DC: Government Printing Office, 1934), as found in ITEM S-18 (Ships & Ships' Machinery), Box 14, RG 19 Records of the Bureau of Ships, NACP; GE Instruction Materials, ITEM S-15 (Ship Machinery Design History and Data Files), Box 9, RG 19, NACP.

11. The majority of this information is present in RG 19, NACP.

12. This quote is originally from the general board records on the high steam study: General Board of the Navy, "Steam Pressures and Temperatures," in General Board Study No. 420–13, General Board Subject File 1900–1947, Box 104, RG 80, NAB. Bowen also uses this quote in his autobiography *Ships, Machinery, and Mossbacks*, 95, as a block quote from the same general board source.

13. Norman Friedman brings up the issue of high steam briefly using Bowen's story in chapter 5 of *U.S. Destroyers* ("Leaders and the Interwar Period, 1917–1940") and in chapter 7 of that same volume ("The Destroyer Escorts, 1941–1945"), in which he makes a rare mention of the shortage of turbines and reduction gears during World War II but goes no further. Evans and Peattie, in their masterful work on the Japanese Navy, *Kaigun*, naturally focus primarily on the Japanese experimentation with high steam and only briefly touch upon the capabilities of the US Navy for a point of comparison. For his part, Albert Nofi's analysis of the US Navy's Fleet Problems in *To Train the Fleet for War* relates the story of the range deficiency of US Navy destroyers rather than the change to high steam itself throughout his work. This is particularly apparent in the case of Fleet Problem XIV in 1933, during which many of the Navy's destroyers were afforded only a limited role due to their range. Friedman, *U.S. Destroyers: An Illustrated Design History*, 88, 95–97, 143–44; David C. Evans and Mark R. Peattie, *Kaigun: Strategy, Tactics, and Technology in the Imperial Japanese Navy, 1887–1941* (Annapolis, MD: Naval Institute Press, 1997), 246–48; Albert A. Nofi, *To Train the Fleet for War: The US Navy Fleet Problems, 1923–1940* (Newport, RI: Naval War College, 2010), 168.

14. Worrall Reed Carter and Thomas Wildenberg's analyses of Pacific Fleet logistics during World War II are related to our focus through their concern with the movement of fuel oil. Within their discussions, they present some of the only postwar negative takes on Admiral Bowen's activities, particularly his notoriously adversarial

management style. Thomas Heinrich, on the other hand, comes the closest any scholar has to a direct analysis of high steam. Heinrich's attempt to break into what he calls the "black box" of military shipbuilding in the mid-twentieth century is a critical aid to our analysis here, but he still heavily relies upon Bowen's autobiography for the majority of his information regarding high steam. There are, however, tantalizing hints of the problems high steam introduced in his discussions of production issues during World War II. Worrall Reed Carter, *Beans, Bullets, and Black Oil: The Story of Pacific Fleet Logistics Afloat in the Pacific During World War II* (Washington, DC: Department of the Navy, 1953); Thomas Wildenberg, *Gray Steel and Black Oil: Fast Tankers and Replenishment at Sea in the U.S. Navy, 1912–1992* (Annapolis, MD: Naval Institute Press, 1996); Thomas Heinrich, *Warship Builders: An Industrial History of U.S. Naval Shipbuilding, 1922–1945* (Annapolis, MD: Naval Institute Press, 2020).

15. The majority of these authors have not been as interested in manpower mobilization as much as industrial mobilization. A rare, recent exception to this rule is Stanford Edward Fisher, "Sustaining the Pacific Carrier Air War: The Development of U.S. Naval Aviation Maintenance and the Enlisted Aircraft Technician in World War II" (PhD diss., University of Maryland College Park, 2019).

16. Given Karsten's former background as a junior naval officer and the political and academic climate of the early 1970s, there is naturally also reason to suspect an agenda behind the conclusions he presents. Peter Karsten, *The Naval Aristocracy: The Golden Age of Annapolis and the Emergence of American Navalism* (Annapolis, MD: Naval Institute Press, 1972).

17. There are many sections in Chisholm's work that contain references such as, "Conflicts consequent upon the need for technical specialization originating with steam propulsion had not and would not go away, as much as the Navy tried to finesse them." Chisholm himself, however, is far more interested in the specialist conflict of interest created by naval aviation. Donald Chisholm, *Waiting for Dead Men's Shoes: Origins and Development of the US Navy's Officer Personnel System, 1793–1941* (Palo Alto, CA: Stanford University Press, 2002), 700.

18. Alan S. Milward, *War, Economy, and Society, 1939–1945* (Berkeley: University of California Press, 1999); and Paul A. C. Koistinen, *Arsenal of World War II: The Political Economy of American Warfare, 1940–1945* (Lawrence: University Press of Kansas, 2004).

19. Louis C. Hunter, *A History of Industrial Power in the United States, 1780–1930, Volume Two: Steam Power* (Charlottesville: University Press of Virginia, 1985).

20. Thomas P. Hughes, *Networks of Power: Electrification in Western Society, 1880–1930* (Baltimore, MD: Johns Hopkins University Press, 1985).

21. Richard F. Hirsch, *Technology and Transformation in the American Electric Utility Industry* (New York: Cambridge University Press, 1989).

22. Bowen, *Ships, Machinery, and Mossbacks*.

CHAPTER 1

1. John T. Kuehn, *Agents of Innovation: The General Board and the Design of the Fleet that Defeated the Japanese Navy* (Annapolis, MD: Naval Institute Press, 2008); John T. Kuehn, *America's First General Staff: A Short History of the Rise and Fall of the General Board of the U.S. Navy, 1900–1950* (Annapolis, MD: Naval Institute Press, 2017).

2. For example, managing the throttles was necessary in response to ordered changes in speed and/or available steam, something that was rare when generating power. While this was a common (and critical) requirement in a warship and required a dedicated sailor, it was somewhat less so in a merchant vessel and could be one of several tasks performed by a single individual. Roscoe, *United States Destroyer Operations in World War II*, 12–14.

3. Hunter, *A History of Industrial Power in the United States*, 2–8.

4. Hunter, *A History of Industrial Power in the United States*, 2–8.

5. Watt was, first and foremost, a businessman. He and his partners thus jealously guarded their patents and attempted to prevent the rise of any competitors that improved upon his designs.

6. Hunter, *A History of Industrial Power in the United States*, 601.

7. The need for an external supply of water actually posed a significant problem for early marine adoption of steam propulsion. Hunter, *A History of Industrial Power in the United States*, 7–8.

8. Hunter, *A History of Industrial Power in the United States*, 329–33.

9. Hunter, *A History of Industrial Power in the United States*, 335–40.

10. Another Englishman, Arthur Woolf, is credited with the creation of the compound engine.

11. Hunter, *A History of Industrial Power in the United States*, 594–97.

12. Hughes, *Networks of Power*, 1.

13. Hughes, *Networks of Power*, 209.

14. Hirsch, *Technology and Transformation in the American Electric Utility Industry*, 19–21.

15. Hirsch, *Technology and Transformation in the American Electric Utility Industry*, 20.

16. Hughes, *Networks of Power*, 209.

17. Specifically, the turbines in question were capable generating 5,000 kilowatts of power at a time when 1,000 was considered the maximum that was wise or safe. Hughes, *Networks of Power*, 216–21.

18. The blades themselves are also referred to as "buckets" in this configuration.

19. Charles A. Parsons, *The Steam Turbine: The Rede Lecture, 1911* (Cambridge: Cambridge University Press, 1911), 21–24.

20. Hughes, *Networks of Power*, 216–21.

21. Hirsch, *Technology and Transformation in the American Electric Utility Industry*, 1–2.

22. Hunter, *A History of Industrial Power in the United States*, 685.

23. Hunter, *A History of Industrial Power in the United States*, 685–88.

24. Hughes, *Networks of Power*, 368–69.

25. N. E. Funk, "Higher Steam Pressures," *Journal of the American Society for Naval Engineers* 40, no. 2 (May 1, 1928): 256–65.

26. The same amount of gas (in this case steam) compressed beyond typical pressures in use at the time could be contained in smaller machinery. Naturally, the side effect was the need for higher quality materials to contain these pressures.

27. Hunter, *A History of Industrial Power in the United States*, 631–33.

28. Direct drive meaning there was no intervening gearing or transferring of motion

between the engine and the means of propulsion. Hunter, *A History of Industrial Power in the United States*, 20–25.

29. Hunter, *A History of Industrial Power in the United States*, 641.

30. Hunter, *A History of Industrial Power in the United States*, 644–46.

31. Torpedo boats and torpedo-boat destroyers were then the fastest reciprocating-engine powered vessels in the world. In extreme cases, they were capable of near to 30 knots—but this was often not sustainable for any length of time.

32. Ingvar Jung, *The Marine Turbine, Part 2, 1928–1980: Development of Naval Turbines and the Engines of the Great Atlantic Liners* (Greenwich, London: National Maritime Museum, 1986).

33. It is also important to note that impulse turbines have even *higher* ideal RPM, which, while not a problem for a shore-based station, is a severe handicap when attempting to adapt the same machinery to a ship. Parsons, *The Steam Turbine*.

34. Edgar J. March, *British Destroyers, 1892–1953* (London: Billing & Sons Limited, 1966), 55–62.

35. Jung, *The Marine Turbine, Part 2*.

36. Though "best" isn't really saying a whole lot at this stage in turbine development. Jung, *The Marine Turbine, Part 2*.

37. March, *British Destroyers, 1892–1953*, 39, 113; Friedman, *U.S. Destroyers*, 26.

38. Though this concept would intermittently make appearances in various designs in the continued pursuit for added economy.

39. March, *British Destroyers, 1892–1953*, 116–23; W. W. Smith, "The Economic Advantages of the Reduction Gear as Applied in the Propulsion of Naval Vessels," *Journal of the American Society for Naval Engineers* 23, no. 1 (February 1911): 126–43; Jung, *The Marine Turbine, Part 2*.

40. March, *British Destroyers, 1892–1953*, 226–30; Friedman, *U.S. Destroyers*, 461–62; Evans and Peattie, *Kaigun*, 176–77.

41. It is also worth mentioning that the additional need for motors separate from the rest of the propulsion system had the tendency to make turbo-electric systems heavier and less efficient than geared turbines. C. R. Waller, "What Is the Most Economical Drive for Ships?" *Journal of the American Society for Naval Engineers* 41, no. 2 (May 1929): 267–79.

42. Frank O. Braynard, *By Their Works Ye Shall Know Them: The Life and Ships of William Francis Gibbs, 1886–1967* (New York: Gibbs & Cox, 1968), 12–22.

43. Reportedly, Gibbs even went so far as to sneak into the French liner *Normandie*'s engine spaces with an aide, where he then proceeded to dodge crew members for several hours. After World War II, these efforts would produce the fastest passenger liner ever built: the SS *United States*, which as of the time of writing this book lies rusting at a pier in Philadelphia. Braynard, *By Their Works Ye Shall Know Them*, 151–69.

44. Matson Lines in particular received many design proposals for diesel-propelled ships. Braynard, *By Their Works Ye Shall Know Them*, 42–44.

45. Braynard, *By Their Works Ye Shall Know Them*, 35–41.

46. Gibbs appears to have been joined in this opinion by most naval engineers of the time. In fact, the entire May 1928 issue of the *Journal of the American Society for Naval Engineers* is dedicated to this subject. Braynard, *By Their Works Ye Shall Know Them*, 35–41; J. B. Stillman, "Marine Boilers for High Pressures," *Journal of the American*

Society for Naval Engineers 40, no. 1 (May 1928), 286–96. See also American Society for Naval Engineers, "World Trend Is Toward Geared Turbines and High-Pressure Steam," *Journal of the American Society for Naval Engineers* 47, no. 4 (November 1935): 627–31.

47. Braynard, *By Their Works Ye Shall Know Them*, 54.
48. Braynard, *By Their Works Ye Shall Know Them*, 54.
49. It also helped that Gibbs had also long been known to the Navy thanks to his association with IMM and the *Leviathan*. Braynard, *By Their Works Ye Shall Know Them*, 12–22.
50. Julius Augustus Furer, *Administration of the Navy Department in World War II* (Washington, DC: Government Printing Office, 1959), 214–16.
51. Braynard, *By Their Works Ye Shall Know Them*, 63–72.

CHAPTER 2

1. Kenneth J. Hagan, *This People's Navy: The Making of American Sea Power* (New York: The Free Press, 1991), 179–80.
2. Hagan, *This People's Navy*, 180–82.
3. *Maine* is often referred to as a battleship as well as an armored cruiser depending on the source consulted. This is because it was intended to serve in both roles—that is, to fight enemy capital ships but also to raid enemy commerce. *Maine* was not well designed for either role. Norman Friedman, *U.S. Battleships: An Illustrated Design History* (Annapolis, MD: Naval Institute Press, 1985), 17–23, 424–25.
4. The US Navy had nominally shared the coastal defense mission with the army from the earliest days of American independence. The American infatuation (or perhaps obsession) with coastal fortifications thus had a significant impact on the navy's budget throughout this period. Friedman, *U.S. Battleships*, 25–29, 425–26.
5. While the term "Open Door" was only applied with Secretary of State John Hay's "Open Door Note" of September 1899, it merely represented the first official spelling out of a US commercial interest that had existed for decades. It also depended on the cooperation of all of the major powers active in the region. Gregory Moore, *Defining and Defending the Open Door Policy: Theodore Roosevelt and China, 1901–1909* (New York: Lexington Books, 2015), 80–81; William R. Braisted, *The United States Navy in the Pacific, 1897–1909* (Austin: University of Texas Press, 1958), 15–17.
6. Braisted, *The United States Navy in the Pacific, 1897–1909*, 42–50.
7. The *Indiana*s were also compromised by carrying a full load of coal, as poor placement of their armored belt resulted in it being underwater in that condition. Friedman, *U.S. Battleships*, 17–23.
8. The primary focus of range concerns prior to 1916 were with the fleet's battleships, which were the primary source of combat power. The concept of a balanced fleet—and thus, the need to worry about the ability for smaller ships to *also* reach the Philippines quickly—did not really become clear until late in World War I.
9. Braisted, *The United States Navy in the Pacific, 1897–1909*, 10–15; Walter LaFeber, *The Clash: US-Japanese Relations throughout History* (New York: W. W. Norton, 1997), 53–54.
10. LaFeber, *The Clash*, 55–57. A complete examination of the complex Japanese-American rivalry over Hawaii is beyond the scope of this book. For a thorough

exploration of the facets of this issue, see William Michael Morgan, *Pacific Gibraltar: US-Japanese Rivalry Over the Annexation of Hawaii, 1885–1898* (Annapolis, MD: Naval Institute Press, 2011).

11. Evans and Peattie, *Kaigun*, 11–13, 57–65.

12. Evans and Peattie, *Kaigun*, 57–65.

13. Braisted, *The United States Navy in the Pacific, 1897–1909*, 170–80.

14. Evans and Peattie, *Kaigun*, 129–32.

15. Evans and Peattie, *Kaigun*, 141–51.

16. Erika Lee, "The 'Yellow Peril' and Asian Exclusion in the Americas," in *Pacific Historical Review* 76, no. 4 (November 2007): 543, 550–56; Braisted, *The United States Navy in the Pacific, 1897–1909*, 191; LaFeber, *The Clash*, 88–90.

17. For additional details on the bureau system, see the introduction.

18. Despite having no formally defined powers, the board's advice was nearly *always* followed between 1900 and 1941. For additional information on the General Board of the Navy, see chapter 5 and the work of historian John Kuehn on the subject. Lee, "The 'Yellow Peril' and Asian Exclusion in the Americas," 550–54; Braisted, *The United States Navy in the Pacific, 1909–1922*, 4; Edward S. Miller, *War Plan Orange: The US Strategy to Defeat Japan, 1897–1945* (Annapolis, MD: Naval Institute Press, 2007), 14–16.

19. Miller, *War Plan Orange*, 1–2.

20. Miller, *War Plan Orange*, 31–33.

21. Braisted, *The United States Navy in the Pacific, 1909–1922*, 34–35; Miller, *War Plan Orange*, 15, 33–35.

22. Miller, *War Plan Orange*, 35, 65–76.

23. The terms used here to describe the opposing approaches to the second phase of War Plan Orange are borrowed from Edward Miller. Miller, *War Plan Orange*, 36, 77–85.

24. Miller, *War Plan Orange*, 33–36, 77–85.

25. This plan also marked a definitive pivot from the primary driver of US Far East policy being the Open Door to a "nebulous restraining force" on Japanese ambition. While Filipino independence was promised as early as the Jones Act in 1916 (as a major part of the US population wished to be rid of Philippine obligations), it would be a long process. Throughout, a continued US military presence in the Philippines would, at the very least, require its own protection against Japanese aggression. Additionally, popular theory through 1934 was that independence granted too quickly would lead to aggression by more powerful neighbors like Japan, making war even more likely as the United States was forced to protect its ward. Braisted, *The United States Navy in the Pacific, 1909–1922*, 34–35; Miller, *War Plan Orange*, 15, 24–26, 68–70.

26. Miller, *War Plan Orange*, 75–76. This would of course also affect Japanese plans (and resulting ship designs) for a Blue-Orange War. See chapter 3 for details.

27. Initially, the Treaty system imposed a tonnage cap only on battleships and aircraft carriers, triggering a renaissance in cruiser and destroyer production. The result was the imposition of a similar tonnage cap on those classes of warships in the 1930 London Naval Treaty. Kuehn, *Agents of Innovation*, 28–56.

28. That the ban on fortifications was a rebuke of bastion advocates is without doubt; the 1922 treaty was the only one of the system negotiated purely by diplomats, with naval officers relegated to a purely advisory role. Miller, *War Plan Orange*, 74–76.

29. Miller, *War Plan Orange*, 82–85.
30. Miller, *War Plan Orange*, 86–87, 122–31, 180–83.

CHAPTER 3

1. Throughout the interwar period and World War II, the Italian Regia Marina (Royal Navy) utilized three-drum boiler designs licensed from the British companies Thornycroft and Yarrow, while their single-reduction turbines were designed by Parsons. All of their warships built after 1927 therefore relied upon similar machinery to that which the British Royal Navy utilized, with steam characteristics reaching a maximum of around 400 PSI, 640°F in the 3,084-ton *Capitani Romani*-class light cruisers laid down beginning in 1939. These ships were a response to the French *Le Fantasque* and *Mogador*-class large destroyers and derived their designs from the destroyer *Tashkent* built in Italy for the Soviet Navy in 1937–1938. Italy only managed to build a handful of warships during the war itself. Maurizio Brescia, *Mussolini's Navy: A Reference Guide to the Regia Marina, 1930–1945* (Barnsley, UK: Seaforth Publishing, 2012), 100–103; John Jordan and Jean Moulin, *French Destroyers: Torpilleurs d'Escadre & Contre-Torpilleurs, 1922–1956* (Annapolis, MD: Naval Institute Press, 2015), 116.

2. Parsons or Parsons-licensed equipment even powered the majority of US Navy warships until the 1930s.

3. These vessels came into existence in the late nineteenth century as "torpedo-boat destroyers," intended to counter small and fast torpedo craft with their rapid-fire artillery. As time went on, these vessels evolved into dedicated escorts (a role for which they are most famous), intended to defend their charges against all types of threats. By the time of World War I, these now highly versatile vessels were often referred to simply as "destroyers."

4. At this early stage of the use of the turbine at sea, both efficiency and durability tended to be major headaches. They had become a particular focus of Parsons's research and development as a result. As mentioned previously, cross-compounding offered one potential solution, at least to the efficiency problem, by permitting the customization of two or three separate turbines for the best utilization of the highest, intermediate, and lowest pressures that a given vessel's boilers could produce, without taking up excessive space with a single large turbine. Eventually, each turbine would gain the ability to be bypassed for better economy at different speeds—but this feature would become only gradually more developed over the course of the next thirty years. After World War I, cross-compounding was gradually adopted by all the world's navies in conjunction with single-reduction gearing, largely as a space-saving measure. Parsons, *The Steam Turbine*; and March, *British Destroyers, 1892–1953*, 116–23.

5. March, *British Destroyers, 1892–1953*, 120, 498.
6. March, *British Destroyers, 1892–1953*, 117.
7. March, *British Destroyers, 1892–1953*, 116–23.
8. March, *British Destroyers, 1892–1953*, 500.
9. March, *British Destroyers, 1892–1953*, 247–50; Evans and Peattie, *Kaigun*, 246; John Jordan, *Warships After London* (Annapolis, MD: Naval Institute Press, 2020), 35–36.
10. March, *British Destroyers, 1892–1953*, 500.
11. March, *British Destroyers, 1892–1953*, 500.
12. Evans and Peattie, *Kaigun*, 475.

13. Evans and Peattie, *Kaigun*, 247.
14. Kampon was the short name for the Imperial Japanese Navy Technical Department. Evans and Peattie, *Kaigun*, 182.
15. Granted, the Americans had different priorities. Evans and Peattie, *Kaigun*, 182, 247–48.
16. Evans and Peattie, *Kaigun*, 220.
17. Evans and Peattie, *Kaigun*, 246–48.
18. Evans and Peattie, *Kaigun*, 247–48.
19. Jordan and Moulin, *French Destroyers*, 193–96.
20. Jordan and Moulin, *French Destroyers*, 9, 16.
21. Jordan and Moulin, *French Destroyers*, 15–20.
22. The lack of standardization in turbine design was a characteristic of French shipbuilding of this era, which relied heavily upon private yards that, in turn, produced their contract's turbines based upon the license they held. Jordan and Moulin, *French Destroyers*, 20–26, 35, 41–46, 52–53.
23. Jordan and Moulin, *French Destroyers*, 62, 79–80, 95–97.
24. Jordan and Moulin, *French Destroyers*, 116–17.
25. While renegotiation of the Treaty system in 1930 was a component of these stoppages, the unstable domestic environment of interwar France played a major role in and of itself. For more information, see Jordan and Moulin, *French Destroyers*, 122.
26. Jordan and Moulin, *French Destroyers*, 137–55.
27. Jordan and Moulin, *French Destroyers*, 160–65.
28. Jordan and Moulin, *French Destroyers*, 176.
29. Jordan and Moulin, *French Destroyers*, 160–65.
30. The small size and operational flexibility of the Sural boiler were the benefits of an automatic regulation system and increased pressures in the combustion chamber ("Sural" was short for *suralimenté*, "supercharged"). This was believed to hold so much promise that this same type of boiler was subsequently adopted for the pair of *Richelieu*-class battleships ordered late in the 1930s. Only *Richelieu* was completed before the end of World War II. The battleship was commissioned under the Vichy regime, where it saw limited service until its 1943 defection to the Allies. Jordan and Moulin, *French Destroyers*, 184; J. P. Ricard, "The Sural Boiler," *Journal of the American Society for Naval Engineers* 58, no. 1 (February 1946), 70–74.
31. Though "too late" in this context means too late in the building program rather than too late in time. Few French warships were completed after the middle of the 1930s, when the United States was only beginning to commit to high steam.
32. *Mogador*, at least, appears to have actually proved quite rugged in service. *Richelieu* seems to have had a reasonably similar record. Jordan and Moulin, *French Destroyers*, 154–55, 160–65.
33. Jordan and Moulin, *French Destroyers*, 184.
34. M. J. Whitley, *Destroyer! German Destroyers in World War II* (Annapolis, MD: Naval Institute Press, 1983), 20–21.
35. This was due in large part to the numbers of the French and British making any action beyond those seas seem highly unlikely. Whitley, *Destroyer!*, 19–20.
36. DeSchiMAG, or Deutsche Schiff- und Maschinenbau Aktiengesellschaft, was an eight-company cooperative led by the AG Weser company.

37. Hamburg America's proper name was Hamburg-Amerikanishe Packetfahrt-Aktien-Gesellschaft—hence, HAPAG. Additionally, that the first modern battleship built by Germany after World War I was also named *Scharnhorst* was no coincidence. SS *Scharnhorst* and its sister SS *Gneisenau* were considered to be testbeds for the propulsion systems under consideration for use in warships, and experience with them led directly to the propulsion systems eventually installed in the *Scharnhorst*-class battleships. While SS *Scharnhorst* was equipped with high-pressure turbo-electric drive, SS *Gneisenau* had traditional reduction-gearing linking its turbines and shafts. *Scharnhorst* was determined to be the most successful for a balance of long range and power despite it only reaching 21 knots, far too slow for a major warship of the day. Whitley, *Destroyer!*, 29, and American Society for Naval Engineers, "The Machinery of the Scharnhorst, Potsdam, and Gneisenau," *Journal of the American Society for Naval Engineers* 49, no. 2 (May 1937): 251–54.

38. While shore and sea testing was organized for the machinery of the Type 34, 34A and 36 destroyers, shore testing was cut short while sea testing took place after some of the Type 34s were already afloat—far too late for a machinery redesign. Additionally, the German Navy relied almost entirely on shipyards and academics for its machinery designs, preferring to stay almost entirely out of the business itself. Whitley, *Destroyer!*, 29.

39. These were colloquially known as "flash" boilers. Whitley, *Destroyer!*, 29–34, 261; General Board Study No. 420–13, 12, General Board Subject File 1900–1947, Box 104, RG 80, NAB.

40. The Vulcan clutch apparently generated unacceptably high amounts of drag during limited shore tests, hence the entire apparatus's omission in later ships. Whitley, *Destroyer!*, 32.

41. Whitley, *Destroyer!*, 29–34.

42. Their range proved to be significantly shorter than expected due to the difficulties of accessibility. Maintenance was not *quite* as much of an issue in the cases of the heavy cruisers or battleships, simply because they did not need to sortie anywhere near as frequently as the destroyers.

CHAPTER 4

1. Kuehn, *Agents of Innovation*, 8–15; Kuehn, *America's First General Staff*, 1–8.

2. This included the transformation of the marines into a true amphibious force, as well as many more radical studies, such as a hybrid cruiser-carrier warship. Kuehn, *Agents of Innovation*, 1–6.

3. American Society for Naval Engineers, "World Trend Is Toward Geared Turbines and High-Pressure Steam," 627–31; J. H. King, "Marine Boilers for Higher Pressures and Temperatures and Their Contribution to Greater Economy," *Journal of the American Society for Naval Engineers* 40, no. 2 (May 1928): 238–55.

4. For a direct discussion of the implications of the United States' strategic position between 1899 and 1941, see chapter 2 of this work. For more information on US war planning, see Miller, *War Plan Orange*.

5. Fleet Problems covered many subjects but were largely intended to function as a test of both strategic ideas and tactical operations. Nofi, *To Train the Fleet for War*, 1.

6. While this was initially planned as a nonstop deployment of the fleet to the

Philippines, it gradually evolved into a campaign plan that necessitated the capture of islands for refueling. Miller argues that this directly evolved into the American campaign in the Pacific War as it happened. Miller, *War Plan Orange*.

7. Despite the knowledge that underway refueling was important to any future war effort, it was rarely practiced throughout the bulk of the interwar period due to the fiscal and material limitations on the navy. Thus, while the navy built a number of ships capable of serving as fleet "oilers" early in this period, most were either not in commission or not properly outfitted to carry out their task. All of these early vessels were obsolete at the beginning of World War II. See chapter 10 for more information. David Fuquea, "Advantage Japan: The Imperial Japanese Navy's Superior High Seas Refueling Capability," *Journal of Military History* 84, no. 1 (January 2020): 223–25.

8. Unfortunately, this was not the case. See chapter 9.

9. Nofi, *To Train the Fleet for War*, 168.

10. John G. Howell Jr., "Notes on Engineering Practices," Bureau of Ships General Correspondence A5 (Trial Data), Box 27, RG 19, NACP.

11. Twelve knots is chosen here as it was the established "fleet standard cruising speed" until 1936. Office of the Chief of Naval Operations, *FTP 136: Cruising Radii of U.S. Naval Vessels from Actual Steaming Data, 1933* (Washington, DC: Government Printing Office, 1935), 79, as found in US Navy Technical Publications, Box 62, RG 38: Records of the Office of the Chief of Naval Operations, NACP.

12. Friedman, *U.S. Destroyers*, 462.

13. The *Clemson* class had a mix of different turbines depending on which yard manufactured a given ship. The majority used Parsons reaction turbines, but some used subcontracted impulse turbines. Jung, *The Marine Turbine, Part 2*, 12.

14. Bowen, *Ships, Machinery, and Mossbacks*, 53.

15. Nofi, *To Train the Fleet for War*, 168. Claims to this effect are also everywhere in the general board's records. Several examples are Chairman of the General Board to the Secretary of the Navy, "1936 Building Program—Characteristics of Destroyers and Submarines," March 19, 1935; "General Board Study 420-9: Characteristics of Destroyers Building Program of 1939," General Board Subject File 1900–1947, Box 95, RG 80, NAB; Gibbs & Cox, Inc. to Chairman of the General Board, "Memorandum supplementing the Testimony to be given by Mr. William Francis Gibbs in accord with Invitation to the firm of Gibbs & Cox, Inc. from the General Board for its opinion with respect to Pressures and Temperatures," November 9, 1938, General Board Study 420-13, General Board Subject File 1900–1947, Box 104; RG 80; Bureau of Engineering Memorandum to the General Board of the Navy, "General Engineering Matters," November 30, 1938, General Board Study 420-13, General Board Subject File 1900–1947, Box 104, RG 80, NAB.

16. As discussed in the next chapter, 1899 marked an enormous milestone in the history of the Naval Academy. Robinson's attendance in its immediate aftermath likely had a major influence on the rest of his career.

17. Robinson actually began his career by favoring gunnery, but after six years in service he realized that most of his strengths (and interests) actually lay with engineering. S. M. Robinson, "The Reminiscences of Samuel Murray Robinson," interview by William J. Cromie, *Naval History Project*, Columbia Digital Library Collections, September 30–October 1, 1963, Oral history transcript, 1–7.

18. Robinson, "The Reminiscences of Samuel Murray Robinson," 10–17.

19. While working in the design division of BuEng, Robinson made a point of frequently visiting and getting to know his counterparts in the Bureau of Construction and Repair. This sort of practice was a trend that can be traced throughout his career. Robinson, "The Reminiscences of Samuel Murray Robinson," 14, 20–25.

20. It is worth mentioning that, due to the dramatic drop-off in shipbuilding during the 1920s, very few shipbuilders retained any kind of in-house drafting capability at all. Thus, building to a unified working plan wasn't simply a good idea for standardization but also avoided the problem of trying to work up individual drafting divisions for every company involved. Furer, *Administration of the Navy Department in World War II*, 214–16; Heinrich, *Warship Builders*, 37, 60–61.

21. In 1963, Robinson would assert that the main purpose of the adoption of high steam was actually to increase speed and decrease machinery weight. Evidence from the 1930s proves that even if these advantages were initially *his* motivation, they would quickly become secondary to increases in operational range after 1934. Office of the Chief of Naval Operations, *FTP 136*, 88; Robinson, "The Reminiscences of Samuel Murray Robinson," 18.

22. Uncontrolled superheat is exceptionally dangerous to turbines, particularly at low rotational speeds. Office of the Chief of Naval Operations, *FTP 136*, 192.

23. Bowen, *Ships, Machinery, and Mossbacks*, 61–62; Friedman, *U.S. Destroyers*, 461–63.

24. Friedman, *U.S. Destroyers*, 465–66; Office of the Chief of Naval Operations, *FTP 136*, 91.

25. This was, in the case of the later US destroyers, extended to three separate turbines of varying pressure for each propeller shaft—high pressure, low pressure, and cruising—whereas previously there had been only a single turbine. Bureau of Naval Personnel, *Introduction to Engineering and Damage Control with Notes on Ship Construction and Installations* (Washington, DC: Bureau of Naval Personnel, 1945), 198–206.

26. Excessive rotational speed of a propeller causes excessive cavitation and, by extension, inefficiency and wear. C. J. Odend'hal, "The Effects of Turbulence and Cavitation Upon Erosion and Corrosion," *Journal of the American Society for Naval Engineers* 50, no. 2 (May 1938): 231–39.

27. Jung, *The Marine Turbine, Part 2*, 32.

28. Impulse turbines combined with double-reduction gears actually used as much as ten times fewer blades than the *Farragut* and *Porter* classes. Bowen, *Ships, Machinery, and Mossbacks*, 66.

29. This is mentioned offhand in a number of different places, including Office of the Chief of Naval Operations, *FTP 218*, 1; Chief of BuShips to Supervisor of Shipbuilding, USN at New York, Quincy, and Camden, "Cruising Turbines—In Case of Casualty Disengaging from High Pressure Turbines—Provision in Ships now in the Design Stage," January 31, 1941, BuShips General Correspondence S41-1 (Main Propulsion, Turbines), Box 401, RG 19, NACP; Chief of BuShips to Manager of Research Laboratories Division, General Motors Corporation, March 10, 1944, BuShips General Correspondence S41-1 (Main Propulsion, Turbines), Box 405, RG 19, NACP.

30. For their part, the Royal Navy had largely experimented only with cruising "wheels," or small segments of other turbines meant to be used in cruising conditions.

As discussed previously, these high-steam systems, such as those on *Acheron*, only increased fuel efficiency by some 7 percent.

31. In fact, the "Big Three" had been in a tug-of-war with BuEng over increasing steam requirements as far back as 1926, when BuEng had attempted to specify 450 PSI steam for the *Northampton*-class cruisers. The bureau had backed down on that occasion, resulting in those ships' continued reliance on standard lower-pressure machinery. Heinrich, *Warship Builders*, 75.

32. Bowen repeatedly mentions this throughout his autobiography but particularly focuses on this situation here. Bowen, *Ships, Machinery, and Mossbacks*, 56–59.

33. Bowen, *Ships, Machinery, and Mossbacks*, 57; Friedman, *U.S. Destroyers*, 88.

34. This isn't to say that these companies had never supplied such equipment to the navy before (because they had) but rather that after this period they came to *dominate* said supply. Bowen, *Ships, Machinery, and Mossbacks*, 66–67.

35. Bureau of Engineering to the General Board of the Navy, November 30, 1938; General Board Study No. 420-13, General Board Subject File 1900–1947, Box 104, RG 80, NAB.

36. Bowen discusses this issue at length. Bowen, *Ships, Machinery, and Mossbacks*, 52–54, 92, 125.

37. Bowen, *Ships, Machinery, and Mossbacks*, 192.

38. *Somers* actually achieved an estimated range of 10,500 miles on trials. Gibbs & Cox, Inc. to the General Board, "Memorandum Supplementing the Testimony to Be Given by Mr. William Francis Gibbs," 1–11; Office of the Chief of Naval Operations, *FTP 136*; Friedman, *U.S. Destroyers*, 463.

39. While *Somers* had these as well, they don't seem to have become standard on smaller destroyers until the *Gleaves* class. Hardesty testifies to this, and Gibbs describes boiler changes in appendix C, 7. Jung, *The Marine Turbine, Part 2*, 17; General Board Study No. 420-13, General Board Subject File 1900–1947, Box 104, RG 80, NAB.

40. The navy briefly experimented with even higher pressures and temperatures in USS *Dahlgren* (DD-187) in 1939, but the life of this effort was brief thanks to the political climate of the time. Bowen, *Ships, Machinery, and Mossbacks*, 92, 125.

41. Bowen, *Ships, Machinery, and Mossbacks*, 77.

42. In the end, steam conditions for *North Carolina* would be set at 565 PSI, 850°F. Given the advanced stage of design that the ship had reached when this decision was made, the turbines that were installed would not be capable enough to take full advantage of this setup. Friedman, *U.S. Battleships*, 243–79.

43. Bowen, *Ships, Machinery, and Mossbacks*, 69–77.

44. This threat, and the changes that ensued, resulted in a large-scale shift from the shipyard as manufacturer of an entire ship to a "shipyard as assembly yard" concept, where numerous subcontracted parts (notably including the new compound-impulse turbines) were brought and joined together. Bowen, *Ships, Machinery, and Mossbacks*, 56–58.

CHAPTER 5

1. General Board of the Navy to the Secretary of the Navy, "An Estimate on Temperature and Pressure," 1–3.

2. Bowen himself was quite taken with this particular quote and used it for several

different purposes all pertaining to his "victory" in the general board hearing. Bowen, *Ships, Machinery, and Mossbacks*, 95.

3. Karsten, *The Naval Aristocracy*, 65.

4. Karsten, *The Naval Aristocracy*, 67; Chisholm, *Waiting for Dead Men's Shoes*, 419–36.

5. Critically, it should be noted that this was *not* an aversion to technology itself. As Fred Harrod notes in his study of the enlisted force of the early twentieth century, a change in policy or a new idea *never* had an immediate, transformative effect on the navy. Old ideas (and differently trained men) persisted long after (or sometimes even in spite of) official changes. Harrod, *Manning the New Navy*, ix–x; Chisholm, *Waiting for Dead Men's Shoes*, 419–36, 700; Bowen, *Ships, Machinery, and Mossbacks*, 6–20.

6. For quite some time, being appointed to the academy ultimately required a significant amount of political pull. By our period in question, this gradually grew to rely more on the entrance exam, which only really came into force around the late nineteenth century. Chisholm, *Waiting for Dead Men's Shoes*, 5–6; W. K. Thompson, "The Naval Officer Training Program," *Journal of Educational Sociology* 16, no. 9 (May 1943): 557.

7. Interestingly, enlisted personnel around this time moved in the opposite direction. The substantial increase in demand for bluejackets created by naval expansion in the 1890s and first two decades of the 1900s resulted in a move from relying on the recruitment of experienced (often multinational) sailors from America's coasts to the much more readily available uneducated landsmen from the vast interior of the United States. Rather than spend four years on the education of these men, as was the case with officers, they were trained for specific roles based on a combination of their education and experience. After 1902, advanced training for many jobs was provided by dedicated schools that followed immediately after "basic." Karsten, *The Naval Aristocracy*, 23–40; Harrod, *Manning the New Navy*, 89–92.

8. C. N. Smith, "Selection, Training, and Morale of Navy Personnel," *Annals of the American Academy of Political and Social Science* 220, no. 1 (March 1942): 57–60.

9. Thompson, "The Naval Officer Training Program," 557–58.

10. Bowen, *Ships, Machinery, and Mossbacks*, 6.

11. Thompson, "The Naval Officer Training Program," 557–58; Memorandum of 22 September 1932, Program Records Relating to Officer Training, Box 10, Training Division, RG 24 Records of the Bureau of Naval Personnel, NACP; Ford L. Wilkinson, "The US Naval Postgraduate School," *Scientific Monthly* 66, no. 3 (March 1948): 183.

12. This problem persisted well into the 1930s. "Memorandum for Chief of Bureau: Engineer Officers Afloat," February 19, 1931, Program Records Relating to Officer Training, Box 10, Training Division, RG 24, NACP; Robinson, "The Reminiscences of Samuel Murray Robinson," 12–13.

13. Bowen, *Ships, Machinery, and Mossbacks*, 19.

14. Bowen, *Ships, Machinery, and Mossbacks*, 18.

15. This and subsequent postgraduate education details are cited from Bowen's autobiography due to their consolidated state there, but the details are corroborated by numerous other sources such as Chisholm's *Waiting for Dead Men's Shoes*. Bowen, *Ships, Machinery, and Mossbacks*, 19–20.

16. There was even a fear that, although it was popular with those who embraced it,

the EDO concept might be eliminated. No one had forgotten the fate of the old engineering corps in 1917 or soon after. Bowen, *Ships, Machinery, and Mossbacks*, 18–19; Robinson, "The Reminiscences of Samuel Murray Robinson," 12–13.

17. This term is borrowed from Seymour Papert by way of Mark Hagerott. Hagerott's work covers the eventual victory of specialists over generalists during the height of Hyman Rickover's power in the Cold War. Mark R. Hagerott, "Commanding Men and Machines: Admiralship, Technology, and Ideology in the 20th Century U.S. Navy" (PhD diss., University of Maryland College Park, 2008), 2.

18. Bethlehem had, in fact, succeeded in obtaining permission to build the first six *Benson*-class destroyers with older, low-pressure machinery and was indicating it planned to continue such efforts in the future. Bowen, *Ships, Machinery, and Mossbacks*, 82–84.

19. The fear that the navy's newest warships would be unstable would, in fact, be borne out: numerous destroyers of the *Sims* class would fail their inclining (stability) tests during acceptance trials in early 1939, a fact later attributed to underestimation of machinery weight by BuEng and too much added topweight by BuC&R. Bureau of Ships, "An Administrative History of the Bureau of Ships During World War II," 25–33; General Board of the Navy to the Secretary of the Navy, "An Estimate on Temperature and Pressure," 1.

20. Not only were all of these men "generalist" officers, but, like Bowen, the admirals had also all graduated from the Naval Academy between 1895 and 1905—right in the midst of the unification of the ranks. Bureau of Navigation, *Navy Directory: Officers of the United States Navy and Marine Corps* (Washington, DC: Government Printing Office, 1938), 241.

21. The navy department was not the easiest building to navigate at this time, judging from the board secretary's directions to witnesses to "just ask the guard" where to find them. The format and proceedings of the general board itself are described at length by John Kuehn in his two invaluable books on the subject. W. R. Purnell to R. R. Adams, November 26, 1938, General Board Study No. 420-13, General Board Subject File 1900–1947, Box 104, RG 80, NAB; Kuehn, *Agents of Innovation*, 15–21; Kuehn, *America's First General Staff*, 1–8.

22. Naval History and Heritage Command, *Dictionary of American Naval Fighting Ships Volume VII* (Washington, DC: Department of the Navy, 1981), 141.

23. Kuehn, *Agents of Innovation*, 18.

24. General Board of the Navy to the Secretary of the Navy, "An Estimate on Temperature and Pressure," 2.

25. General Board of the Navy, "Steam Pressures and Temperatures," in General Board Study No. 420-13, General Board Subject File 1900–1947, Box 104, RG 80, NAB.

26. Additionally, Dalton appears to have just come off an instructor assignment to the Naval Postgraduate School the previous year. Bureau of Navigation, *Navy Directory: Officers of the United States Navy and Marine Corps* (Washington, DC: Government Printing Office, 1937), 222, 247.

27. Kuehn, *Agents of Innovation*, 15–21.

28. Both Bowen and Gibbs & Cox testified to this effect. Bowen went so far as to call back to the Fleet Problems of the previous decade. Interestingly, Bowen also

remarks on the need for destroyers to be able to develop full power on short notice. General Board of the Navy, "Steam Pressures and Temperatures," 11.

29. The rise of the fast carrier and the eventual evolution of the Fast Carrier Task Force only exacerbated this problem. Testimony of William Francis Gibbs, General Board Study No. 420-13, General Board Subject File 1900-1947, Box 104, RG 80, NAB.

30. General Board of the Navy, "Steam Pressures and Temperatures," 7-11; H. L. Brinser's to General Board of the Navy, "21 November 1938 Memorandum for the General Board," General Board Study No. 420-13, General Board Subject File 1900-1947, Box 104, RG 80, NAB.

31. General Board of the Navy, "Steam Pressures and Temperatures," 7-11.

32. Heinrich, *Warship Builders*, 81; Friedman, *U.S. Battleships*, 243-79; General Board of the Navy, "Steam Pressures and Temperatures," 14-18.

33. General Board of the Navy, "Steam Pressures and Temperatures," 11.

34. General Board of the Navy, "Steam Pressures and Temperatures," 11.

35. General Board of the Navy, "Steam Pressures and Temperatures," 1.

36. General Board of the Navy, "Steam Pressures and Temperatures," 8; Bowen, *Ships, Machinery, and Mossbacks*, 17-18.

37. Gibbs & Cox, Inc. to the General Board, "Memorandum Supplementing the Testimony to Be Given by Mr. William Francis Gibbs," 1-11.

38. General Board of the Navy, "Steam Pressures and Temperatures," 9.

39. General Board of the Navy, "Steam Pressures and Temperatures," 8.

40. H. G. Bowen to T. C. Hart, "Summary of Destroyer Casualties," November 28, 1938, General Board Study No. 420-13, General Board Subject File 1900-1947, Box 104, RG 80, NAB; General Board of the Navy to the Secretary of the Navy, "An Estimate on Temperature and Pressure," 1-3.

41. General Board of the Navy, "Steam Pressures and Temperatures," 16.

42. Gibbs & Cox, Inc. to the General Board, "Memorandum Supplementing the Testimony to Be Given by Mr. William Francis Gibbs," 1-11.

43. It is worth mentioning that Gibbs & Cox cited ruggedness as its *first* priority, which was natural for civilian requirements and for the designer ultimately responsible for putting high-steam technology aboard American warships for the first time. Gibbs & Cox, Inc. to the General Board, "Memorandum Supplementing the Testimony to Be Given by Mr. William Francis Gibbs," 1-11.

44. General Board of the Navy, "Steam Pressures and Temperatures," 9.

45. General Board of the Navy, "Steam Pressures and Temperatures," 18; Bowen, *Ships, Machinery, and Mossbacks*, 68.

46. Such reports were often demanded by Congress due to the rapid increase in warship costs during this era as well as the public backlash against perceived "merchants of death" from World War I, embodied particularly by the congressional Nye committee in the mid-1930s. Heinrich, *Warship Builders*, 25-28; BuShips General Correspondence L4 (Contracts), RG 19, NACP; ITEM S-62 (Correspondence Relating to Congressional Affairs and Public Relations), RG 19, NACP.

47. Gibbs & Cox, Inc. to the General Board, "Memorandum Supplementing the Testimony to Be Given by Mr. William Francis Gibbs," 1-11.

48. General Board of the Navy, "Steam Pressures and Temperatures," 6.

49. General Board of the Navy, "Steam Pressures and Temperatures," 8-9.

50. General Board of the Navy, "Steam Pressures and Temperatures," 19; Gibbs & Cox, Inc. to the General Board, "Memorandum Supplementing the Testimony to Be Given by Mr. William Francis Gibbs," appendix C, 8.

51. Though not a common subject, the *Journal of the American Society for Naval Engineers* published at least one article on this subject in the decade preceding the general board study. Bowen was heavily involved in the society during this time, serving on its board several times and as its leader in 1938. Donald, "Boiler Room Operation on Naval Vessels," 608–19; Bruce Meader, *ASNE, the First 100 Years: The History of the American Society for Naval Engineers, 1888–1988* (Alexandria, VA: American Society for Naval Engineers, 1988).

52. General Board of the Navy, "Steam Pressures and Temperatures," 1–20; J. E. Maher to T. C. Hart, "Statement from Commander J. E. Maher, Commanding Officer, USS Somers," November 20, 1938; General Board Study No. 420–13, General Board Subject File 1900–1947, Box 104, RG 80, NAB.

53. The general board and BuC&R requested opposition testimony from a number of sources, a summary of which can also be found within General Board of the Navy, "Steam Pressures and Temperatures," 1–20.

54. These sources were generally either US diplomatic agents who were stationed in the nations in question or third-party diplomats willing to share what they had been told or observed. This was added to the officially published records of foreign warships to (inaccurately) paint a foreboding picture of success with high steam in foreign navies. Director of Naval Intelligence to the General Board, "Merits of Various High Pressure and High Temperature Steam Installations for Warships," October 26, 1938, General Board Study No. 420–13, General Board Subject File 1900–1947, Box 104, RG 80, NAB.

55. The estimate was written by Admiral Frank Sadler, who may have been Hart's choice to facilitate the study had Cox not been brought in to do so instead. General Board of the Navy to the Secretary of the Navy, "An Estimate on Temperature and Pressure," 3.

56. The matter of production decision-making of this type is, unfortunately, a subject too broad for discussion here.

CHAPTER 6

1. As mentioned in the previous chapter, these were Admiral Sadler's words, which Hart signed and dispatched to the secretary of the navy. General Board of the Navy to the Secretary of the Navy, "An Estimate on Temperature and Pressure," 2.

2. While there are numerous other examples of issues large and small resulting from divided design responsibilities, high steam and several failed inclining tests were dangerous enough problems to spur reform. Bureau of Ships, "An Administrative History of the Bureau of Ships During World War II."

3. Naturally, Bowen believed that he deserved the job of head of BuShips. Unfortunately for him, this did not come to pass. Bowen, *Ships, Machinery, and Mossbacks*, 116–24; Rodney P. Carlisle, *Where the Fleet Begins: A History of the David Taylor Research Center, 1898–1998* (Washington, DC: Naval Historical Center, 1998), 152–57; Bureau of Ships, "An Administrative History of the Bureau of Ships During World War II"; Robinson, "The Reminiscences of Samuel Murray Robinson," 18–25.

4. Manning Ancell and Christine Miller, *The Biographical Dictionary of World War II Generals and Flag Officers: The US Armed Forces* (Westport, CT: Greenwood Press, 1996).

5. Ancell and Miller, *The Biographical Dictionary of World War II Generals and Flag Officers*.

6. Carlisle, *Where the Fleet Begins*, 152–57; US Congress, House of Representatives, Committee on Naval Affairs, Investigation of the Naval Defense Program: Hearings before the Committee on Naval Affairs, 76th Cong., 2nd sess., 1942, 671–723.

7. Bowen was convinced that his treatment following the general board hearing was a result of a continuing grudge held against him by "reactionary" general line officers. Bowen, *Ships, Machinery, and Mossbacks*, 122–26.

8. Today, the ORI is known as the Office of Naval Research. Carlisle, *Where the Fleet Begins*, 152–57.

9. Miller, *War Plan Orange*, 267–85.

CHAPTER 7

1. Such as the removal of the Chiefs of BuEng and BuC&R and their merger, for example. General Board of the Navy to the Secretary of the Navy, "An Estimate on Temperature and Pressure," 1–3.

2. For more on the dangers of this kind of disorganization, see G. A. H. Gordon, *British Seapower and Procurement Between the Wars: A Reappraisal of Rearmament* (Annapolis, MD: Naval Institute Press, 1988). While the general board usually stepped in to fulfill this purpose for the US Navy, it was not specifically mandated to do so. Additionally, research shows that by the 1940s, the board was being increasingly marginalized (hence, perhaps, its hesitance to make a stand on the high-steam issue). Kuehn, *America's First General Staff*, 1–8; Koistinen, *Arsenal of World War II*, 44, 106.

3. While twelve units of the preceding class (*Sims*) were built between 1937 and 1940, ninety-two ships of the *Benson* and *Gleaves* classes were completed in total between 1938 and 1943. See table 7.1 for details on destroyer contracts by year.

4. Bureau of Ships, "An Administrative History of the Bureau of Ships During World War II," 31–33; Robinson, "The Reminiscences of Samuel Murray Robinson," 20–25.

5. Robinson, "The Reminiscences of Samuel Murray Robinson," 20–25.

6. G. B. Ogle, Bureau of Ships, to Chief of the Bureau of Ships, "Main Turbine Delivery & Requirement Dates for Navy Destroyers," June 11, 1941, Bureau of Ships General Correspondence S41-1 (Main Propulsion, Turbines), RG 19, NACP.

7. Bureau of Ships, "An Administrative History of the Bureau of Ships During World War II," 134, 182–83, 204–6.

8. Bowen, *Ships, Machinery, and Mossbacks*, 51, 68; Bureau of Ships, "An Administrative History of the Bureau of Ships During World War II," 134, 182–83, 204–6.

9. An enlightening overview of carbon molybdenum steel as it related to turbine production can be found in an article from a 1935 issue of the *Journal of American Society for Naval Engineers*. Turbine casing production was a difficult and time-consuming process for low steam, but high steam and its requirement of the difficult-to-handle carbon molybdenum steel significantly complicated the process. Hans Naegeli and A. C. Jones, "Carbon-Molybdenum Cast Steel for Steam Service," *Journal of the American Society for Naval Engineers* 47, no. 2 (May 1935): 205–19.

10. Some insight into the importance of machine tools to armament production is provided by Milward, *War, Economy, and Society*, 187–90; Bureau of Ships, "An Administrative History of the Bureau of Ships During World War II," 134, 182–83, 204–6.

11. It is worth noting that this shortage is briefly mentioned by Friedman in his examination of the destroyer escort program but is not elaborated upon. According to Milward, US and German exports represented nearly 80 percent of the value of all machine tools involved in international trade prior to World War II. Massive increases in demand in 1940–1941, as well as the termination of trade with Germany, meant that US turbine contractors were required to rely wholly upon domestic production for their special-purpose machine tools once the war began. Friedman, *U.S. Destroyers*, 143–44; and Milward, *War, Economy, and Society*, 35.

12. Precision machining of a single bull gear, for example, was an exhausting exercise in patience that could take more than two weeks of constant work. Heinrich, *Warship Builders*, 211; Bureau of Ships, "An Administrative History of the Bureau of Ships During World War II," 179–81, 204–6.

13. Captain C. M. Simmers, Supervisor of Shipbuilding, calling Mr. Neuhaus, Progress Branch, Bureau of Ships, "Prospective Shipment Dates for Turbines—Destroyers—1650-Ton—Bethlehem Steel Co.," 2:30 PM, May 13, 1941, Bureau of Ships General Correspondence S41-1 (Main Propulsion, Turbines), RG 19, NACP.

14. G. B. Ogle, Bureau of Ships, to Chief of the Bureau of Ships, "Main Turbine Delivery & Requirement Dates for Navy Destroyers," 1–2; Bureau of Ships, "An Administrative History of the Bureau of Ships During World War II," 183, 217.

15. G. B. Ogle, "Main Turbine Delivery & Requirement Dates for Navy Destroyers," 1–2.

16. G. B. Ogle, "Main Turbine Delivery & Requirement Dates for Navy Destroyers," 1–2.

17. Chief of the Bureau of Ships to all Supervisors of Shipbuilding, USN and all Commandants, US Navy Yard, "Shore Spares—Suspension of Manufacture of," November 17, 1941, as reproduced in Bureau of Ships, "An Administrative History of the Bureau of Ships During World War II," 83–84. There are also numerous records of turbines and components, "shipped less spares" within Bureau of Ships General Correspondence S41-1 (Main Propulsion, Turbines), RG 19, NACP.

18. Bureau of Ships, "An Administrative History of the Bureau of Ships During World War II," 179–81, 206.

19. Bowen, *Ships, Machinery, and Mossbacks*, 102.

CHAPTER 8

1. Chisholm, *Waiting for Dead Men's Shoes*, 419–36.

2. As stated in the footnotes of chapter 5, the move to specialization for the enlisted was a response both to the rapid advance of technology and to the navy's typical recruiting grounds moving from the coasts (where most recruits were familiar with the sea) to the interior of the United States (where many landsmen had never even *seen* the sea before enlisting). Harrod, *Manning the New Navy*, 89–92.

3. Some engineering aspects *had* gotten simpler; for example, there were fewer turbine blades in a high-steam installation than in a low-steam one. However, there were also *more* turbines to service (three per shaft instead of one!) and more components to

regularly check and repair (such as superheater and advanced feedwater systems). See chapter 4 for more details.

4. This tunnel vision is a fact that a few scholars have already picked up on. Wildenberg, *Grey Steel and Black Oil*, 78.

5. This totaled about 600,000 long tons of capital ships. Chisholm, *Waiting for Dead Men's Shoes*, 622.

6. A trickle of NROTC officers were commissioned to help make up the shortfall during this period, but it remained a relatively insubstantial number. Chisholm, *Waiting for Dead Men's Shoes*, 630–31, 698.

7. Chisholm, *Waiting for Dead Men's Shoes*, 620–21, 700–701. The records of the Bureau of Navigation for this period also show a high frequency of references to the shortage of officers in postgraduate training. "Memorandum for Chief of Bureau: Officer Training," November 25, 1939, Program Records Relating to Officer Training, Box 10, Training Division, RG 24, NACP.

8. Specifically, the Vinson-Trammell Act of 1934 provided for replacement vessels. The years 1938 through 1940, a time when Japan had repudiated the Treaty system and clearly developed into a dangerous naval threat, played host to the Naval Act of 1938, the Third Vinson Act of 1940, and the Two-Ocean Navy Act of 1940.

9. This was a unique event in the navy's modern history up to that point, but no one in a command position seems to have thought out the potential repercussions at the time. Chisholm, *Waiting for Dead Men's Shoes*, 629–36, 685–90.

10. Qualified here meaning *more* qualified than those who were ultimately promoted. Chisholm, *Waiting for Dead Men's Shoes*, 620–23.

11. Smith, "Selection, Training, and Morale of Navy Personnel," 57–60, and "Memorandum for Chief of Bureau: Officer Training," November 25, 1939, Program Records Relating to Officer Training; Manuscript of the Administrative History of the Bureau of Naval Personnel in World War II, Historical Records of Navy Training Activities, Box 22, Training Division, RG 24, NACP, 178.

12. This manual is particularly referenced in "Battle Force Letter No. 2–40: Training of Officers in Engineering," August 16, 1940, Program Records Relating to Officer Training, Box 10, Training Division, RG 24, NACP. It is additionally critical to note that if the system was working as intended, this letter never would have been issued.

13. Nominally intended for enlisted personnel, *The Bluejacket's Manual* nevertheless generally found its way into the hands of a majority of officers as well. US Navy, *The Bluejacket's Manual* (Annapolis: Naval Institute Press, 1940).

14. By "educational leave," I refer here to the occasional practice of sending junior officers to civilian universities for postgraduate work. Additionally, the enlisted system would likely have also collapsed without the ad-hoc development of "wildcat" training. "Chapter 2: Officer Training; I—A Broad View," Manuscript of the Administrative History of the Bureau of Naval Personnel in World War II, Historical Records of Navy Training Activities, Box 22, Training Division, RG 24; NACP, 105; "Chapter 3: Operational Training," Manuscript of the Administrative History of the Bureau of Naval Personnel in World War II, Historical Records of Navy Training Activities, Box 22, Training Division, RG 24, NACP, 295.

15. The story of the Bureau of Navigation's leadership throughout this period reads almost like a "who's who" of soon-to-be-famous line officers, including William D.

NOTES / 197

Leahy (1933-1935), Adolphus Andrews (1935-1938), James O. Richardson (1938-1939), and Nimitz (1939-1941). Considering the fact that all of these men proved to be capable leaders, their relative inaction while in charge of BuNav speaks volumes about the quality of the information they worked from. The struggles of the bureau to initially respond are detailed in "Chapter One—Curriculum Section, Part B—Special Studies in Development of Curriculum" and "Chapter One—Curriculum Section, 1. Recruit Training," Manuscript of the Administrative History of the Bureau of Naval Personnel in World War II, Historical Records of Navy Training Activities, Box 21, Training Division, RG 24, NACP, 1-39. Additional sources for this include "(3) The Naval Reserve Officers' Training Corps," Manuscript of the Administrative History of the Bureau of Naval Personnel in World War II, Historical Records of Navy Training Activities, Box 10, Training Division, RG 24, NACP, 1-7; "Memorandum for Captain Callaghan: Naval Training," July 12, 1940, Program Records Relating to Officer Training, Box 10, Training Division, RG 24, NACP; Smith, "Selection, Training, and Morale of Navy Personnel," 57-60.

16. "I. Pre-V-12 Programs," Manuscript of the Administrative History of the Bureau of Naval Personnel in World War II, Historical Records of Navy Training Activities, Box 23, Training Division, RG 24, NACP, 1-14.

17. The acquisition of teachers, classroom facilities, and necessary material proved the primary downfall of this early effort. "Line Officer Training," Manuscript of the Administrative History of the Bureau of Naval Personnel in World War II, Historical Records of Navy Training Activity, Box 21, Training Division, RG 24, NACP, 160-64; "I. Pre-V-12 Programs," Manuscript of the Administrative History of the Bureau of Naval Personnel, 1-14.

18. Programs were of different lengths depending on the origins of the individuals in question: previously enlisted, NROTC, etc. Page 176 of "Chapter 2: Officer Training: II—The General Officer Training Programs: 4—Scheduling: Pre-Midshipmen's & General Line Schools," Manuscript of the Administrative History of the Bureau of Naval Personnel in World War II, Historical Records of Navy Training Activities, Box 22, Training Division, RG 24, NACP; "Chapter 2: Officer Training—I. A Broad View," Manuscript of the Administrative History of the Bureau of Naval Personnel, 103-6; "Line Officer Training," Manuscript of the Administrative History of the Bureau of Naval Personnel, 157-60.

19. "Chapter 2: Officer Training—I. A Broad View," Manuscript of the Administrative History of the Bureau of Naval Personnel, 103-6; "Line Officer Training," Manuscript of the Administrative History of the Bureau of Naval Personnel, 157-60.

20. It has also created an utter nightmare of paperwork for historians to sort through. "Chapter 3: Operational Training," Manuscript of the Administrative History of the Bureau of Naval Personnel, 295.

21. "Chapter 3: Operational Training," 295.

22. In fact, the expansion of specialty courses was apparently so rapid that they nearly got out of hand as the wildcat training they were intended to supplant. "Line Officer Training," Manuscript of the Administrative History of the Bureau of Naval Personnel, 146-66.

23. Bureau of Naval Personnel, *Introduction to Seamanship* (Washington, DC: Bureau of Naval Personnel, 1943); Bureau of Naval Personnel, *Introduction to Ordnance and Gunnery* (Washington, DC: Bureau of Naval Personnel, 1943).

24. The Administrative History actually dwells on this failure for a considerable amount of space. "Line Officer Training," Manuscript of the Administrative History of the Bureau of Naval Personnel, 164–67.

25. "Line Officer Training," 164; Bureau of Naval Personnel, *Introduction to Engineering and Damage Control with Notes on Ship Construction and Installations*.

26. NROTC, though integrated, was allowed to retain its own identity and would reemerge after the war. As discussed in the final chapter, BuPers would make good on an attempt to return to the status quo by offering a "full" naval education to all war-trained officers by the 1950s. "Line Officer Training," Manuscript of the Administrative History of the Bureau of Naval Personnel, 142–56; "Status of Officer Training at Present and During the Ensuing Peacetime Period," March 30, 1946, Program Records Relating to Officer Training, Box 10, Training Division, RG 24, NACP.

27. Naturally, this also served the secondary purpose of making it quite clear which bureau-standardized training courses were most desirable. "Journal of Officer Classification and Selection" (1944) as found in Program Records Relating to the V-12 Program, 1942–48, Box 3, Training Division, RG 24, NACP; Memorandum of September 22, 1932, Program Records Relating to Officer Training, Box 10, Training Division, RG 24, NACP.

28. Telegram from COMPHIBSPAC to COMTRACOMDPHIBSPAC, March 14, 1946; Engineers (General), Program Records Relating to Officer Training, Box 6, Training Division, RG 24, NACP.

CHAPTER 9

1. Office of the Chief of Naval Operations, *FTP 143: War Instructions* (Washington, DC: Government Printing Office, 1940) as found in US Navy Technical Publications, Box 46, RG 38, NACP.

2. "Excessive Fuel Consumption," December 16, 1941, Bureau of Ships General Correspondence A5 (Trial Data), Box 27, RG19, NACP.

3. Nofi, *To Train the Fleet for War*.

4. Office of the Chief of Naval Operations, *FTP 143: War Instructions*.

5. Many of these engineering efficiency scores are readily available in A5 (Trial Data) of the BuShips General Correspondence collection at the National Archives in College Park, MD, with Box 27 of particular interest. The original, handwritten calculations of individual ships' theoretical peacetime and wartime ranges from BuEng are also available in quantity in ITEM S-15 (Ship Machinery Design History and Data Files, Boxes 1–9) of the records of BuShips at the same location. These are the numbers that were lifted directly for the last revisions of *FTP 136* and are criticized in the text of *FTP 218*.

6. While this of course isn't necessarily true for *all* wars, it was very much the reality for the US Navy's Pacific War after the middle of 1943. Regardless, ships must always be loaded for the possibility that combat might dramatically increase the material requirements of any individual deployment. March, *British Destroyers*, 39; Wildenberg, *Gray Steel and Black Oil*, 172–73, 179–89.

7. Naturally, though readily available to commanders, these resources were generally at least "Restricted." Office of the Chief of Naval Operations, *FTP 143(A), War Instructions* (Washington, DC: Government Printing Office, 1944). Like *FTP 146*, this

manual is available in Box 46 of the US Navy Technical Publications Collection of RG 38, the Records of the Office of the Chief of Naval Operations.

8. *FTP 136* has a number of revisions, all of which are stored at the National Archives in College Park, MD, in the US Navy Technical Publications Collection of RG 38, the Records of the Office of the Chief of Naval Operations (Boxes 45 and 46). Office of the Chief of Naval Operations, *FTP 136*, V.

9. If the reader is uncertain of what "average" conditions mean, they are far from alone. This was one of the problems with *FTP 136*. *FTP 136*, v–vi.

10. With the possible exception of fouling, which is emphasized in the manual due to its own high degree of variability. The value given here is considered to be worst-case and would not regularly be in play. *FTP 136*, vii–viii.

11. "Battle Force Letter No. 2–40: Training of Officers in Engineering," August 16, 1940, Program Records Relating to Officer Training, Box 10, Training Division, RG 24, NACP.

12. This letter was composed as Kimmel prepared to execute the relief of Wake Island, an operation that was canceled after significant delays were encountered while Fletcher's Task Force 14 (built around the carrier USS *Saratoga*, CV-3) attempted to refuel in rough seas from an older fleet oiler. Wake was occupied by the Japanese soon after. "Pacific Fleet Confidential Letter 18CL-41: Excessive Fuel Consumption," December 16, 1941, Bureau of Ships General Correspondence A5 (Trial Data), Box 27, RG19, NACP; Wildenberg, *Gray Steel and Black Oil*, 169–72.

13. Specifically, a drastic reduction in the amount of evasive maneuvering in normal situations (such as zigzagging to throw off potential submarine attacks) and in the activity of task force escort vessels (such as destroyer pursuit of underwater sound contacts). Either of these drastic measures could have severe consequences for the safety of the fleet as a whole. Office of the Chief of Naval Operations, *FTP 218*, 1.

14. "Pacific Fleet Confidential Letter 18CL-41: Excessive Fuel Consumption"; Wildenberg, *Gray Steel and Black Oil*, 169–72.

15. These changes are discussed at some length in the entire archive of General Board Study No. 420–13, but for specific discussion of the subject, see General Board of the Navy, "Steam Pressures and Temperatures," 1–20; "Battle Force Letter No. 2–40: Training of Officers in Engineering."

16. Office of the Chief of Naval Operations, *FTP 218*, 1.

17. "Pacific Fleet Confidential Letter 18CL-41: Excessive Fuel Consumption."

18. "Battle Force Letter No. 2–40: Training of Officers in Engineering."

19. Office of the Chief of Naval Operations, *FTP 218*. This manual is readily available at the National Archives in College Park, MD, in the US Navy Technical Publications Collection of RG 38, the Records of the Office of the Chief of Naval Operations (Box 62).

20. Wildenberg, *Gray Steel and Black Oil*, 11–13.

21. BuShips's predecessor organizations had been responsible for compiling the data that had produced the original range calculations in *FTP 136*. Office of the Chief of Naval Operations, *FTP 136*; Office of the Chief of Naval Operations, *FTP 218*. In theory, this information should also be present in Bureau of Ships, "Research Memorandum 3-44: War Service Fuel Consumption: Theory and Construction of Underway Tables and Charts," but unfortunately this document appears to have been lost.

22. Office of the Chief of Naval Operations, *FTP 218*, 1–15.

23. Office of the Chief of Naval Operations, *FTP 218*, 1; ITEM S-15 (Ship Machinery Design History and Data Files), RG 19, NACP.

24. Office of the Chief of Naval Operations, *FTP 218*, 1.

25. Office of the Chief of Naval Operations, *FTP 218*, 1.

26. Office of the Chief of Naval Operations, *FTP 218*, 1–11.

27. Emphasis original. Office of the Chief of Naval Operations, *FTP 218*, 1.

28. This is mentioned offhand in a number of different places, including Office of the Chief of Naval Operations, *FTP 218*, 1; Chief of BuShips to Supervisor of Shipbuilding, USN at New York, Quincy, and Camden, "Cruising Turbines—In case of Casualty Disengaging from High Pressure Turbines—Provision in Ships now in the Design Stage," January 31, 1941, Bureau of Ships General Correspondence S41-1 (Main Propulsion, Turbines), Box 401, RG 19, NACP; Chief of BuShips to Manager of Research Laboratories Division, General Motors Corporation, March 10, 1944, Bureau of Ships General Correspondence S41-1 (Main Propulsion, Turbines), Box 405, RG 19, NACP.

29. It is important to note at this juncture as well that, while many ship classes would have needed to have their range tables modified during the course of the war due to refits changing their basic characteristics, *FTP 218* does not consider the modifications of this type to have been responsible for any part of the causes of confusion but instead to have been merely a complicating factor. Office of the Chief of Naval Operations, *FTP 218*, 1–15.

30. This vastly reduced range due to the nonuse of cruising turbines is clear merely from comparing post-1934 warship classes between the two main FTPs we have been discussing. See the sample tables earlier in the chapter for one example, USS *Somers* herself. Office of the Chief of Naval Operations, *FTP 218*, and Office of the Chief of Naval Operations, *FTP 136*.

31. Numerous discussions in Bureau of Ships General Correspondence A5 (Trial Data). There were also contracts out (with GE) for a rapidly declutchable cruising turbine, but this project does not seem to have come to fruition. Chief of BuShips to Manager of Research Laboratories Division, General Motors Corporation, March 10, 1944, Bureau of Ships General Correspondence S41-1 (Main Propulsion, Turbines), Box 405, RG 19, NACP.

32. This is clear throughout the early years of the Orange Plan. Miller, *War Plan Orange*.

33. This is a clear theme throughout the secondary literature concerning the war plans of both nations. Evans and Peattie, *Kaigun*; Miller, *War Plan Orange*; Office of the Chief of Naval Operations, *FTP 218*, 1.

34. Office of the Chief of Naval Operations, *FTP 218*, 1.

CHAPTER 10

1. The preference for modern, high-steam vessels is most clear when considered in the context of the US fleet's older battleships. These were relegated to the West Coast during the fuel shortages of the early war despite the majority of them being fit for combat within months of the attack on Pearl Harbor. The rationale behind the idling of these assets was the source of a brief exchange between scholars Thomas Hone and

David Fuquea in the late 1990s. Within, Fuquea downplayed the role of logistical problems in sidelining the battleships after the first few months of war, arguing instead that they languished largely due to a command belief that they could not survive modern combat. Hone countered this argument by clearly demonstrating the severity of both the fuel *and* tanker shortage during the early war period, as well as listing the reasons why it was preferred to use those limited assets in conjunction with younger vessels equipped with modern high-steam machinery. David C. Fuquea, "Task Force One: The Wasted Assets of the United States Pacific Battleship Fleet," *Journal of Military History* 61, no. 4 (October 1997): 707–34; Thomas C. Hone, "Letters to the Editor," *Journal of Military History* 62, no. 2 (April 1998): 471–73.

2. General Board of the Navy, "Steam Pressures and Temperatures," 1–20; Gibbs & Cox, Inc. to the General Board, "Memorandum Supplementing the Testimony to Be Given by Mr. William Francis Gibbs," 1–11.

3. "Fuel Oil for Use in National Emergency," June 14, 1940, Bureau of Ships General Correspondence JJ7–3 (Oil, Fuel), Box 73, RG19, NACP, 1–3.

4. Bureau of Engineering, "Navy Department Specification 7-O-1d: Oil, Fuel," 1933, ITEM S-28 (Specifications and Standard Development Case Files), Box 4, RG19, NACP.

5. What these "metallurgical purposes" were is not entirely clear from the documentation but likely refers both to experimental and lubrication use. Bureau of Engineering, "Navy Department Specification 7-O-1d: Oil, Fuel," 1933, ITEM S-28 (Specifications and Standard Development Case Files), Box 4, RG19, NACP.

6. For some of the myriad of communications regarding the preferences for and allocation of different fuel categories, see Bureau of Ships General Correspondence JJ7–3 (Oil, Fuel), Box 75, RG19, NACP.

7. Bureau of Engineering, "Bureau of Engineering Specification 7-O-1d: Oil, Fuel," August 15, 1938, ITEM S-28 (Specifications and Standard Development Case Files), Box 4, RG19, NACP; Husband E. Kimmel, "Fuel Oil for Use in National Emergency," July 13, 1940, Bureau of Ships General Correspondence JJ7–3 (Oil, Fuel), Box 73, RG19, NACP.

8. Bureau of Ships, "Bureau of Ships Ad Interim Specification: 7-O-1 (INT) Oil, Fuel, Boiler," February 1, 1944, ITEM S-28 (Specifications and Standard Development Case Files), Box 4, RG19, NACP.

9. A review of all available fuel sources from the East and West Coasts accompanies this information. Bureau of Ships, "Fuel Oil—Navy Special Grade," April 10, 1942, Bureau of Ships General Correspondence JJ7–3 (Oil, Fuel), Box 75, RG19, NACP; Bureau of Supplies and Accounts, "Requirements of Fuel Oil Under Navy Contracts for Period July 1, 1942, to June 20, 1943 Inclusive," March 18, 1942, Bureau of Ships General Correspondence JJ7–3 (Oil, Fuel), Box 75, RG19, NACP.

10. This is explained both in the fuel requirements and in reply to queries by oil companies. Bureau of Ships. "Fuel Oil—Navy Special Grade"; and Bureau of Supplies and Accounts, "Requirements of Fuel Oil Under Navy Contracts for Period July 1, 1942, to June 20, 1943 Inclusive."

11. Office of the Chief of Naval Operations, *FTP 218*, 1.

12. Wildenberg, *Gray Steel and Black Oil*, 5, 27–45.

13. The history of this process, and of the United States' oiler fleet itself, was all

but lost before the publication of Thomas Wildenberg's *Gray Steel and Black Oil* in the late 1990s. It is likely that the lack of this knowledge may have also played a part in the adoption of Bowen's high-steam narrative. Wildenberg, *Gray Steel and Black Oil*, 5, 27–45.

14. Replacing or augmenting the logistics force in any way also took a back seat to more "glamourous" combat forces between the world wars. Such a trend is, unfortunately, not historically uncommon. Wildenberg, *Gray Steel and Black Oil*, 273.

15. This was made particularly clear in Fleet Problem IX of 1929, during which the carrier *Lexington*'s escorting destroyers could not accompany their charge on its final run to the target for lack of fuel, leaving the carrier in the company only of the light cruiser *Omaha* (which was short of fuel itself). Lack of standardized procedures for and experience with at-sea refueling vastly exacerbated this problem. Wildenberg, *Gray Steel and Black Oil*, 27–45, 81; Nofi, *To Train the Fleet for War*; Fuquea, "Advantage Japan," 223–25.

16. Wildenberg, *Gray Steel and Black Oil*, 53–55.

17. The genesis of the national defense tanker lies primarily with Maritime Commission member Rear Admiral Emory S. Land. While critical, Land's role in the development of the US Navy's fast fleet oilers is superbly treated elsewhere and lies beyond the scope of this work. Wildenberg, *Gray Steel and Black Oil*, 74–82, 93–100.

18. Namely, under light load and in calm seas. In service, speeds generally stuck to around 18 knots at best. Wildenberg, *Gray Steel and Black Oil*, 107, 275.

19. Perhaps contrary to what one might think, the conversion of a tanker to a fleet oiler went far beyond the simple installation of refueling gear—it also required the installation of weapons, fire control equipment, damage control measures, and the substantially increased support facilities required by the crew needed to man it all. This was, as a result, an extensive and time-consuming process. Wildenberg, *Gray Steel and Black Oil*, 108–21.

20. Despite the fact that acting as a tanker took up the majority of its time, *Cimarron* nevertheless managed to serve the fleet in its intended role for both the Tokyo raid and the Battle of Midway in 1942. Wildenberg, *Gray Steel and Black Oil*, 170.

21. Wildenberg, *Gray Steel and Black Oil*, 175–76; Fuquea, "Advantage Japan," 223–25.

22. Carter, *Beans, Bullets, and Black Oil*, 17–22.

23. A respectable amount of attention has been paid to the role of the tanker shortage in this particular development, but the extent of its origins had not been fully explored before this study. For additional information on the marginalization of combat assets due to the supply issue, see Hone, "Letters to the Editor," 471–73; Wildenberg, *Gray Steel and Black Oil*; Carter, *Beans, Bullets, and Black Oil*; Office of the Chief of Naval Operations, *FTP 218*, 1–11.

24. Wildenberg, *Gray Steel and Black Oil*, 172–73.

25. Thomas C. Hone, "Replacing Battleships with Aircraft Carriers in the Pacific in World War II," *Naval War College Review* 66, no. 1 (Winter 2013): 58–59.

26. Specifically, this was one of the actions that led to Kimmel's fleet memorandum regarding excessive fuel consumption. "Pacific Fleet Confidential Letter 18CL-41: Excessive Fuel Consumption."

27. Wildenberg, *Gray Steel and Black Oil*, 170.

28. Hone, "Letters to the Editor," 471–73.

29. It bears mentioning that it was this style of operations that had resulted in the *Cimarron*-class oiler *Neosho* ending up as the target of Japanese carrier aircraft at the Battle of the Coral Sea in May 1942 due to the oiler's proximity to the battle zone. Wildenberg, *Gray Steel and Black Oil*, 170; Office of the Chief of Naval Operations, *FTP 218*, 1.

30. Wildenberg, *Gray Steel and Black Oil*, 81.

31. While the navy had long focused on the Pacific with War Plan Orange, the importance of preserving Britain and "Europe First" forced the shift to the "Rainbow" plans. This was also done partly due to the fact that said vessels, once converted, would be able to effectively refuel their own escorts. See Wildenberg, *Gray Steel and Black Oil*, 161–65; and Miller, *War Plan Orange*, 267–312.

32. Wildenberg, *Gray Steel and Black Oil*, 179–80; Carter, *Beans, Bullets, and Black Oil*, 105–13.

33. Wildenberg, *Gray Steel and Black Oil*, 179–89, 275.

34. Chief of the Bureau of Ships to all Supervisors of Shipbuilding, "Shore Spares—Suspension of Manufacture of," 83–84.

35. There are numerous discussions of this within the archival records, particularly in the form of rejection notifications and lengthy complaints about the inspection process on the part of the various contractors. Many of these are found in Bureau of Ships General Correspondence A5-7 (Main Propulsion, Turbines), RG 19, NACP. Additionally, the subject is touched upon (as mentioned in chapter 5) throughout the general board hearing. General Board of the Navy, "Steam Pressures and Temperatures," 1–20.

36. Robinson, "The Reminiscences of Samuel Murray Robinson," 24–36.

37. Koistinen, *Arsenal of World War II*, 106–8.

38. Robinson, "The Reminiscences of Samuel Murray Robinson," 28–37; Koistinen, *Arsenal of World War II*, 134, 182–83, 204–6. The activities of the Office of Procurement and Material were critical to the overall war effort and, accordingly, fill eighteen volumes at the Navy Department Library. Much has and still can be written about this agency, but the bulk of its activities are beyond the scope of this book. For more information, see Office of Procurement and Material, "Office of Procurement and Material: Industrial Mobilization," vols. 1–2 (2a-b), Rare Book Room, Navy Department Library in Washington, DC; Office of Procurement and Material, "Office of Procurement and Material: Production Branch," vols. 1–4 (4a-d), Rare Book Room, Navy Department Library in Washington, DC; Office of Procurement and Material, "Office of Procurement and Material: Coordination of Material Procurement," vols. 1–7 (6a-g), Rare Book Room, Navy Department Library in Washington, DC.

39. Chief of the Bureau of Ships to Inspector of Machinery, USN, "DD445 Class Destroyers—High Pressure and Cruising Turbine Spindle Forgings for—Shipment of From Allis-Chalmers Manufacturing Company to Westinghouse Company," October 20, 1942, Bureau of Ships General Correspondence S41-1 (Main Propulsion, Turbines), RG 19, NACP.

40. Inspector of Machinery, USN, to Westinghouse Electric & Manufacturing Company, "Substance of Telephone Conversation—Lt. Commander Ogle, Bureau of Ships to Captain Wille, USN, 2:50 PM, May 29, 1942," Bureau of Ships General

Correspondence S41-1 (Main Propulsion, Turbines), RG 19, NACP; Inspector of Machinery, USN, to Westinghouse Electric & Manufacturing Company, "Substance of Telephone Conversation—Lt. Commander Ogle, Bureau of Ships to Captain Wille, USN, 3:20 PM, May 29, 1942, Bureau of Ships General Correspondence S41-1 (Main Propulsion, Turbines), RG 19, NACP; F. J. Wille, Inspector of Machinery, USN to Chief of the Bureau of Ships, "Main Propulsion Equipment—2150 Ton Destroyers," February 4, 1942, Bureau of Ships General Correspondence S41-1 (Main Propulsion, Turbines), RG 19, NACP.

41. Numerous examples of this appear in the records, most of which are found in Bureau of Ships General Correspondence S41-1 (Main Propulsion, Turbines), Boxes 401-10, RG 19, NACP. One example is Inspector of Machinery, USN to Westinghouse Electric & Manufacturing Company, "Manufacturing of Turbine Blading of DD-445 Class, 2150-Ton Destroyers, High-Pressure and Cruising Turbines for the Account of the Westinghouse Electric & Manufacturing Company," May 27, 1942, Bureau of Ships General Correspondence S41-1 (Main Propulsion, Turbines), RG 19, NACP.

42. G. B. Ogle, Bureau of Ships, to Chief of the Bureau of Ships, "Main Turbine Delivery & Requirement Dates for Navy Destroyers," 1-2; Commandant, US Navy Yard, New York, to Chief of the Bureau of Ships, "Manufacture of Turbine Blading by Navy Yard, New York for Westinghouse Elec. & Mfg. Co.," April 17, 1942, Bureau of Ships General Correspondence S41-1 (Main Propulsion, Turbines), RG 19, NACP; Bureau of Ships, "An Administrative History of the Bureau of Ships During World War II," 182-83.

43. See Bureau of Ships General Correspondence S41-1 (Main Propulsion, Turbines), Boxes 401-10. Captain N. L. Rawlings, USN, "Development of Additional Sources for the Manufacture of High Pressure Main Propulsion Turbines for 2100 Ton Destroyers," February 16, 1942, Bureau of Ships General Correspondence S41-1 (Main Propulsion, Turbines), RG 19, NACP; Inspector of Machinery, USN to Westinghouse Electric & Mfg. Co., "Norfolk Navy Yard," January 8, 1942, Bureau of Ships General Correspondence S41-1 (Main Propulsion, Turbines), RG 19, NACP; Commandant Norfolk Navy Yard calling Chief of the Bureau of Ships, "Manufacture of Turbine Blades at Norfolk Navy Yard for Allis-Chalmers and Westinghouse Electric & Mfg. Co. on usual deposit basis," January 19, 1942, Bureau of Ships General Correspondence S41-1 (Main Propulsion, Turbines), RG 19, NACP.

44. Elliott Company to the Bureau of Ships, "Development of Additional Sources for the Manufacture of High Pressure Main Propulsion Turbines for 2100 Ton Class Destroyers," March 3, 1942, Bureau of Ships General Correspondence S41-1 (Main Propulsion, Turbines), RG 19, NACP.

45. See chapter 7 as well as Chief of the Bureau of Ships to all Supervisors of Shipbuilding, "Shore Spares—Suspension of Manufacture of," 83-84. There are also numerous records of turbines and components, "shipped less spares" within Bureau of Ships General Correspondence S41-1 (Main Propulsion, Turbines), RG 19, NACP.

46. Additional attempts by BuShips to standardize propulsion design continued throughout World War II. Chief of the Bureau of Ships to the Controller of Shipbuilding, War Production Board, "Standardization of Geared Turbine Propulsion Equipment for Naval Vessels," June 7, 1943, Bureau of Ships General Correspondence S41-1 (Main Propulsion, Turbines), Box 404, RG 19, NACP.

47. As mentioned previously, engines were not usually installed in destroyers until after their launch as one of the final stages of production. Thus, seizure of an engine from a nearly completed vessel was not a well-liked practice, though it did occur for all types of vessels, such as shown in commandant, Norfolk Navy Yard, calling the chief of the Bureau of Ships, "Consolidated Steel Corporation—Spare Parts for Type DA Engines," June 22, 1943, Bureau of Ships General Correspondence S41-1 (Main Propulsion, Turbines), RG 19, NACP.

48. Inspector of Machinery, USN, to Westinghouse Electric & Manufacturing Company, "Substance of Telephone Conversation—Lt. Commander Ogle, Bureau of Ships to Captain Wille, USN, 2:50 PM, 29 May 1942."

49. Nearly every case in the records of the Bureau of Ships contains unprovoked direct assurances by the contractor that the contract may be moved forward immediately should battle damage require it. Bureau of Ships General Correspondence L4 (Contracts), RG 19, NACP.

50. Examples abound of this within the Bureau of Ships General Correspondence L4 (Contracts) and S41-1 (Main Propulsion, Turbines). This particular example is quoted from Bureau of Ships, "Negotiations with Westinghouse Electric & Manufacturing Company for One Set of Main Propulsion Turbines and Reduction Gears for the DD231 Class of Destroyer," January 7, 1944, Bureau of Ships General Correspondence S41-1 (Main Propulsion, Turbines), RG 19, NACP, 2.

51. Bureau of Ships, "An Administrative History of the Bureau of Ships During World War II," 183–84.

52. Bureau of Ships, "An Administrative History of the Bureau of Ships During World War II," 183–84.

53. Friedman, *U.S. Destroyers*, 137–61, 352.

54. G. B. Ogle, Bureau of Ships, to Chief of the Bureau of Ships, "Main Turbine Delivery & Requirement Dates for Navy Destroyers," 1–2; W. J. Kastor, Order Service Manager, Steam Division, Westinghouse Electric & Manufacturing Co., to Inspector of Machinery, US Navy, "Propulsion Equipment—2150 Ton Destroyers." Both mention that subcontracting could rectify the shortages, but such a move would not entirely eliminate the delay.

55. Again, this issue is mentioned by Friedman but is not elaborated upon outside of allusions to this issue as the reason for the initial use of diesel engines in destroyer escorts. Friedman, *U.S. Destroyers*, 143–44.

56. Bureau of Ships, "An Administrative History of the Bureau of Ships During World War II," 182.

57. Friedman, *U.S. Destroyers*, 137–61, 478–81, 518–37.

58. Of course, they did still need to be capable of about 15 knots to be considered safe from submarine attack. Wildenberg, *Gray Steel and Black Oil*, 54; Carter, *Beans, Bullets, and Black Oil*, 105–13.

59. Bureau of Ships, "An Administrative History of the Bureau of Ships During World War II," 182–84.

60. General Board of the Navy, "Steam Temperatures and Pressures," 1–20.

61. The propulsion study is filed under its own reference item in the navy finding aid at the National Archives in College Park and thus will be cited by that identifier. ITEM S-24 Propulsion Study Information, RG19, NACP.

62. This is stated a number of times in the study. ITEM S-24 Propulsion Study Information.

63. ITEM S-24 Propulsion Study Information; Bowen, *Ships, Machinery, and Mossbacks*, 47–126.

64. ITEM S-24 Propulsion Study Information.

65. These records can be found in two primary locations: Bureau of Ships General Correspondence L4 (Contracts), RG 19, NACP; Bureau of Ships General Correspondence S41-1 (Main Propulsion, Turbines), RG 19, NACP.

66. Checking for and dealing with shock damage was a major component of the US's damage control practice during the World War II era. Bureau of Naval Personnel, *Introduction to Engineering and Damage Control with Notes on Ship Construction and Installations*.

CONCLUSION

1. William Peerenboom and George Philipps, "Reminiscences of High Steam," interview by Tyler Pitrof, April 15, 2021.

2. Quote of William Peerenboom. Peerenboom and Philipps, "Reminiscences of High Steam."

3. Generally, gunnery and operations remained the places to be if you were pursuing the promotion. This was the consensus reached between William Peerenboom and George Philipps. Peerenboom and Philipps, "Reminiscences of High Steam."

4. In our discussion, both Bill Peerenboom and George Philips were effusive in their praise of postwar engineering sailors. George in particular stopped our conversation to make it clear that these men were "absolutely professionals in the area through knowledge, experience, and the ability to teach. They made sure their underlings did things right." To this, Bill added, "You did not want to run afoul of the Chief Boiler Technician!" Peerenboom and Philipps, "Reminiscences of High Steam."

5. Peerenboom and Philipps, "Reminiscences of High Steam."

6. Although this seems to have often gotten off track with auxiliary machinery. Peerenboom and Philipps, "Reminiscences of High Steam."

7. This was partly due to the need to be ready to operate at high power at short notice but also to ensure that the ship remained in ballast without having to pump seawater into fuel storage tanks—a procedure that was, to put it politely, laborious to reverse. Peerenboom and Philipps, "Reminiscences of High Steam."

8. Jordan and Moulin, *French Destroyers*, 184; Whitley, *Destroyer!*, 29–34.

Bibliography

ARCHIVAL
Bureau of Ships. "An Administrative History of the Bureau of Ships During World War II," vols. 1–2/89a–b. Manuscript, Navy Department Library Rare Book Room, Washington, DC, 1952.
Publications of the Federal Government: Record Group 287, National Archives at College Park, MD.
Records of the Bureau of Ships: Record Group 19, National Archives at College Park, MD.
Records of the Bureau of Naval Personnel: Record Group 24, National Archives at College Park, MD.
Records of the Office of the Chief of Naval Operations: Record Group 38, National Archives at College Park, MD.
Records of the General Board of the Navy: Record Group 80, National Archives Building, Washington, DC.

ARTICLES
American Society for Naval Engineers. "The Machinery of the Scharnhorst, Potsdam, and Gneisenau." *Journal of the American Society for Naval Engineers* 49, no. 2 (May 1937): 251–54.
———. "World Trend Is Toward Geared Turbines and High-Pressure Steam." *Journal of the American Society for Naval Engineers* 47, no. 4 (November 1935): 627–31.
Donald, H. G. "Boiler Room Operation on Naval Vessels." *Journal of the American Society for Naval Engineers* 41, no. 4 (November 1929): 608–19.
Fuquea, David C. "Advantage Japan: The Imperial Japanese Navy's Superior High Seas Refueling Capability." *Journal of Military History* 84, no. 1 (January 2020): 213–35.
———. "Task Force One: The Wasted Assets of the United States Pacific Battleship Fleet." *Journal of Military History* 61 no. 4 (October 1997): 707–34.
Funk, N. E. "Higher Steam Pressures." *Journal of the American Society for Naval Engineers* 40, no. 2 (May 1, 1928): 256–65.
Griswold, A. Whitney. "The Influence of History Upon Sea Power: A Comment on American Naval Policy." *Journal of the American Military Institute* 4, no. 1 (Spring 1940): 1–7.
Hardy, A. C. "The French Liner *Normandie*: A Visit to the World's Largest Electrically-Propelled Ship and the First Liner Over 1000 Feet in Length to Go into Commission." *Journal of the American Society for Naval Engineers* 47, no. 2 (May 1935): 276–83.

Hone, Thomas C. "Letters to the Editor." *Journal of Military History* 62, no. 2 (April 1998): 471–73.

———. "Replacing Battleships with Aircraft Carriers in Pacific in World War II." *Naval War College Review* 66 (2013): 56–76.

King, J. H. "Marine Boilers for Higher Pressures and Temperatures and Their Contribution to Greater Economy." *Journal of the American Society for Naval Engineers* 40, no. 2 (May 1928): 238–55.

Lee, Erika. "The 'Yellow Peril' and Asian Exclusion in the Americas." *Pacific Historical Review* 76, no. 4 (November 2007): 537–62.

Naegeli, Hans, and A. C. Jones. "Carbon-Molybdenum Cast Steel for Steam Service." *Journal of the American Society for Naval Engineers* 47, no. 2 (May 1935): 198–219.

Odend'hal, C. J. "The Effects of Turbulence and Cavitation Upon Erosion and Corrosion." *Journal of the American Society for Naval Engineers* 50, no. 2 (May 1938): 231–39.

Pate, James E. "Mobilizing Manpower." *Social Forces* 22, no. 2 (December 1943): 154–62.

Pumphrey, Lowell M. "Planning for Economic Warfare." *Military Affairs* 5, no. 3 (Autumn 1941): 145–51.

Raudzens, George. "War-Winning Weapons: The Measurement of Technological Determinism in Military History." *Journal of Military History* 54, no. 4 (October 1990): 403–34.

Ricard, J. P. "The Sural Boiler." *Journal of the American Society for Naval Engineers* 58, no. 1 (February 1946): 70–74.

Robinson, Samuel M. "The Stopping of Ships." *Journal of the American Society for Naval Engineers* 50, no. 3 (August 1938): 325–40.

Roland, Alex. "Technology, Ground Warfare, and Strategy: The Paradox of American Experience." *Journal of Military History* 55, no. 4 (October 1991): 447–68.

Sackett, R. L. "The Supply of Technical Men to the Armed Forces and to Industry." *Science* 96, no. 2503 (December 1942): 553–54.

Smith, C. N. "Selection, Training, and Morale of Navy Personnel." *Annals of the American Academy of Political and Social Science* 220, no. 1 (March 1942): 57–66.

Smith, W. W. "The Economic Advantages of the Reduction Gear as Applied in the Propulsion of Naval Vessels." *Journal of the American Society for Naval Engineers* 23, no. 1 (February 1911): 126–43.

Stillman, J. B. "Marine Boilers for High Pressures." *Journal of the American Society for Naval Engineers* 40, no. 2 (May 1928): 286–96.

Thompson, W. K. "The Naval Officer Training Program." *Journal of Educational Sociology* 16, no. 9 (May 1943): 557–61.

US Navy. "War Information [The Navy College Training Program]." *American Mathematical Monthly* 50, no. 10 (December 1943): 645–50.

Waller, C. R. "What Is the Most Economical Drive for Ships?" *Journal of the American Society for Naval Engineers* 41, no. 2 (May 1929): 267–79.

Wickenden, William E. "Engineering Education." *Annals of the American Academy of Political and Social Science* 231, no. 1 (January 1944): 100–102.

Wilkinson, Ford L. "The US Naval Postgraduate School." *Scientific Monthly* 66, no. 3 (March 1948): 183–94.

Willey, Malcolm M. "The College Training Programs of the Armed Services." *Annals of the American Academy of Political and Social Science* 231, no. 1 (January 1944): 14–28.

Wright, J. M. P. "Review of Ships, Machinery and Mossbacks by Harold G. Bowen." *Military Affairs* 19, no. 3 (Autumn 1955): 160–61.

Zook, George F. "How the Colleges Went to War." *Annals of the American Academy of Political and Social Science* 231, no. 1 (January 1944): 1–7.

BOOKS

Admiralty. *Stokers' Manual 1912 (For Engine-Room Ratings Not Entitled to the Steam Manuals and Seamen Under Training in Mechanical and Stokehold Work)*. London: Eyre and Spottiswoode, 1912.

Ancell, Manning, and Christine Miller. *The Biographical Dictionary of World War II Generals and Flag Officers: The US Armed Forces*. Westport, CT: Greenwood Press, 1996.

Black, Newton Henry, and Harvey Davis. *Practical Physics for Secondary Schools: Fundamental Principles and Applications to Daily Life*. London: Macmillan, 1913.

Bowen, Harold G. *Ships, Machinery, and Mossbacks: The Autobiography of a Naval Engineer*. Princeton, NJ: Princeton University Press, 1954.

Braisted, William R. *The United States Navy in the Pacific, 1897–1909*. Austin: University of Texas Press, 1958.

———. *The United States Navy in the Pacific, 1909–1922*. Austin: University of Texas Press, 1971.

Braynard, Frank O. *By Their Works Ye Shall Know Them: The Life and Ships of William Francis Gibbs, 1886–1967*. New York: Gibbs & Cox, 1968.

Brescia, Maurizio. *Mussolini's Navy: A Reference Guide to the Regia Marina, 1930–1945*. Barnsley, UK: Seaforth Publishing, 2012.

Bureau of Engineering. *Manual of Engineering Instructions*. Washington, DC: Bureau of Engineering, 1921.

———. *Special Specifications for Propelling Machinery with Boilers, Auxiliary Machinery, and Electric Plant for U.S. Destroyers DD 381 and DD 383*. Washington, DC: Government Printing Office, 1934.

Bureau of Naval Personnel. *Introduction to Ordnance and Gunnery*. Washington, DC: Bureau of Naval Personnel, 1943.

———. *Introduction to Seamanship*. Washington, DC: Bureau of Naval Personnel, 1943.

———. *Introduction to Engineering and Damage Control with Notes on Ship Construction and Installations*. Washington, DC: Bureau of Naval Personnel, 1945.

———. *Principles of Naval Engineering*. Washington, DC: Government Printing Office, 1958.

Bureau of Navigation. *Navy Directory: Officers of the United States Navy and Marine Corps*. Washington, DC: Government Printing Office, 1937.

———. *Navy Directory: Officers of the United States Navy and Marine Corps*. Washington, DC: Government Printing Office, 1938.

———. *Navy Directory: Officers of the United States Navy and Marine Corps*. Washington, DC: Government Printing Office, 1939.

Carew, Michael G. *Becoming the Arsenal: The American Industrial Mobilization for World War II, 1938–1942*. Lanham, MD: University Press of America, 2009.

Carlisle, Rodney P. *Where the Fleet Begins: A History of the David Taylor Research Center, 1898–1998*. Washington, DC: Naval Historical Center, 1998.

Carter, Worrall Reed. *Beans, Bullets, and Black Oil: The Story of Fleet Logistics Afloat in the Pacific During World War II*. Washington, DC: Department of the Navy, 1953.

Chisholm, Donald. *Waiting for Dead Men's Shoes: Origins and Development of the US Navy's Officer Personnel System, 1793–1941*. Palo Alto, CA: Stanford University Press, 2002.

Evans, David C., and Mark R. Peattie. *Kaigun: Strategy, Tactics, and Technology in the Imperial Japanese Navy, 1887–1941*. Annapolis, MD: Naval Institute Press, 1997.

Evers, Henry. *Steam and the Steam Engine: Land and Marine*. Glasgow: Williams Collins, 1875.

Friedman, Norman. *U.S. Battleships: An Illustrated Design History*. Annapolis, MD: Naval Institute Press, 1985.

———. *U.S. Cruisers: An Illustrated Design History*. Annapolis, MD: Naval Institute Press, 1987.

———. *U.S. Destroyers: An Illustrated Design History*. Annapolis, MD: Naval Institute Press, 2004.

Furer, Julius Augustus. *Administration of the Navy Department in World War II*. Washington, DC: Government Printing Office, 1959.

Gordon, G. A. H. *British Seapower and Procurement Between the Wars: A Reappraisal of Rearmament*. Annapolis, MD: Naval Institute Press, 1988.

Hagan, Kenneth J. *This People's Navy: The Making of American Sea Power*. New York: Free Press, 1991.

Harrod, Frederick S. *Manning the New Navy: The Development of a Modern Naval Enlisted Force, 1899–1940*. Westport, CT: Greenwood Press, 1978.

Heinrich, Thomas. *Warship Builders: An Industrial History of US Navy Shipbuilding, 1922–1945*. Annapolis, MD: Naval Institute Press, 2020.

Hirsch, Richard F. *Technology and Transformation in the American Electric Utility Industry*. New York: Cambridge University Press, 1989.

Hughes, Thomas P. *Networks of Power: Electrification in Western Society, 1880–1930*. Baltimore, MD: Johns Hopkins University Press, 1985.

Hunter, Louis C. *A History of Industrial Power in the United States, 1780–1930, Volume Two: Steam Power*. Charlottesville: University Press of Virginia, 1985.

Hutton, Frederick Remsen. *The Mechanical Engineering of Power Plants*. New York: John Wiley & Sons, 1897.

Jordan, John. *Warships After London*. Annapolis, MD: Naval Institute Press, 2020.

Jordan, John, and Jean Moulin. *French Destroyers: Torpilleurs d'Escadre & Contre-Torpilleurs, 1922–1956*. Annapolis, MD: Naval Institute Press, 2015.

Jung, Ingvar. *The Marine Turbine, Part 2, 1928–1980: Development of Naval Turbines and the Engines of the Great Atlantic Liners*. Greenwich, London: National Maritime Museum, 1986.

Karsten, Peter. *The Naval Aristocracy: The Golden Age of Annapolis and the Emergence of American Navalism*. Annapolis, MD: Naval Institute Press, 1972.

Kludas, Arnold. *Record Breakers of the North Atlantic: Blue Riband Liners, 1838–1952*. London: Chatha, 2000.

Koistinen, Paul A. C. *Arsenal of World War II: The Political Economy of American Warfare, 1940–1945*. Lawrence: University Press of Kansas, 2004.

Kuehn, John T. *Agents of Innovation: The General Board and the Design of the Fleet That Defeated the Japanese Navy*. Annapolis, MD: Naval Institute Press, 2008.

———. *America's First General Staff: A Short History of the Rise and Fall of the General Board of the U.S. Navy, 1900–1950*. Annapolis, MD: Naval Institute Press, 2017.

LaFeber, Walter. *The Clash: US-Japanese Relations throughout History*. New York: W. W. Norton & Company, 1997.

Mahan, Alfred Thayer. *Naval Strategy: Compared and Contrasted with the Principles and Practice of Military Operations on Land*. Boston: Little, Brown, and Company, 1911.

March, Edgar J. *British Destroyers, 1892–1953*. London: Billing & Sons Limited, 1966.

McBride, William. *Technological Change and the United States Navy, 1865–1945*. Baltimore, MD: Johns Hopkins University Press, 2011.

Meader, Bruce. *ASNE, the First 100 Years: The History of the American Society for Naval Engineers, 1888–1988*. Alexandria, VA: American Society for Naval Engineers, 1988.

Miller, Edward S. *War Plan Orange: The US Strategy to Defeat Japan, 1897–1945*. Annapolis, MD: Naval Institute Press, 2007.

Mills, Geofrey T., and Hugh Rockoff, eds. *The Sinews of War: Essays on the Economic History of World War II*. Ames: Iowa State Press, 1993.

Milton, J. H. *Marine Steam Boilers*. Bungay, UK: Richard Clay and Company, Ltd., 1953.

Milward, Alan S. *War, Economy, and Society, 1939–1945*. Berkeley: University of California Press, 1999.

Moore, Gregory. *Defining and Defending the Open Door Policy: Theodore Roosevelt and China, 1901–1909*. New York: Lexington Books, 2015.

Morgan, William Michael. *Pacific Gibraltar: US-Japanese Rivalry Over the Annexation of Hawaii, 1885–1898*. Annapolis, MD: Naval Institute Press, 2011.

Nofi, Albert A. *To Train the Fleet for War: The US Navy Fleet Problems, 1923–1940*. Newport, RI: Naval War College, 2010.

Parsons, Charles A. *The Steam Turbine: The Rede Lecture, 1911*. Cambridge, UK: Cambridge University Press, 1911.

Poolman, Kenneth. *The Winning Edge: Naval Technology in Action, 1939–1945*. Annapolis, MD: Naval Institute Press, 1997.

Reckner, James R., ed. *A Sailor's Log: Water-Tender Frederick T. Wilson, USN, on Asiatic Station, 1899–1901*. Kent, OH: Kent State University Press, 2004.

Roscoe, Theodore. *United States Destroyer Operations in World War II*. Annapolis, MD: Naval Institute Press, 1953.

Sumida, Jon T. *Inventing Grand Strategy and Teaching Command: The Classic Works of Alfred Thayer Mahan Reconsidered*. Washington, DC: Woodrow Wilson Center Press, 1997.

Whitley, M. J. *Destroyer! German Destroyers in World War II*. Annapolis, MD: Naval Institute Press, 1983.

Wildenberg, Thomas. *Gray Steel and Black Oil: Fast Tankers and Replenishment at Sea in the U.S. Navy, 1912–1992*. Annapolis: Naval Institute Press, 1996.
United States Navy. *The Bluejacket's Manual*. Annapolis: Naval Institute Press, 1940.
Unknown Author. *Blue Book of American Shipping*. Cleveland, OH: Marine Review, 1897.
United States Naval Institute. *Naval Machinery*. Menasha, WI: George Banta Publishing Company, 1941.

OTHER

Fisher, Stanford Edward. "Sustaining the Pacific Carrier Air War: The Development of U.S. Naval Aviation Maintenance and the Enlisted Aircraft Technician in World War II." PhD diss., University of Maryland College Park, 2019.
Hagerott, Mark R. "Commanding Men and Machines: Admiralship, Technology, and Ideology in the 20th Century U.S. Navy." PhD diss., University of Maryland College Park, 2008.
Peerenboom, William, and George Philipps. "Reminiscences of High Steam." Interview by Tyler Pitrof. April 15, 2021.
Pitrof, Tyler. "Adapting to Innovation: The US Navy, High-Steam Destroyers, and the Second World War." Master's thesis, University of Maryland College Park, 2013.
Robinson, S. M. "The Reminiscences of Samuel Murray Robinson." Interview by William J. Cromie. *Naval History Project*, Columbia Digital Library Collections, September 30–October 1, 1963. Oral history Transcript.
US Congress. House of Representatives. Committee on Naval Affairs. *Investigation of the Naval Defense Program: Hearings before the Committee on Naval Affairs*. 76th Cong., 2nd sess., March 23 and 25, and April 13, 1942.

Index

Acheron, 51, 53, *60*, 189n30
Allis-Chalmers, 113, 118, *119*, 163
Andrews, Adolphus, 197n15

Babcock & Wilcox, 25–26, 52, 71, 74, *76*, 89, 93, 101
Baker, Commander Charles A., 87
Bethlehem Shipbuilding Corporation, 66, 67, 74, 80, 87, 116, 118–20 191n18
"Big Three" shipyards, 65–67, 73–74, 80, 87, 89, 98, 113, 118, 189n31
Blohm and Voss, 58–59
bluejackets, 123, 126, 190n7; *Bluejacket's Manuel, The*, 126, 196n13
Board of Inspection and Survey (INSURV); opposition to BuEng, 80, 87, 89, 94–96, 101; staffing, 85–86
boiler, 11–12, 14, 17, 20–21, 28, 33, 50, 69, 74–76, 84, 89, 93, 116–17, 130, 140–42, 149, 154, 170, 172, 177n6; Admiralty Three-Drum, 51–52; air-encased, 6, 55, 76, 189n39; Benson, 59; definition, 20; fire-tube, 21–22, 25, 28; "flash," 186n39; fuel, 20; Ro-Gō Kampon, 53; Sural, 57, 185n30; Thornycroft, 51, 56, 184n1; Type M Express boiler, *76*; Wagner, 58; water-tube, 6, 21–22, 25, 29; Yarrow, 51, 56, 65, 184n1
Bowen Sr., Vice Admiral Harold G., 4–6, 12–14, 85–86, 135, 171–75, 177n6, 189n32 189n36 (chap. 4), 189n2 (chap. 5), 193n51; autobiography, 2, 7, 9, 50, 81–83, 91, 173–75; chief of Bureau of Engineering, 1, 20, 34–35, 36, 48, 49, 61, 62, 74–75, 110, 113–15, 120–21, 122, 135, 154, 173; education, 4–5, 67, 83–84, 162, 190n15, 191n20; post-controversy career, 109, 193n3, 194n7 (chap. 6); role in the high-steam controversy, 1, 6–8, 77, 81, 87, 89, 91–104, 105–7, 116, 123, 153, 169, 173–74, 191n28; scholarly perception of, 2–3, 8–11, 178n13, 178n14, 201n13; subject matter expert, 2, 98–104, 110, 116–17, 122–26
Brinser, Rear Admiral Harry L., 80, 81, 86–87, 91, 94–96, *95*, 101–2; biography, 85–86; post-controversy career, 108
Bureau of Construction and Repair (BuC&R), 15, 123, 126, 189n31, 191n19; function, 63, 69, 114, 135, 149, 154; merger with BuEng, 105–6, 115, 130, 194n1; opposition to BuEng, 77, 81, 87, 89, 193n53; staffing, 85–86, 108, 162, 188n19
Bureau of Engineering (BuEng), 1–3, 12, 15, 34, 36, 48, 62–68, 73–74, *78–79*, *86*, 89, 135, 149, 174–75, 191n19, 196n12, 201n5; function, 7, 62–63, 105, 114, 122–23, 153–54, 174–75; merger with BuC&R, 106, 115, 194n1; staffing, 5, 68, 85–86
Bureau of Naval Personnel (BuPers), 10, 128; function, 129; wartime educational adjustments, 129–31, 198n26; wartime teaching manuals, 129, 206n66
Bureau of Navigation (BuNav), 15, 127–28, 196n15, 197n15; function, 63, 122–26, 197n20, 197n22, 198n24. *See also* Bureau of Naval Personnel (BuPers)

Bureau of Ships (BuShips), 119, 130, 142–49, 162, 167–69, 173, 193n3, 201n6, 201nn9–10, 203n35, 204n46, 205nn49–50, 205–6nn61–62; function, 115–18, 139, 154, 162–66, 168–70, 198n5, 200n31; origins, 106, 109, 115, 199n21
bureau system, 2, 18, 43, 63, 77, 87, 115, 162; definition, 15

carrier raid, 158, 160
Carter, Worrall Reed, 9, 178n14
Chicago Edison Company, 23–24
Cimarron (oiler), 157, *159*, 166–67, *169*, 202n20, 203n29
Chisholm, Donald, 10, 179n17, 190nn5–6, 190n15, 196nn5–7, 196nn9–10
Clemson (destroyer), 65–67, *66*, 70, 76, *78–79*, 87, *100*, *108*, 187n13
Cobra (destroyer), 30
Cochrane, Rear Admiral Edward L., 162–66, 169
college training programs; V-1, 127–30; V-5, 127; V-7, 127–30, 197nn17–18; V-12, 130–31, 198n27
Consolidated Steel Corporation, 119
Cox, Rear Admiral Ormond L., 89, 92–94, 99
Curtis, C. G., 23–24, 71

Dahlgren, 189n40
Dalton, Lieutenant Charles M., 1–2, 89–92, 96–98, 101–2, 191n26
DeLaval Company, 98, 113, 164
DeSchiMAG, 58–59, 185n36
destroyer, 9, 13, 30, *32*, 34, 50–60, 65–80, 92–102, 106–8, 111, 114–21, *138*, 143, *144–45*, 155–56, 164–65, 172–73, 177n6, 178n13, 181n31, 183n27, 184nn1–2, 186n38, 188n25, 189n39, 191nn18–19, 191n28, 202n15, 205n47; challenges of design, 64–65, 181n31; role, 91–92, 158, 184n3, 186n42, 199n13
destroyer escort, 166–69; impact of high steam, 167–68, 195n11, 205n55; role, 167
Dewey, Commodore George, 39, 43
diesel propulsion, 33–34, 152–53, 167–69, 181n44, 205n55
displacement, 15–16, 77, 138, *144–48*
Dreadnought (battleship), 30, 124
DuBose, Rear Admiral William G., 77, 81, *86*, 87, 106; biography, 85; post-controversy career, 108–9, 115

Engineering Duty Only (EDO), 3, 123, 128, 130, 179n17, 190n16; definition, 84–85; educational requirements, 85; lacking proficiency, 7, 133, 139–41
engineer officer, 4; dislike by general line, 81–83; history, 82–86, 122–23, 179n17; postwar education, 171–72; training, 84–85, 122–31, 140; wartime shortage, 7, 102, 131
enlisted sailors, 190n7, 195n2, 196n14; lack of sources, 4; qualifications for engineering, 172, 206n4
Ericsson, John, 27–28
Espionage Act, 74, 80, 98, 113

Farragut (destroyer), 62, 69–70, 75, 77, *78–79*, 97, *100*, 106, *138*, 188n28
Federal Shipbuilding and Drydock Company, 34
Fisher, Stanford Edward, 179n15
Fleet Problems, 64, 67, 91–92, 134, 156, 178n13, 186n5, 191n28, 202n15
fleet standard cruising speed, 156–57, 187n11
Forrestal, Secretary of the Navy James, 109
Friedman, Norman, 9, 178n13, 195n11, 205n55
FTP 136: Cruising Radii of U.S. Naval Vessels from Actual Steaming Data, 135–36, *137*, 138–39, 142–43, 160, 172
FTP 143: War Instructions, 135, 139
FTP 218: War Service Fuel Consumption of U.S. Naval Surface Vessels, *137*, 143,

144–47, 148–49, 155, 160, 200n29, 200n30
fuel economy. *See* operational range
fuel oil, 93, 152–56, 161, 178n14; conversion from coal, 31, 155–56; quality standards, 153–54. *See also* oiler
Fulton, Robert, 27
Fuquea, David, 187n7, 201n1, 202n15

General Board of the Navy, 69, 156, 199n13; bureau oversight, 63, 194n2; high-steam hearing, 1–2, 80, 81–82, 86–104, 105–6; organization, 63, 87–88; origins, 43, 183n18; role in high-steam adoption, 2, 103–4, 105–7; technologically progressive, 18, 47, 63; war planning, 43–46, 64
General Electric Company, 26, 34, 71, 74, 89, 98, 113, 116–18, *119*, 200n31
general line officer, 2, 62, 85, 87, 89, 194n7 (chap. 6); definition, 83; dislike of engineering, 13, 81–83, 172; prewar education and training, 2, 84, 111, 123–26, 130–31, 196n14; postwar education, 130–31, 171–72, 198n26
Gibbs, William Francis, 33–34, 89, 96–98, 101–2, 109, 168, 181n43, 181n46, 182n49, 189n39
Gibbs & Cox, Inc., 6, 34–35, 63, 71, *71*, 101, 191n28, 192n43
Great Depression, 33, 67, 110, 121, 124
Gulf Shipbuilding Corporation, 119

Hagerott, Mark, 191n17
Hamburg America Line (HAPAG), 59, 186n37
Hardesty Jr., Lieutenant Charles J., 1–2, 89–94, 97–99, 101, 189n39
Harrod, Frederick S., 4, 177n5, 190n5
Hart, Admiral Thomas C., 2, 81, 87–88, 96–98, 100–104, 105, 114, 193n1, 193n55; biography, 87–89; opposition to BuEng, 80, 88–89; post-controversy career, 107–8

Heinrich, Thomas, 9, 11, 179n14, 189n31, 192n46, 195n12
high steam, 1–3, 6–7, 12; American interest, 34–35; American system, 6–7, 173–74, 192n43, 193n2, 195n3, 200n1; British system, 51–52, *60*, 188n30; complexities, 7–8; controlled superheat, 75–76; definition, 15; durability, 96–98, 166, 169–70; economizer, 69–70; expectations, 2–3, 67, 96, 110, 133, 149, 152, 173–74; French system, 57–58, *60*, 185n31; German system, 59–60; influence of shore-based power generation, 7–8, 17–18, 19, 22–26, 94–95, 105–6, 121, 164; integral superheat, 50–51, 52, 53, 56, 59, 69; lack of scholarly understanding, 8–10, 173–74, 178n13, 178n14, 201n13; material requirements, 6, 99–100, 117, 194n9 (chap. 7); merchant shipping, 20, 33–34, 121, 180n2; postwar use, 171–73; production capacity, 98, 113–18; production struggles, 113, 116–21, 150, 161–62, 165–66; shortcomings, 3, 149–51, 152, 174–75; subcontracting, 74, 98, 116–18, 163–66, 189n44; training requirements, 100–102, 122; versus turbo-electric, 152, 167, 170, 181n41, 186n37; wartime construction, 166–69
high-steam study, 80, 123–26; Bowen testimony, 91–92, 98, 101–2, 191n28; controversy, 1–3; cost, 99–100; education and training, 100–102; fallout, 103–4, 105–7; fuel, 93–94; manpower, 100–101; Office of Naval Intelligence influence, 103, 193n54; operational range, 91–93; opposition testimony, 94–95; origin, 87, 89–91; production, maintenance, and supply, 94–98
Hone, Thomas, 200–201n1, 202n23
Hopkins (destroyer), 5, 84, 177n6
Horne, Admiral Frederick J., 87, 97

216 / INDEX

Imperial Japanese Navy (IJN), 41–42, 46, 52–54, 60, 121, 150, 171; anticipated enemy, 43, 52–53; propulsion limitations, 53
Indiana (battleship), 38–39, 182n7
Introduction to Engineering and Damage Control, 129–30, 142, 170, 171

Jacobs, Rear Admiral Randall, 129
Japan, 12–13, 40–41, 64, 103, 108, 110, 111, 114, 120, 133, 138, 140–41, 149–50, 157–58, 196n8, 199n12; American relations, 36, 40–47, 182n10, 183n25; reliance on British naval technology, 41

Kanawaha (oiler), 156, *159*
Kantai Kessen, 42, 53, 150
Karsten, Peter, 10, 179n16, 190n7
Kimmel, Admiral Husband E., 139–41, 148–49, 199n12, 202n26
King, Admiral Ernest J., 141–42
King Edward (steamer), 30
Knox, Secretary of the Navy Frank, 109, 162
Kriegsmarine, 58–61; high-steam shortcomings, 59–61, 173
Kuehn, John, 183n18, 186n2, 191n21

Leahy, William D., *86*, 196–97n15
London Naval Treaty, 47, 70
low steam, 55, 66–67, 80, 94, 152, 184n2, 194n9 (chap. 7), 195n3; definition, 15

machine tools, 117–19, 164, 166, 195nn10–12
Mahan (destroyer), 70–74, *78–79*, 96
Maine (armored cruiser), 37, 182n3
Malolo (steamer), 33–34, 109
Manual of Engineering Instructions, 126, 129
Marine Nationale (MN), 54–58, 60; *contre-torpilleurs* (*CT*) and *torpilleurs d'escadre* (*TE*), 54–55; high-steam shortcomings, 56, 57–58, 173
McKinley, President William, 39, 40, 43

Milward, Alan S., 11, 195nn10–11
Mogador-class, 56, 57, 59, 184n1, 185n32
Monitor (ironclad), 28, 37, 82
Munroe, Vice Admiral William R., 103

national defense tanker program, 154, 156–57, 202n17
Naval Act of 1916, 125, 182n8
Naval Reserve Officer Training Corps (NROTC), 83, 123, 127, 130–31, 196n6, 198n26
navy yards, 5, 68–69, 108, 119–20, 163–64
Neches (oiler), 158–60, *159*
Neosho (oiler), *159*, 161, 203n29
New York Shipbuilding Corporation, 66, 67, 74, 80
Newcomen, Thomas, 20
Newport News Shipbuilding and Drydock Company, 66, 67, 74, 80
Nimitz, Admiral Chester W., 127, 129, 141–42, 197n15
North Carolina (battleship), 65, 77, 93, 189n42
North River Steamboat, 27

Office of Procurement and Material (OP&M); function, 162–63, 203n38; mitigating production problems, 163–67
Office of the Chief of Naval Operations (OPNAV), 2, 47, 108, 114, 135, 139, 141, 198–99nn7–10, 199n13, 200nn28–30, 200n33
officer corps, 7, 77; education of, 82–85, 122–31; interwar nature, 89, 123–25, 150; wartime expansion, 126–27, 139
oiler: early-war deficiency, 156–58, *159*, 187n7; early war use, 141, 158, 160; fast fleet, 156–58; impact of high steam, 141, 157, 160; late-war use, 160–61; slow, 156, 158, 160–61; versus tanker, 155, 157, 202n19
Open Door Policy, 38–40, 182n5, 183n25
operational range, 6–7, 64, 91–93, 157–58; definition, 16, 93; engineering efficiency scores, 134–38, 142,

148–50, 172; mitigating variables, 134–51, 199n10; postwar, 172–73; reconceptualization, 141–49; wartime flaws, 133–35, 198n6, 199n13

Pacific War, 2–3, 36, 44–47, 53, 61, 91, 111, 133, 138–43, 150, 157–61, 164–66, 169–70, 172–73, 186n6, 198n6
Papert, Seymour, 191n17
Parsons, Ltd., 29, 50–51, 55–57, *65*, 66, 67, 70, 71, 74, 80, 87, 100, 113, 187n13
Parsons, Sir Charles A., 22, *23*, *24*, 29–30, 50, 184nn1–2, 184n4
Peerenboom, William, 206nn3–4, 206nn6–7
Perry, Commodore Matthew C., 40–41
Pershing, General of the Armies John "Black Jack," 48–49
Philippines; American acquisition, 12, 38–39; significance to war planning, 36, 39–40, 42–47, 64, 110, 133, 150, 182n8, 183n25, 186n6
Philipps, George, 206nn3–4, 206nn6–7
Pickens, Admiral Andrew C., 87
postgraduate training, 68, 84–85, 124–25, 127, 196n14
propeller (screw), 27–28, 178n9, 188n26; rotational efficiency, 29–30, 70, 72, *73*, 143, 148
propulsion battle damage study, 169–70
Purnell, Rear Admiral William R.; board secretary, 87, *90*, 90–91, 94, 102; post-controversy career, 108

reduction gear: direct drive, 27–31, 180n28; double reduction, 34, 71, 72, *73*, 75, 92–93, 142, 150, 188n28; single reduction, 31, *32*, 34, 66, 70, 72
Reichsmarine. *See* Kriegsmarine
Regia Marina (Italian Royal Navy), 49, 103, 184n1
replenishment group, 160–61, 167–69, 173
Richardson, James O., 197n15
Richelieu-class, 185n30, 185n32
Robinson, Vice Admiral Samuel Murray, 135, 142; as director of Office of Procurement and Material, 162–63, 167; biography, 67–69, 74, 187nn16–17, 188n19; post-controversy career, 115–16, 118–20, 162–64; role in high steam, 5–6, 36, 48, 62, 63, 67, 70, 87, 106, 173, 188n21
Roosevelt, President Franklin D., 48, 124
Royal Navy, 41, 42, 50–52, 66; high-steam adoption, 52; high-steam experiments, 50–51; turbine adoption, 29–30, 50. *See also Acheron*

Sadler, Admiral Frank H., 87, 193n55 (chap. 5), 193n1 (chap. 6)
Santa Rosa (passenger liner), 34
Seattle-Takoma Shipbuilding Corporation, *119*
shore spares, 120–21, 161–62, 164–65
Snyder, Admiral Charles P., 138
Somers (destroyer), 1, *65*, 74–77, *75*, *78–79*, 89, 92–101, *100*, *137*, 144–45, 189n38, 200n30; high-steam template, 76–77, 103–4, 106–7, 116–17, 173, 189n39
Spanish-American War, 38–39, 42–43, 64
Standard Oil Company, 157
Standley, Admiral William H., 47–48
steam power: adoption for steam propulsion, 19–20, 26–27, 180n7, 180n26; condenser, 21; early power generation, 22–26; evolution of power grids, 24–26; reciprocating engines, 20–22, 37
Swanson, Claude, Secretary of the Navy, 2, 81, *86*, 87–88, 103–4, 109, 160

Townsend, Admiral Julius C., 87
Treaty system, 51, 77, 111, 185n25; definition, 47–48; impact on high steam, 62–63, 114–15; impact on naval design, 6, 55, 67, 183n27, 196n8; impact on officer corps, 123–26; origin, 46–47, 49. *See also* Washington Naval Treaty
Trevithick, Richard, 21

Tsushima, Battle of, 36, 40–42, 44, 53
turbine, 22, 26, 29–34, 49, 53, 180nn17–18, 181n36, 185n22, 188n22, 188n25; adoption for marine propulsion, 29–30; cross-compound, 31, 50, 59, 69–72, *107*, 188n25; cruising, 6–7, 51, 56, 57, 71–73, 75, 92–93, 133, 149–51, 172, 200n30; efficiency shortcomings, 23, 24–25, 29–30, 184n4; impulse, 23–24, 56, 71–72, 75, 181n33, 188n28; manufacturing difficulties, 31, 98, 113–18; production capacity, 97–98, 113–18, 163–67; reaction, 22, *23*, 66–67, 71; shore-based power, 22–26. See also *Turbinia* (steam launch)
Turbinia (steam launch), 29–30
turbo-electric propulsion, 33–34, 167–70; versus high steam, 152, 167, 170, 181n41, 186n37
Two-Ocean Navy Act (Vinson-Walsh Act), 111, 116, 126, 196n8
Type 1934 (destroyer), 58, 59–60, 69–70, 73, 186n38

United States Naval Academy, 4, 66, 82–84, 123, 130, 171–72, 190n6, 191n20
underway refueling, 18, 48, 64, 91, 110, 142, 155–56, 187n7. See also oiler

Van Keuren, Rear Admiral Alexander, 115–16, 162

Vinson, Congressman Carl, 116, 124–26
Vinson-Trammell Act, 196n8
Vinson-Walsh Act. *See* Two-Ocean Navy Act (Vinson-Walsh Act)
Viper (destroyer), 30
Virginius Affair, 37–38
Vulcan clutch, 56–57, 59, 186n40

War Plan Orange, 36, 43–47, 109–10, 133, 156–58, 160, 183n23, 183nn25–26, 183n28, 186n6, 200n32, 203n31; cautionaries versus thrusters, 45, 47–48, 183n28; influence on high steam, 64, 150
Warrington (destroyer), 1, 89, 92–101, *137*
warship procurement process, 118, 205n47; America interwar period, 69, 188n20
Washington Naval Treaty, 6, 12, 16, 46–47, 49, 64, 123–24, 168
Watt, James, 20, 180n5
Westinghouse Electric Corporation, 26, 74, 98, 113, 118, *119*, 164, 165
wildcat training, 126–31, 173–74, 196n14, 197n22
Wildenberg, Thomas, 9, 178n14, 201–2nn13–15, 202nn17–20, 203n31, 205n58
Wilson, Frederick T., 4, 177n5
Wood, Major General Leonard, 47–48.
Woolf, Arthur, 180n10
World War II. *See* Pacific War